IDEAS THAT MATTER

A Sourcebook for Speakers

LESTER THONSSEN

AND

WILLIAM L. FINKEL

THE CITY COLLEGE OF NEW YORK

THE RONALD PRESS COMPANY · NEW YORK

Library of Congress Catalog Card Number: 61–8423
PRINTED IN THE UNITED STATES OF AMERICA

Preface

> If there is a first principle in intellectual education it
> is this—that the discipline which does good to the
> mind is that in which the mind is active, not that in
> which it is passive. The secret for developing the
> faculties is to give them much to do, and much in-
> ducement to do it.
>
> —JOHN STUART MILL

Designed as a sourcebook for speakers, *Ideas That Matter*
contains 163 short, provocative passages on a wide variety of
subjects in the arts, science, education, and public affairs. The
selections serve as an introduction to ideas that have persistently
attracted informed men and women. They are intended to stimu-
late thought, to indicate areas for intensive and extensive exploration, and to serve as the basis for the development of original
talks.

With few exceptions, the passages contain ideas that cut
across different fields of study. A selection on an ethical concept,
for example, may bear on politics, art, or criticism; a passage on
poetry may touch upon a subject in science. This affords the
student an opportunity to extend his mind beyond the borders of
his own specialty and gain some insights into other areas.

The selections deal with persistent and unresolved questions.
They invite a variety of answers, sometimes contradictory ones.
Speeches on these passages call for a full measure of individual
contribution. All of the excerpts are short. The student cannot
simply repeat what he reads—there is not enough in a single
passage for a sustained speaking assignment. The selection merely
contains suggestions for examination and development. What is
added by the student is the heart of the speech.

Speeches deriving from ideas in this book also require personal involvement. The selections contain partial and partisan attempts at answers to which the student is required to make an active response by amplifying, challenging, or refuting. None of the excerpts is intended to do the student's thinking for him; all are chosen to provoke him to think for himself.

The approach set forth in this work has been used in the classroom for many years. In the hope that our experience may prove helpful to others, we include in the Appendixes certain suggestions for the use of the readings. Appendix A is a guide to major ideas in the selections. The questions are purely exploratory. Teachers and students may use them as points of departure, as gross indicators of contents. Appendix B lists a few projects in speaking and discussion. Appendix C contains fifty sentences and short expressions which may also be used as springboards for the preparation of original talks. They are provocative, undeveloped ideas which deal with urgencies, doubts, and paradoxes in modern life.

Lester Thonssen
William L. Finkel

February, 1961

Contents

Science

portant than knowledge is the life of the emotions.   THOMAS H.
HUXLEY: Is the study of physical science competent to confer culture?
JOHN BURROUGHS: After science has done its best, the mystery is as
great as ever.   EDGAR A. SINGER, JR.: A child might have grasped
this idea which brought a world to an end.   FREDERICK J. E. WOOD-
BRIDGE: Man's history must also be written in terms of aspiration.

Social Disciplines

A. Reason, Ideals, and Action   85

WILLIAM K. CLIFFORD: It is always wrong to believe anything upon insufficient evidence.   WILLIAM JAMES: There are cases where faith in a fact can help create the fact.   HAROLD CHILD: A Utopia begs the question of moral improvement.   C. DELISLE BURNS: An ideal cannot be understood by mere intellectual analysis.   WALTER LIPPMANN: When there is panic in the air, there is no chance for the constructive use of reason.   P. W. BRIDGMAN: Social scientists lack a disinterested point of view.   GEORGE STUART FULLERTON: Man lives first and thinks afterwards.   GEORGE SANTAYANA: Importance springs from the cry of life, not from reason.   L. T. HOBHOUSE: The psychologist descends upon the mother with the intellectualist fallacy. CRANE BRINTON: Those who think ideals are of no use are very much mistaken.   IRWIN EDMAN: To be effective, moral standards must have emotional support.   LEO TOLSTOY: Every human action is conceived by us as a combination of free will and necessity.   F. ERNEST JOHNSON: Facts may get in the way of truth.   WILLIAM E. H. LECKY: Reasoning which in one age would make no impression whatever, in the next age is received with enthusiastic applause.   JAMES BRYCE: There is little individual thinking in political opinion.   FRANK L. LUCAS: Language has often mastered mankind.

B. Leaders, Reformers, and Ordinary Citizens   110

WOODROW WILSON: Nations are renewed from the bottom, not from the top.   WILLIAM BENNETT MUNRO: It must follow that if you differ from the reformer, you are wrong.   FREDERICK J. E. WOODBRIDGE: Those doing the work of the world do not like to be told how to do it by others who are not doing that work.   SIDNEY HOOK: Politics is a messy business, and life is short.   JAMES BRYCE: Why are great men not chosen as Presidents?   CHARLES W. ELIOT: In a democracy, public offices are not the places of greatest influence.   SYDNEY SMITH: Our ancestors are younger than we are.   VISCOUNT HALDANE: Leadership always depends on personality.   SIDNEY HOOK: A democracy must be suspicious of great men.   ARTHUR M. SCHLESINGER, JR.: Why should our age be without great men?

Artistic Experience

Art is one of the conditions of human life.   WILLIAM ALLEN WHITE:
One man's answer to the question "What is Art?" is as good as another's, and probably better.   SUSANNE K. LANGER: It is not enough
to know why Leonardo's women smile mysteriously.   MORRIS R.
COHEN and ERNEST NAGEL: May not logical tests enable us to find
out whether some moral and aesthetic opinions have more evidence
in their favor than others?   JOHN CIARDI: All good poets write for
the vertical audience.   ROBERT LYND: Indiscriminate praise is one of
the deadly sins of criticism.   LONGINUS: Lofty genius is far removed
from flawlessness.   CHARLES MORGAN: If art has anything to teach,
it is that no one has a monopoly of vision.   RALPH BARTON PERRY:
It is proper to subject art to moral criticism.   AARON COPLAND: Our
concert halls have been turned into musical museums.   WILLIAM
HAZLITT: The principle of universal suffrage is not applicable to
matters of taste.

C. Literature and Science   247

JAMES B. CONANT: Philosophers, writers, and artists affect our daily
lives more profoundly than scholars and scientists.   JOHN HALL
WHEELOCK: Words too often violate the innocent nobility of things.
GILBERT MURRAY: Unlike great works of science, great works of literature do not become obsolete.   WALTER PATER: Art and literature
bring a sense of freedom into a world ruled by natural laws.   J.
BRONOWSKI: In the moment of creation—in art or in science—the heart
misses a beat.   THOMAS LOVE PEACOCK: As science and knowledge
advance, poetry becomes increasingly unnecessary and increasingly
inferior.   PERCY BYSSHE SHELLEY: For want of the poetical faculty,
man, having enslaved the elements, remains himself a slave.   GEORGE
SANTAYANA: Where it is believed that only experimental science can
yield knowledge, poetry will be rather despised.   G. H. HARDY: The
mathematician's patterns, like the painter's or the poet's, must be
beautiful.

SCIENCE

A. Science and the Social Order

J. Bronowski: *People who are by no means fools really believe that we should be better off without science.*

The sense of doom in us today is not a fear of science; it is a fear of war. And the causes of war were not created by science; they do not differ in kind from the known causes of the War of Jenkins' Ear or the Wars of the Roses, which were carried on with only the most modest scientific aids. No, science has not invented war; but it has turned it into a very different thing. The people who distrust it are not wrong. The man in the pub who says "It'll wipe out the world," the woman in the queue who says "It isn't natural"—they do not express themselves very well; but what they are trying to say does make sense. Science has enlarged the mechanism of war, and it has distorted it. It has done this in at least two ways.

First, science has obviously multiplied the power of the warmakers. The weapons of the moment can kill more people more secretly and more unpleasantly than those of the past. This progress, as for want of another word I must call it—this progress has been going on for some time; and for some time it has been said, of each new weapon, that it is so destructive or so horrible that it will frighten people into their wits, and force the nations to give up war for lack of cannon fodder. This hope has never been fulfilled, and I know no one who takes refuge in it today. The acts of men and women are not dictated by such simple compulsions; and they themselves do not stand in any simple relation to the decisions of the nations which they compose. Grapeshot

Reprinted by permission of the publishers from J. Bronowski, *The Common Sense of Science* (Cambridge, Mass.: Harvard Univ. Press and London: William Heinemann, Ltd., 1953), pp. 140–42.

and TNT and gas have not helped to outlaw war; and I see no sign that the hydrogen bomb or a whiff of bacteria will be more successful in making men wise by compulsion.

Secondly, science at the same time has given the nations quite new occasions for falling out. I do not mean such simple objectives as someone else's uranium mine, or a Pacific Island which happens to be knee-deep in organic fertilizer. I do not even mean merely another nation's factories and her skilled population. These are all parts of the surplus above our simple needs which they themselves help to create and which gives our civilization its character. And war in our world battens on this surplus. This is the object of the greed of nations, and this also gives them the leisure to train and the means to arm for war. At bottom, we have remained individually too greedy to distribute our surplus, and collectively too stupid to pile it up in any more useful form than the traditional mountains of arms. Science can claim to have created the surplus in our societies, and we know from the working day and the working diet how greatly it has increased it in the last two hundred years. Science has created the surplus. Now put this year's budget beside the budget of 1750, anywhere in the world, and you will see what we are doing with it.

I myself think there is a third dimension which science has added to modern war. It has created war nerves and the war of nerves. I am not thinking about the technical conditions for a war of nerves: the camera man and the radio and the massed display of strength. I am thinking of the climate in which this stage lightning flickers and is made to seem real. The last twenty years have given us a frightening show of these mental states. There is a division in the mind of each of us, that has become plain, between the man and the brute; and the rift can be opened, the man submerged, with a cynical simplicity, with the meanest tools of envy and frustration, which in my boyhood would have been thought inconceivable in a civilized society. I shall come back to this cleavage in our minds, for it is much more than an item in a list of war crimes. But it is an item. It helps to create the conditions for disaster. And I think that science has contributed to it. Science; the fact that science is there, mysterious, powerful; the fact that most people are impressed by it but ignorant and helpless—all this seems to me to have contributed to the division in our minds. And scientists cannot escape the responsibility for this. They have enjoyed acting the mysterious stranger, the powerful voice without emotion, the expert and the god. They have failed to make themselves comfortable in the talk of people in the street; no one taught them the knack, of course, but they were not keen to learn. And now they find the distance which they enjoyed has turned to distrust, and the awe has turned to fear; and people who are by no means fools really believe that we should be better off without science.

Raymond S. Fosdick: *Should not research be subject to some kind of restraint?*

To the layman it seems as if science were facing a vast dilemma. Science is the search for truth, and it is based on the glorious faith that truth is worth discovering. It springs from the noblest attribute of the human spirit. But it is this same search for truth that has brought our civilization to the brink of destruction; and we are confronted by the tragic irony that when we have been most successful in pushing out the boundaries of knowledge we have most endangered the possibility of human life on this planet. The pursuit of truth has at last led us to the tools by which we can ourselves become the destroyers of our own institutions and all the bright hopes of the race. In this situation what do we do— curb our science or cling to the pursuit of truth and run the risk of having our society torn to pieces?

It is on the basis of this dilemma that serious questions are forming in the public mind. Unless research is linked to a humane and constructive purpose should it not be subject to some kind of restraint? Can our scientists afford to be concerned solely with fact and not at all with value and purpose? Can they legitimately

From "A Layman Looks at Science" from *The Scientists Speak*, ed. Warren Weaver (New York: Boni & Gaer, 1947), pp. 349–51. Courtesy United States Rubber Company.

claim that their only aim is the advancement of knowledge regardless of its consequences? Is the layman justified in saying to the scientist: "We look to you to distinguish between that truth which furthers the well-being of mankind and that truth which threatens it"?

One of the scientists who played a leading role in the development of the atomic bomb said to the newspapermen: "A scientist cannot hold back progress because of fears of what the world will do with his discoveries." What he apparently implied was that science has no responsibility in the matter and that it will plunge ahead in the pursuit of truth even if the process leaves the world in dust and ashes.

Is that the final answer? Is there no other answer? Frankly, as a layman I do not know. Offhand, this disavowal of concern for the social consequences of science seems callous and irresponsible. But we may be facing a situation where no other answer is realistic or possible. To ask the scientist to foresee the use—the good or evil of the use—to which his results may be put is doubtless beyond the realm of the attainable. Almost any discovery can be used for either social or antisocial purposes. The German dye industry was not created to deal with either medicine or weapons of war; and yet out of that industry came our sulfa-drugs and mustard gas. When Einstein wrote his famous transformation equation in 1905 he was not thinking of the atomic bomb, but out of that equation came one of the principles upon which the bomb was based.

Willard Gibbs was a gentle spirit whose life was spent in his laboratory at Yale University and who never dreamed that his work in mathematical physics might have even a remote relationship to war; and yet it is safe to say that his ideas gave added power to the armaments of all nations in both World War I and World War II.

I suspect that the way out of the dilemma is not as simple as the questions now being asked seem to imply. The good and the evil that flow from scientific research are more often than not indistinguishable at the point of origin. Generally they are byproducts, or they represent distortions of original purpose, none of which could have been foreseen when the initial discovery was made. We are driven back to a question of human motives and desires. Science has recently given us radar, jet propulsion and power sources of unprecedented magnitude. What does society want to do with them? It can use them constructively to increase the happiness of mankind, or it can employ them to tear the world to pieces. There is scarcely a scientific formula or a process or a commodity which cannot be used for war purposes, if that is what we elect to do with it. In brief, the gifts of science can be used by evil men to do evil even more obviously and dramatically than they can be used by men of good will to do good.

P. W. Bridgman: *The stupid have no right to exploit the bright.*

The assumption of the right of society to impose a responsibility on the scientist which he does not desire obviously involves acceptance of . . . the right of the stupid to exploit the bright. There are, I believe, specific objections to the application of this philosophy in the present situation. . . . It is not necessary. Society can deal with the issues raised by scientific discoveries by other methods than by forcing the scientist to do something uncongenial, something for which he is often not fitted. The course of action that can accomplish this seems to me the only self-respecting one. The applications made of scientific discoveries are very seldom made by the scientists themselves, but are usually made by the industrialists. It is the manufacture and sale of the invention that should be controlled rather than the act of inventing. This could surely be accomplished by specific action rather than by throwing out baby and bath together. One can think of revisions in the patent laws, for instance, that would be pertinent. Or society can control the situation by other means already in its possession. If it had not wanted to construct an atomic bomb, it

Reprinted from "Scientists and Social Responsibility" in *Scientific Monthly*, LXV, (August 1947), 151–52. Used by permission of The American Association for the Advancement of Science.

need not have signed the check for the two billion dollars which alone made it possible. Without this essential contribution from society the atomic bomb would have remained an interesting blueprint in the laboratory.

Why is it that there is such popular clamor for dealing with this situation by the tremendously clumsy and backhanded method of imposing responsibility on the individual scientist, a method which involves the sacrifice of fundamental principles and the development of social mechanisms of more than doubtful practicality? I suspect the clamor arises from the unconscious operation of very human motives. The cry of responsibility is often no more than the cry of a lazy man to get someone else to do for him what he ought to do for himself. There may perhaps be a small element of despair in the clamor. It is obvious that if society would only abolish war, 99 percent of the need for the control of scientific discoveries would vanish. Furthermore, it is obvious enough that the abolition of war is the business of everyone. The difficulties of doing this, however, appear to have become so enormous that the average man may well despair of being able to accomplish it himself. Into this situation comes the vision that if only some *deus ex machina* would stop scientific discoveries from being put to bad uses we could all be at peace in our minds. Whereupon the human race, with its capacity for wishful thinking and rationalization, needs only this hint to invent the legend of the responsibility of the scientists for the uses society makes of their discoveries. Let society deal with this situation by the means already in its hands, means by which it deals with similar situations. If it truly believes that the peculiar qualifications necessary to deal with the misuse of scientific discovery are to be found among the scientists, which I, for one, very much doubt, then let it create mechanisms and make opportunities by which those scientists who can do this sort of work well will be attracted to this field, rather than to insist on its right to the indiscriminate concern of all scientists with this problem. And let the scientists, for their part, take a long-range point of view and not accept the careless imposition of responsibility, an acceptance which to my mind smacks too much of appeasement and lack of self-respect.

Alfred Zimmern: *The drift to disaster will become irre-sistible.*

Too deeply absorbed in his highly skilled task and too remote from the point at which his specialism branched off from the main high-road, he [the scientist] too often forgets to pause and reflect . . . on the relation between his inquiry and the general interests of mankind. . . .

It is this tendency in modern science to pursue facts for the sake of facts, to exalt the means and forget the end, which has given rise to the accusation so often levelled against it as an agency of materialism. No impeachment could be more untrue either of the spirit of the pioneers of the scientific method or of its leading exponents in every generation. Nevertheless, there is unhappily a large element of truth in the criticism. Science has done damage to the spiritual interests of mankind not by what it has achieved but by what it has forgotten in the moment of achievement . . . What produced the Great War? Historians may investigate the conflicts of interest which acted both as its determining and its predisposing causes. But those conflicts of interest were no fiercer or more deeply rooted than many similar conflicts between rival peoples in earlier ages. Athens and Sparta, Rome and Carthage, stood ranged against one another in a far more permanent opposition than the peoples of the Entente and of the Central Powers. Yet the Peloponnesian and Carthaginian wars were mere local skirmishes which slew men by hundreds, whilst the war between the Entente and the Central Powers involved three-quarters of the globe and drove millions to their doom.

What is the cause of this cruel and unreasonable disproportion? Science is the cause. It is Science which has changed the life and habits of mankind and created an interdependent world society. It is Science again which has provided the weapons which have

From *Learning and Leadership* (London: Oxford Univ. Press, 1928), pp. 76–80, 82–86. Used by permission.

transformed war from a contest of chivalry to a collective mas-
sacre.

Science, we say, is the cause. But in what sense? Does the work
of scientific invention, after six or seven generations of development, reveal a process of growth, with an organic life and meaning of its own . . . Has the Industrial Revolution been a great
achievement of international intellectual cooperation, directed
towards the welfare of mankind? Or has Science merely lent her
brain, as the unskilled workman lends his labour, to be the instrument of the purposes of others? Science carried out the Industrial
Revolution. But did she will it? Science carried out the destruction
of the Great War. But did she will it?

To ask these questions is to answer them. Science, by its very
nature as an intellectual power, abhors violence and upheaval.
Between Science and Revolution, Science and Warfare, there is
no possible kinship. Both in her aims and her methods, Science is
utterly opposed to them. Her home is in a realm of the spirit into
which the powers of disorder not only do not penetrate but of
which they cannot even conceive the existence. How then can
we explain the ghastly paradox that Reason has become the servant of Unreason, and Science, who should be ministering to the
amelioration of human existence, is found playing the horrid role
of 'procuress to the lords of hell'?

The answer is that Science is helpless. She has lost control over
the results of her own thinking. Content to add knowledge to
knowledge, she hands on her discoveries to others, to make of
them what they will. And those others, for whom she has become
indispensable, whose lives and habits and institutions she has
transformed, so far from looking to her for leadership, regard her
as a convenient handmaiden. Did Science will the war? Surely
not.

> Hers not to reason why;
> Hers but to make men die.

Here we reach the uttermost result of the fatal divorce between
the 'how' and the 'why'. For to whom have the diligent servitors
of method handed over the determination of aims? Who, while
the laboratories are reeking with her labours over the 'how', are

taking over from the listless grasp of Science the great issues of human policy? . . . The control that Science has so carelessly abandoned has found no one equipped to accept it. In the abdication of Mind, Matter cannot take command. So to our double question there is a single and ominous answer. Who willed the Industrial Revolution? Nobody. Who willed the World War? Nobody. The two greatest changes in the history of mankind were not brought about by mankind. They were brought about by unreasoning forces—since reason is the prerogative of man, let us boldly say by animal forces, using man's intelligence as their instrument. Mankind, in other words, is no longer master of its destiny. Civilization has ceased to exist. Its outward form survives, the tribute of man's enslaved intelligence to the dark forces which enthral him. But its reality is no more. . . . Civilization, in the true spiritual sense of the term, has ceased to exist. And even its outward semblance, the proud and imposing apparatus of wealth and material power, exists only on sufferance. It has been granted a reprieve until the next war—that war for which Science is preparing and which statesmen are powerless to arrest. . . . Who has increased the carrying power of the aeroplane? Who has improved the construction of bombs? . . . Not the men of action who employ them, not the young heroes who, in devotion to duty, risk their own lives in conveying these means of wholesale destruction, but the men of thought. If the art of war has been brought to a point where it seems destined, unless checked by higher forces, to destroy both itself and civilization through the perfecting of its powers of offence, it is Science, and Science alone, which is responsible.

But Science has never accepted the responsibility. She knows nothing of ends. She is concerned only with means. And, even if she turned her mind to ends, how is she to give voice to her conclusions? Men are not accustomed to listen to her on matters extending beyond the narrow province which she has herself delimited. Moreover, she has no appropriate organ through which to speak. Unskilled in the arts of assemblies and parliaments, she does not know how to set herself to address humanity.

Yet she owes it to herself and to mankind to accept the responsibility which she has too long disclaimed. The men of action, left to themselves for a century and a half, have reduced civilization to a shadow. They are powerless, admittedly powerless, to retrieve what has been lost. It is for the men of thought to assert themselves and insist on a renewal of the collaboration which is the only true basis of civilization. That the task is uncongenial and contrary to lifelong habit and disposition, there is no need to emphasize: nor that the very idea will evoke the ingenious pretexts for evasion with which the intellectual is always so ready when confronted with urgent and disagreeable practical tasks. But to all such arguments Plato has long since given a classic answer: 'You have forgotten, my friend, that it is not the law's concern that any one class in a State should live surpassingly well. Rather it contrives a good life for the whole State, harmonizing the citizens by persuasion and compulsion, and making them share with one another the advantage which each class can contribute to the community . . . You must, therefore, descend by turns to dwell with the rest of the city, and must be accustomed to see these dark objects, for when you are accustomed you will be able to see a thousand times better than those who dwell there . . . because you have seen the truth of what is beautiful and just and good. And so your city and our city will become a waking reality and not a dream like most existing cities, which are peopled by men fighting about shadows and quarrelling for office as though that were a notable good. Whereas the truth surely is this, that that city wherein those who are to rule are least anxious for office must have the best and most stable constitution.'

Thus the recovery of civilization depends . . . on the use made in public affairs of those who know: on adjusting the available resources of good will, expert knowledge and intellectual and moral leadership to the needs of the post-war world. The problem of the recovery of civilization is the problem of the relation between learning and leadership. . . . Unless regular and recognized methods of collaboration are worked out between the thinkers and the doers, between expert knowledge and the representatives of the public interest, power will continue to pass in increasing measure into private and irresponsible hands, and the drift to disaster will become irresistible.

Joseph A. Brandt: *The man of learning must become a man of action.*

The scientific educator, has had no liaison with the people—as he discovered to his dismay after Hiroshima. Not until science had brought about an immediate possibility of the end of the world did it realize that socially it had been going nowhere at all. . . . The life of academic quietism is over. The man of learning, however ill-equipped he may be, must learn to become a man of action, a politician, a man of the people, speaking for people, leading people. . . .

The atomic bomb destroyed something more than Hiroshima and Nagasaki. It blew up the ivory tower. Ultimately, this may be the greatest gain we made by the conquest of the atom. Even when the physical scientists began their work on the atom bomb, they suddenly realized they had taken in their hands the fate of society, of a society which they had not prepared for the ultimate triumph of their scientism. Leaders among them, like Professor Harold C. Urey of Chicago, have gone to the people, to tell them about the fate which may be in store for us. And they are using simple, everyday language, such as the eloquent statement of Mr. Urey to *The New Yorker*: "I've dropped everything to try to carry the message of the bomb's power to the people, because, if we can't control this thing, there won't be any science worthy of the name in the future. I know the bomb can destroy everything we hold valuable and I get a sense of fear that disturbs me in my work. I feel better if I try to do something about it."

From "I Can't Quite Hear You, Doctor" in *Harper's Magazine*, March 1946, pp. 249–50. Used by permission.

John Theodore Merz: *Science and knowledge have overtaken the march of practical life.*

One reason why science forms such a prominent feature in the culture of this age is the fact that only within the last hundred years has scientific research approached the more intricate phenomena and the more hidden forces and conditions which make up and govern our everyday life. The great inventions of the sixteenth, seventeenth, and eighteenth centuries were made without special scientific knowledge, and frequently by persons who possessed skill rather than learning. They greatly influenced science and promoted knowledge, but they were brought about more by accident or by the practical requirements of the age than by the power of an unusual insight acquired by study. But in the course of the last hundred years the scientific investigation of *chemical* and *electric* phenomena has taught us to disentangle the intricate web of the elementary forces of nature, to lay bare the many interwoven threads, to break up the equilibrium of actual existence, and to bring within our power and under our control forces of undreamed-of magnitude. The great inventions of former ages were made in countries where practical life, industry, and commerce were most advanced; but the great inventions of the last fifty years in chemistry and electricity and the science of heat have been made in the scientific laboratory: the former were stimulated by practical wants; the latter themselves produced new practical requirements, and created new spheres of labour, industry, and commerce. Science and knowledge have in the course of this century overtaken the march of practical life in many directions.

From *History of European Thought in the Nineteenth Century* (Edinburgh and London: William Blackwood & Sons, 1896), I, 91–92.

Alfred North Whitehead: *Modern science has imposed on humanity the necessity for wandering.*

One main factor in the upward trend of animal life has been the power of wandering. Perhaps this is why the armour-plated monsters fared badly. They could not wander. Animals wander into new conditions. They have to adapt themselves or die. Mankind has wandered from the trees to the plains, from the plains to the seacoast, from climate to climate, from continent to continent, and from habit of life to habit of life. When man ceases to wander, he will cease to ascend in the scale of being. Physical wandering is still important, but greater still is the power of man's spiritual adventures—adventures of thought, adventures of passionate feeling, adventures of aesthetic experience. . . .

Modern science has imposed on humanity the necessity for wandering. Its progressive thought and its progressive technology make the transition through time, from generation to generation, a true migration into uncharted seas of adventure. The very benefit of wandering is that it is dangerous and needs skill to avert evils. We must expect, therefore, that the future will disclose dangers. It is the business of the future to be dangerous; and it is among the merits of science that it equips the future for its duties. The prosperous middle classes, who ruled the nineteenth century, placed an excessive value upon placidity of existence. They refused to face the necessities for social reform imposed by the new industrial system, and they are now refusing to face the necessities for intellectual reform imposed by the new knowledge. The middle class pessimism over the future of the world comes from a confusion between civilisation and security. In the immediate future there will be less security than in the immediate past, less stability. It must be admitted that there is a degree of insta-

From *Science and the Modern World* (New York: The Macmillan Co., 1925), pp. 290–91. Used by permission.

bility which is inconsistent with civilisation. But, on the whole, the great ages have been unstable ages.

Susanne K. Langer: *The machine is starving the imagination.*

In modern civilization there are two great threats to mental security: the new mode of living, which has made the old nature-symbols alien to our minds, and the new mode of working, which makes personal activity meaningless, inacceptable to the hungry imagination. Most men never see the goods they produce, but stand by a traveling belt and turn a million identical passing screws or close a million identical passing wrappers in a succession of hours, days, years. This sort of activity is too poor, too empty, for even the most ingenious mind to invest it with symbolic content. Work is no longer a sphere of ritual; and so the nearest and surest source of mental satisfaction has dried up. At the same time, the displacement of the permanent homestead by the modern rented tenement—now here, now there—has cut another anchor-line of the human mind. Most people have no home that is a symbol of their childhood, not even a definite memory of one place to serve that purpose. Many no longer know the language that was once their mother-tongue. All old symbols are gone, and thousands of average lives offer no new materials to a creative imagination. This, rather than physical want, is the starvation that threatens the modern worker, the tyranny of the machine. The withdrawal of all natural means for expressing the unity of personal life is a major cause of the distraction, irreligion, and unrest that mark the proletariat of all countries. Technical progress is putting man's freedom of mind in jeopardy.

Reprinted by permission of the publishers from *Philosophy in a New Key* (Cambridge, Mass.: Harvard Univ. Press, copyright 1942, 1951, 1957 by The President and Fellows of Harvard College), pp. 291–92.

J. Bronowski: *The society of scientists survives change without revolution.*

Usually when scientists claim that their work has liberated men, they do so on more practical grounds. In these four hundred years, they say, we have mastered sea and sky, we have drawn information from the electron and power from the nucleus, we have doubled the span of life and halved the working day, and we have enriched the leisure we have created with universal education and high-fidelity recordings and electric light and the lip-stick. We have carried out the tasks which men set for us because they were most urgent. To a world population at least five times larger than in Kepler's day, there begins to be offered a life above the animal, a sense of personality, and a potential of human fulfil-ment, which make both the glory and the explosive problem of our age.

These claims are not confined to food and bodily comfort. Their larger force is that the physical benefits of science have opened a door and will give all men the chance to use mind and spirit. The technical man here neatly takes his model from evolu-tion, in which the enlargement of the human brain followed the development of the hand.

I take a different view of science as a method; to me, it enters the human spirit more directly. Therefore I have studied quite another achievement: that of making a human society work. As a set of discoveries and devices, science has mastered nature; but it has been able to do so only because its values, which derive from its method, have formed those who practice it into a living, stable and incorruptible society. Here is a community where everyone has been free to enter, to speak his mind, to be heard and contradicted; and it has outlasted the empires of Louis XIV and the Kaiser. Napoleon was angry when the Institute he had founded awarded his first scientific prize to Humphry Davy, for

Reprinted by permission of Julian Messner, Inc. from *Science and Human Values* by J. Bronowski; copyright © 1956 by J. Bronowski, pp. 85–88.

this was in 1807, when France was at war with England. Science survived then and since because it is less brittle than the rage of tyrants.

This is a stability which no dogmatic society can have. There is today almost no scientific theory which was held when, say, the Industrial Revolution began about 1760. Most often today's theories flatly contradict those of 1760; many contradict those of 1900. In cosmology, in quantum mechanics, in genetics, in the social sciences, who now holds the beliefs that seemed firm fifty years ago? Yet the society of scientists has survived these changes without a revolution and honors the men whose beliefs it no longer shares. No one has been shot or exiled or convicted of perjury; no one has recanted abjectly at a trial before his colleagues. The whole structure of science has been changed, and no one has been either disgraced or deposed. Through all the changes of science, the society of scientists is flexible and single-minded together and evolves and rights itself. In the language of science, it is a stable society.

The society of scientists is simple because it has a directing purpose: to explore the truth. Nevertheless, it has to solve the problem of every society, which is to find a compromise between man and men. It must encourage the single scientist to be independent, and the body of scientists to be tolerant. From these basic conditions, which form the prime values, there follows step by step the spectrum of values: dissent, freedom of thought and speech, justice, honor, human dignity and self-respect.

J. Robert Oppenheimer: *We are, of course, an ignorant lot.*

We are, of course, an ignorant lot; even the best of us knows how to do only a very few things well; and of what is available in knowledge of fact, whether of science or of history, only the smallest part is in any one man's knowing.

From *Science and the Common Understanding* (New York: Simon and Schuster, Inc., 1953), p. 89. Used by permission.

The greatest of the changes that science has brought is the acuity of change; the greatest novelty the extent of novelty. Short of rare times of great disaster, civilizations have not known such rapid alteration in the conditions of their life, such rapid flowering of many varied sciences, such rapid changes in the ideas we have about the world and one another. What has been true in the days of a great disaster or great military defeat for one people at one time is true for all of us now, in the sense that our ends have little in common with our beginnings. Within a lifetime what we learned at school has been rendered inadequate by new discoveries and new inventions; the ways that we learn in childhood are only very meagerly adequate to the issues that we must meet in maturity.

In fact, of course, the notion of universal knowledge has always been an illusion; but it is an illusion fostered by the monistic view of the world in which a few great central truths determine in all its wonderful and amazing proliferation everything else that is true. We are not today tempted to search for these keys that unlock the whole of human knowledge and of man's experience. We know that we are ignorant; we are well taught it, and the more surely and deeply we know our own job the better able we are to appreciate the full measure of our pervasive ignorance.

J. Bronowski: *It is odd that science should be called amoral.*

It is this last charge, which is commonly brought against science. The claim is not that science is actively anti-moral, but that it is without morality of any kind. The implication is that it thereby breeds in the minds of those who practise it an indifference to morality which comes in time to atrophy in them the power of right judgment and the urge to good conduct.

This charge seems to me as false of the sciences as of the arts. . . .

Reprinted by permission of the publishers from J. Bronowski, *The Common Sense of Science* (Cambridge, Mass.: Harvard Univ. Press and London: William Heinemann, Ltd., 1953), pp. 122–24.

There is indeed no system of morality which does not set a high value on truth and on knowledge, above all on a conscious knowledge of oneself. It is therefore at least odd that science should be called amoral, and this by people who in their own lives set a high value on being truthful. For whatever else may be held against science, this cannot be denied, that it takes for ultimate judgment one criterion alone, that it shall be truthful. If there is one system which can claim a more fanatical regard for truth than Lao-tsze and the Pilgrim Fathers, it is certainly science.

We cannot of course put their truth or any other human values quite so simply as this. We must look round and see whether, either in ethics or in science, truth does not extend beyond a simple truthfulness to fact. And we may take this enquiry into truth as a characteristic test for science, on which we can ground the larger decision, whether science does indeed possess its own values. But do not let us miss the simple point. Whatever else they have also meant by truth, men who take pride in their conduct and its underlying values do not set store by truthfulness in the literal sense. They are ashamed to lie in fact and in intention. And this transcending respect for truthfulness is shared by science. T. H. Huxley was an agnostic, Clifford was an atheist, and I know at least one great mathematician who is a scoundrel. Yet all of them rest their scientific faith on an uncompromising adherence to the truth, and the irresistible urge to discover it. All of them spurn that grey appeal to expediency which is the withering thumb-print of the administrator in committee.

Richard L. Meier: *Two codes of behavior are demanded of scientists.*

The personal ethos for every person is a product of his social origins as modified by his adult experience. Problems of ethics are much more severe if the individual no longer circulates in the

From "The Origins of the Scientific Species" in the *Bulletin of the Atomic Scientists*, VII (June 1951), 172. Used by permission of Educational Foundation for Nuclear Science, Inc.

kind of society to which he became accustomed as a child. Most chemists, engineers, and many biologists have ascended in social status and so have had to learn, in later life, how to behave in new and relatively strange surroundings. As one would expect, the adaptation was usually not complete, a high degree of sophistication in the new role was seldom achieved, and elaborate "holeproof" analyses of right versus wrong were rare. The engineers, because in general they have moved farther up the social scale and have had the least booklearning in cultural subjects, tend to exhibit responsibility only toward their families, their employers, and a close circle of suburban or metropolitan friends. The chemists will go farther and usually become responsible participants in the community, while a large proportion of the physicists struggle to define their responsibilities in terms of ultimates such as Truth, the liberal viewpoint, or the democratic concept. The attitudes of biologists are so diverse it is best not to generalize.

Scientists are bedeviled because two codes of behavior are demanded of them, and society requires that these be kept separate. In the laboratory and design office an attempt is made to exclude emotional bias and moral standards (mainly because experience tells us they lead to errors in logic and fact finding), while in the remainder of daily life a rigorous scientific outlook is quite reprehensible. The mark of the successful scientist is that he has disciplined himself to compartmentalize his life so that neither side will seriously influence the other.

James B. Conant: *That the study of science is the best education for public affairs is a very dubious hypothesis.*

Would it be too much to say that in the natural sciences today the given social environment has made it very easy for even an emotionally unstable person to be exact and impartial in his labo-

From *On Understanding Science* (New Haven, Conn.: Yale University Press, 1947), pp. 7, 9–10. Used by permission.

ratory? The traditions he inherits, his instruments, the high degree of specialization, the crowd of witnesses that surrounds him, so to speak (if he publishes his results)—these all exert pressures that make impartiality on matters of *his* science almost automatic. Let him deviate from the rigorous role of impartial experimenter or observer at his peril; he knows all too well what a fool So-and-so made of himself by blindly sticking to a set of observations or a theory now clearly recognized to be in error. But once he closes the laboratory door behind him, he can indulge his fancy all he pleases and perhaps with all the less restraint because he is now free from the imposed discipline of his calling. . . . As I see it, science today represents the accumulated fruits of one line of descent which migrated, so to speak, into certain fields which were ripe for cultivation. Once science became a self-propagating social phenomenon, those who till these fields have had a relatively easy time keeping up the tradition of their forebears.

Therefore, to put the scientist on a pedestal because he is an impartial inquirer is to misunderstand the situation entirely. Rather, if we seek to spread more widely among the population the desire to seek the facts without prejudice, we should pick our modern examples from the nonscientific fields. We should examine and admire the conduct of the relatively few who in the midst of human affairs can courageously, honestly, and intelligently come to conclusions based on reason without regard for their own or other people's loyalties and interests, and having come to these conclusions, can state them fairly, stick by them, and act accordingly.

To say that all impartial and accurate analyses of facts are examples of the scientific method is to add confusion beyond measure to the problems of understanding science. To claim that the study of science is the best education for young men who aspire to become impartial analysts of human affairs is to put forward a very dubious educational hypothesis at best. Indeed, those who contend that the habits of thought and the point of view of the scientist as a scientist can be transferred with advantage to other human activities have hard work documenting their proposition. Only an occasional brave man will be found nowadays to claim that the so-called scientific method is applicable to the solution of almost all the problems of daily life in the modern world. Yet some proponents of this doctrine have at times gone even further and maintained that only by a widespread application of the scientific method to the problems of society at every level can we hope for peace and sanity. Now, however, such extreme statements are less likely to be coupled with an insistence on the disciplinary value of the physicial sciences. One is more likely to hear that what the layman needs is more education in the social sciences.

Ernest Nagel: *Controlled inquiry cannot be employed for many social problems.*

If the substance of liberalism is its insistence on the use of the method of modern science in dealing with human affairs, is liberalism a philosophy by which men can live? It is well enough to urge the capital importance of responsible inquiry as a condition of intelligent social action, but what shall we be intelligent about? Does liberalism offer a conception of the good society which can capture the imagination and the dedicated service of ordinary men? Does it supply definite objectives, except merely negative ones, toward which a society might direct its resources? Does it provide guidance to the resolution of concrete personal and social problems? Unless liberalism does at least some of these things, so it is frequently argued, its content is purely formal; and in that event, it offers no more intellectual nourishment than antisepsis provides food for the body.

I believe these critical queries to be highly pertinent. For to me also it seems that much of the literature of liberalism is little more than a profound obeisance to modern natural science and an eloquent plea for the extension of its method—a plea that is not invariably associated with clear conceptions as to what that method really is. . . . In any event, what, after all, does the plea

From "Liberalism and Intelligence," The Fourth John Dewey Memorial Lecture, pp. 14–15. Bennington College, Bennington, Vermont. Used by permission of Ernest Nagel.

for extending the method of scientific intelligence come to? No one today seriously maintains that one can employ in the study of human affairs the rigorous experimental controls which characterize inquiries in some of the laboratory sciences, or that one can hope to obtain as the termini of inquiry in the former area conclusions as general and as reliable as are many of the conclusions in the latter. Even in fields of social science in which gifted investigators have pursued the ideals of science with unexcelled zeal, generalized conclusions are rare, frequently trivial, and in all cases hedged with serious qualifications. Moreover, controlled inquiry cannot be employed for many social problems, either because the necessary factual evidence is simply unavailable, or because the problems are so urgent that decision cannot wait upon the completion of competent inquiry into them.

I hope I will not be misunderstood in saying all this. I certainly do not wish to minimize the importance of responsible inquiry in connection with human affairs, or to cast doubt upon the value of a correct logical method when investigating them. On the contrary, I believe that the logical method illustrated in the operations of the natural sciences is the supreme intellectual arbiter wherever questions of knowledge or responsible evaluation are at stake. Like a medieval knight who has chosen his fair lady from all the world, I am prepared to work and fight for my choice of logical method. But I also think that the advocacy of this method is often associated with excessive pretentiousness, as if the mere resolution to employ it were tantamount to assured success in resolving the problems to which the method is relevant. In my opinion, what liberals can and should do is to exemplify in their own studies the actual operation of the method, and thereby to make evident the concrete achievements of scientific intelligence at work.

J. Bronowski: *Science requires more courage than one might think.*

. . . the idea which has given a new vigour to science in our generation is larger than the machinery of cause and effect. . . . It is content to predict the future, without insisting that the computation must follow the steps of causal law. I have called this the idea of chance, because its method is statistical, and because it recognises that every prediction carries with it its own measurable uncertainty. A good prediction is one which defines its area of uncertainty; a bad prediction ignores it. And at bottom this is no more than the return to the essentially empirical, the experimental nature of science. Science is a great many things, and I have called them a great many names; but in the end they all return to this: science is the acceptance of what works and the rejection of what does not. That needs more courage than we might think.

It needs more courage than we have ever found when we have faced our worldly problems. This is how society has lost touch with science: because it has hesitated to judge itself by the same impersonal code of what works and what does not. We have clung to . . . what we have wanted to believe. Here is the crux of what I have been saying. Here is our ultimate hope of saving ourselves from extinction. We must learn to understand that the content of all knowledge is empirical; that its test is whether it works; and we must learn to act on that understanding in the world as well as in the laboratory.

This is the message of science: our ideas must be realistic, flexible, unbigoted—they must be human, they must create their own authority. If any ideas have a claim to be called creative, because they have liberated that creative impulse, it is the ideas of science.

Reprinted by permission of the publishers from J. Bronowski, *The Common Sense of Science* (Cambridge, Mass.: Harvard Univ. Press and London: William Heinemann, Ltd., 1953), pp. 147–48.

B. The Effect of Science on Culture

Hannah Arendt: *It may be wise to distrust the political judgment of scientists.*

. . . the situation created by the sciences is of great political significance. Wherever the relevance of speech is at stake, matters become political by definition, for speech is what makes man a political being. If we would follow the advice, so frequently urged upon us, to adjust our cultural attitudes to the present status of scientific achievement, we would in all earnest adopt a way of life in which speech is no longer meaningful. For the sciences today have been forced to adopt a "language" of mathematical symbols which, though it was originally meant only as an abbreviation for spoken statements, now contains statements that in no way can be translated back into speech. The reason why it may be wise to distrust the political judgment of scientists *qua* scientists is not primarily their lack of "character"—that they did not refuse to develop atomic weapons—or their naïveté—that they did not understand that once these weapons were developed they would be the last to be consulted about their use—but precisely the fact that they move in a world where speech has lost its power. And whatever men do or know or experience can make sense only to the extent that it can be spoken about. There may be truths beyond speech, and they may be of great relevance to man in the singular, that is, to man in so far as he is not a political being, whatever else he may be. Men in the plural, that is, men in so far as they live and move and act in this world, can experience meaningfulness only because they can talk with and make sense to each other and to themselves.

From *The Human Condition* (Chicago: Univ. of Chicago Press, 1958), pp. 3–4. Used by permission.

José Ortega y Gasset: *The specialist is a learned ignoramus.*

Specialisation commences precisely at a period which gives to civilised man the title "encyclopaedic." The Nineteenth Century starts on its course under the direction of beings who lived "encyclopaedically," though their production has already some tinge of specialism. In the following generation, the balance is upset and specialism begins to dislodge culture from the individual scientist. When by 1890 a third generation assumes intellectual command in Europe we meet with a type of scientist unparalleled in history. He is one who, out of all that has to be known in order to be a man of judgment, is only acquainted with one science, and even of that one only knows the small corner in which he is an active investigator. He even proclaims it as a virtue that he take no cognizance of what lies outside the narrow territory specially cultivated by himself, and gives the name of "dilettantism" to any curiosity for the general scheme of knowledge.

What happens is that, enclosed within the narrow limits of his visual field, he does actually succeed in discovering new facts, and advancing the progress of the science which he hardly knows, and incidentally the encyclopedia of thought of which he is conscientiously ignorant. How has such a thing been possible, how is it still possible? For it is necessary to insist upon this extraordinary but undeniable fact: experimental science has progressed thanks in great part to the work of men astoundingly mediocre, and even less than mediocre. That is to say, modern science, the ¬oot and symbol of our actual civilisation, finds a place for the intellectually commonplace man and allows him to work therein with success. The reason of this lies in what is at the same time the great advantage and the gravest peril of the new science, and of the civilisation directed and represented by it, namely, mecha-

Reprinted from *The Revolt of the Masses* by José Ortega y Gasset. By permission of W. W. Norton & Co., Inc. Copyright 1932 by W. W. Norton & Co., Inc. Copyright renewed 1960. Pp. 122–26.

nisation. A fair amount of the things that have to be done in physics or in biology is mechanical work of the mind which can be done by anyone, or almost anyone. For the purpose of innumerable investigations it is possible to divide science into small sections, to enclose oneself in one of these, and to leave out of consideration all the rest. The solidity and exactitude of the methods allow of this temporary but quite real disarticulation of knowledge. The work is done under one of these methods as with a machine, and in order to obtain quite abundant results it is not even necessary to have rigorous notions of their meaning and foundations. In this way the majority of scientists help the general advance of science while shut up in the narrow cell of their laboratory, like the bee in the cell of its hive, or the turnspit in its wheel.

But this creates an extraordinarily strange type of man. The investigator who has discovered a new fact of Nature must necessarily experience a feeling of power and self-assurance. With a certain apparent justice he will look upon himself as "a man who knows." And in fact there is in him a portion of something which, added to many other portions not existing in him, does really constitute knowledge. This is the true inner nature of the specialist, who in the first years of this century has reached the wildest stage of exaggeration. The specialist "knows" very well his own, tiny corner of the universe; he is radically ignorant of all the rest.

Here we have a precise example of this strange new man, whom I have attempted to define, from both of his two opposite aspects. I have said that he was a human product unparalleled in history. The specialist serves as a striking concrete example of the species, making clear to us the radical nature of the novelty. For, previously, men could be divided simply into the learned and the ignorant, those more or less the one, and those more or less the other. But your specialist cannot be brought in under either of these two categories. He is not learned, for he is formally ignorant of all that does not enter into his specialty; but neither is he ignorant, because he is "a scientist," and "knows" very well his own tiny portion of the universe. We shall have to say that he is a learned ignoramus, which is a very serious matter, as it implies that he is a person who is ignorant, not in the fashion of the ignorant man, but with all the petulance of one who is learned in his own special line.

And such in fact is the behaviour of the specialist. In politics, in art, in social usages, in the other sciences, he will adopt the attitudes of primitive, ignorant man; but he will adopt them force-fully and with self-sufficiency, and will not admit of—this is the paradox—specialists in those matters. By specialising him, civilisa-tion has made him hermetic and self-satisfied within his limita-tions; but this very inner feeling of dominance and worth will induce him to wish to predominate outside his specialty. The result is that even in this case, representing a maximum of quali-fication in man—specialisation—and therefore the thing most opposed to the mass-man, the result is that he will behave in almost all spheres of life as does the unqualified, the mass-man.

This is no mere wild statement. Anyone who wishes can ob-serve the stupidity of thought, judgment, and action shown to-day in politics, art, religion, and the general problems of life and the world by the "men of science," and of course, behind them, the doctors, engineers, financiers, teachers, and so on. That state of "not listening," of not submitting to higher courts of appeal which I have repeatedly put forward as characteristic of the mass-man, reaches its height precisely in these partially qualified men. They symbolise, and to a great extent constitute, the actual dominion of the masses, and their barbarism is the most immediate cause of European demoralisation. Furthermore, they afford the clear-est, most striking example of how the civilisation of the last cen-tury, *abandoned to its own devices*, has brought about this rebirth of primitivism and barbarism.

The most immediate result of this *unbalanced* specialisation has been that to-day, when there are more "scientists" than ever, there are much less "cultured" men than, for example, about 1750. And the worst is that with these turnspits of science not even the real progress of science itself is assured. . . .

If the specialist is ignorant of the inner philosophy of the sci-ence he cultivates, he is much more radically ignorant of the his-torical conditions requisite for its continuation; that is to say: how society and the heart of man are to be organised in order that there may continue to be investigators. . . . He . . . believes that

civilisation *is there* in just the same way as the earth's crust and
the forest primeval.

C. P. Snow: *Some people dismiss the scientists as ignorant specialists.*

. . . these [scientists] are very intelligent men. Their culture is
in many ways an exacting and admirable one. It doesn't contain
much art, with the exception, an important exception, of music.
Verbal exchange, insistent argument. Long-playing records.
Colour-photography. The ear, to some extent the eye. Books, very
little, though perhaps not many would go so far as one hero, who
perhaps I should admit was further down the scientific ladder
than the people I've been talking about—who, when asked what
books he read, replied firmly and confidently: 'Books? I prefer to
use my books as tools.' It was very hard not to let the mind wander—what sort of tool would a book make? Perhaps a hammer? A
primitive digging instrument?

Of books, though, very little. And of the books which to most
literary persons are bread and butter, novels, history, poetry,
plays, almost nothing at all. It isn't that they're not interested in
the psychological or moral or social life. In the social life, they
certainly are, more than most of us. In the moral, they are by and
large the soundest group of intellectuals we have; there is a moral
component right in the grain of science itself, and almost all
scientists form their own judgments of the moral life. In the psychological they have as much interest as most of us, though occasionally I fancy they come to it rather late. It isn't that they lack
the interests. It is much more that the whole literature of the traditional culture doesn't seem to them relevant to those interests.
They are, of course, dead wrong. As a result, their imaginative
understanding is less than it could be. They are self-impoverished.

But what about the other side? They are impoverished too—

From *The Two Cultures and the Scientific Revolution* (New York: Cambridge Univ. Press, 1959), pp. 14–16. Used by permission.

perhaps more seriously, because they are vainer about it. They still like to pretend that the traditional culture is the whole of 'culture,' as though the natural order didn't exist. As though the exploration of the natural order was of no interest either in its own value or its consequences. As though the scientific edifice of the physical world was not, in its intellectual depth, complexity and articulation, the most beautiful and wonderful collective work of the mind of man. Yet most non-scientists have no conception of that edifice at all. Even if they want to have it, they can't. It is rather as though, over an immense range of intellectual experience, a whole group was tone-deaf. Except that this tone-deafness doesn't come by nature, but by training, or rather the absence of training.

As with the tone-deaf, they don't know what they miss. They give a pitying chuckle at the news of scientists who have never read a major work of English literature. They dismiss them as ignorant specialists. Yet their own ignorance and their own specialisation is just as startling. A good many times I have been present at gatherings of people who, by the standards of the traditional culture, are thought highly educated and who have with considerable gusto been expressing their incredulity at the illiteracy of scientists. Once or twice I have been provoked and have asked the company how many of them could describe the Second Law of Thermodynamics. The response was cold: it was also negative. Yet I was asking something which is about the scientific equivalent of: *Have you read a work of Shakespeare's?*

I now believe that if I had asked an even simpler question— such as, What do you mean by mass, or acceleration, which is the scientific equivalent of saying, *Can you read?*—not more than one in ten of the highly educated would have felt that I was speaking the same language. So the great edifice of modern physics goes up, and the majority of the cleverest people in the western world have about as much insight into it as their neolithic ancestors would have had.

C. D. Broad: *Physics and death have a long start over psychology and life.*

Now undoubtedly the greatest immediate threat to the further progress of the human mind is the *unequal development* of these three branches of knowledge; *i.e.*, the relatively high degree of our control over inorganic nature, combined with our still very rudimentary knowledge of biology and genetics, and with the complete absence of a scientific psychology and sociology. The first and least obvious danger of this state of affairs is that our environment and mode of life are changed deliberately, profoundly, and very quickly by the application of physical and chemical knowledge. The human organism has had no time to adapt itself spontaneously to these changes; for the spontaneous evolutionary adaptation of organisms is an extremely slow process. It therefore seems not unlikely that there is a great and growing disharmony between human organisms and their environment; and that, unless this can be corrected, the physical and mental qualities of the human race may degenerate. Now it cannot be corrected except by a *deliberate* modification of human organisms, which shall proceed as fast as the deliberate modification of their environment now proceeds. And this is possible only if we have a scientific knowledge of biology, physiology, and genetics comparable in extent and accuracy to our knowledge of physics and chemistry.

The more obvious danger of this unequal development of our knowledge lies in the fact that human control over inorganic nature provides men with means of destroying life and property on a vast scale; whilst the present emotional make-up of men, and their extraordinarily crude and inept forms of social organisation, make it only too likely that these means will be used. This danger, so far as I can see, could be averted only by deliberately altering the emotional constitution of mankind, and deliberately

From *The Mind and Its Place in Nature* (Reprint edition; New York: Humanities Press, Inc., 1951), pp. 664–66. Used by permission of Humanities Press and Routledge & Kegan Paul, Ltd.

constructing more sensible forms of social organisation. And it is quite useless to attempt the latter without the former. In order to do this a vast development of scientific psychology would be needed for two different reasons. In the first place, it would obviously be needed in order to know how to alter the emotional make-up of the individual. But this would not be enough. We might know how to do these things, and yet it might be quite impossible to get people to submit to having these things done to them. For this purpose we should need an enormous development of what Kant calls "the wholesome art of persuasion"; and this could arise only on the basis of a profound theoretical knowledge of the factors which produce, modify, and remove non-rational beliefs.

Conclusion. The conclusion of the whole matter seems to be that perpetual mental progress is certainly not logically impossible, and certainly not causally inevitable, in the sense of being bound to happen whatever we may do. On the other hand, there seems to be no positive reason to believe that it is causally impossible, in the sense that it is bound not to happen whatever we may do. So far as we are concerned, the possibility depends on our getting an adequate knowledge and control of life and mind before the combination of ignorance on these subjects with knowledge of physics and chemistry wrecks the whole social system. Which of the runners in this very interesting race will win, it is impossible to foretell. But physics and death have a long start over psychology and life.

James B. Conant: *We must find ways of balancing the biases of experts.*

There is a fairly common fallacy that if you are dealing with scientific and technical matters, judgment of value rarely, if ever, enters in. Facts speak for themselves in science, we are often told. Anyone who is familiar with the course of scientific research and

From *Modern Science and Modern Man* (New York: Columbia Univ. Press, 1953), pp. 66–67. Used by permission.

development knows this is nonsense. What is true is that the area of debate is fairly definitely circumscribed. The proponent of a process for making a new fabric, for example, is unlikely to quote either Plato or Aristotle on behalf of his proposal. Nor is he likely to appeal to the doctrines set forth in the Declaration of Independence or to the decisions of the Supreme Court. But that does not mean that what is proposed is not controversial. It means simply that the number of people qualified to take part in the controversy is highly limited. And this fact is one pregnant with trouble for our free society. Indeed, among the highly significant but dangerous results of the development of modern science is the fact that scientific experts now occupy a peculiarly exalted and isolated position. Of course, this is an age of experts of all types; one of the vital problems of education is to start a trend of mind among our young people that will lead to a better understanding by one group of experts of what other groups of experts are doing. . . .

The notion that a scientist is a cool, impartial, detached individual is, of course, absurd. The vehemence of conviction, the pride of authorship burn as fiercely among scientists as among any creative workers. Indeed, if they did not, there would be no advance in science. But this emotional attachment to one's own point of view is particularly insidious in science because it is so easy for the proponent of a project to clothe his convictions in technical language. Therefore it is necessary to explore ways and means of balancing the biases of experts whenever their opinions are of prime importance in the making of decisions.

Bertrand Russell: *Even more important than knowledge is the life of the emotions.*

The new powers that science has given to man can only be wielded safely by those who, whether through the study of history or through their own experience of life, have acquired some

Reprinted from *The Scientific Outlook* by Bertrand Russell. By permission of W. W. Norton & Company, Inc., and George Allen & Unwin, Ltd. Copyright 1931, 1959 by Bertrand Russell. Pp. 268–69.

reverence for human feelings and some tenderness towards the emotions that give colour to the daily existence of men and women. I do not mean to deny that scientific technique may in time build an artificial world in every way preferable to that in which men have hitherto lived, but I do say that if this is to be done it must be done tentatively and with a realization that the purpose of government is not merely to afford pleasure to those who govern, but to make life tolerable for those who are governed. Scientific technique must no longer be allowed to form the whole culture of the holders of power, and it must become an essential part of men's ethical outlook to realize that the will alone cannot make a good life. Knowing and feeling are equally essential ingredients both in the life of the individual and in that of the community. Knowledge, if it is wide and intimate, brings with it a realization of distant times and places, an awareness that the individual is not omnipotent or all-important, and a perspective in which values are seen more clearly than by those to whom a distant view is impossible. Even more important than knowledge is the life of the emotions. A world without delight and without affection is a world destitute of value. These things the scientific manipulator must remember, and if he does his manipulation may be wholly beneficial. All that is needed is that men should not be so intoxicated by new power as to forget the truths that were familiar to every previous generation. Not all wisdom is new, nor is all folly out of date.

Thomas H. Huxley: *Is the study of physical science competent to confer culture?*

How often have we not been told that the study of physical science is incompetent to confer culture; that it touches none of the higher problems of life. . . .

. . . . .

From *Science and Education* (New York: D. Appleton & Co., 1893), pp. 140–44. Used by permission of Appleton-Century-Crofts, Inc.

I hold very strongly by two convictions— The first is, that neither the discipline nor the subject-matter of classical education is of such direct value to the student of physical science as to justify the expenditure of valuable time upon either; and the second is, that for the purpose of attaining real culture, an exclusively scientific education is at least as effectual as an exclusively literary education.

I need hardly point out to you that these opinions, especially the latter, are diametrically opposed to those of the great majority of educated Englishmen, influenced as they are by school and university traditions. In their belief, culture is obtainable only by a liberal education; and a liberal education is synonymous, not merely with education and instruction in literature, but in one particular form of literature, namely, that of Greek and Roman antiquity. They hold that the man who has learned Latin and Greek, however little, is educated; while he who is versed in other branches of knowledge, however deeply, is a more or less respectable specialist, not admissible into the cultured caste. The stamp of the educated man . . . is not for him.

. . . . .

Mr. Arnold tells us that the meaning of culture is "to know the best that has been thought and said in the world." It is the criticism of life contained in literature. That criticism regards "Europe as being, for intellectual and spiritual purposes, one great confederation, bound to a joint action and working to a common result; and whose members have, for their common outfit, a knowledge of Greek, Roman, and Eastern antiquity, and of one another. Special, local, and temporary advantages being put out of account, that modern nation will in the intellectual and spiritual sphere make most progress, which most thoroughly carries out this programme. And what is that but saying that we too, all of us, as individuals, the more thoroughly we carry it out, shall make the more progress?"

We have here to deal with two distinct propositions. The first, that a criticism of life is the essence of culture; the second, that literature contains the materials which suffice for the construction of such a criticism.

I think that we must all assent to the first proposition. For culture certainly means something quite different from learning or technical skill. It implies the possession of an ideal, and the habit of critically estimating the value of things by comparison with a theoretic standard. Perfect culture should supply a complete theory of life, based upon a clear knowledge alike of its possibilities and of its limitations.

But we may agree to all this, and yet strongly dissent from the assumption that literature alone is competent to supply this knowledge. After having learnt all that Greek, Roman, and Eastern antiquity have thought and said, and all that modern literatures have to tell us, it is not self-evident that we have laid a sufficiently broad and deep foundation for that criticism of life, which constitutes culture.

Indeed, to any one acquainted with the scope of physical science, it is not at all evident. Considering progress only in the "intellectual and spiritual sphere," I find myself wholly unable to admit that either nations or individuals will really advance, if their common outfit draws nothing from the stores of physical science. I should say that an army, without weapons of precision and with no particular base of operations, might more hopefully enter upon a campaign . . . than a man, devoid of a knowledge of what physical science has done in the last century, upon a criticism of life.

John Burroughs: *After science has done its best, the mystery is as great as ever.*

The ancients had that kind of knowledge which the heart gathers; we have in superabundance that kind of knowledge which the head gathers. If much of theirs was made up of mere childish delusions, how much of ours is made up of hard, barren, and unprofitable details—a mere desert of sand where no green

From "Science and Literature" in *Indoor Studies. The Writings of John Burroughs* (Boston: Houghton Mifflin Company, 1904), VIII: 57–62. Used by permission.

thing grows, or can grow. How much there is in books that one does not want to know, that it would be a mere weariness and burden to the spirit to know; how much of modern physical science is a mere rattling of dead bones, a mere threshing of empty straw. Probably we shall come round to as lively a conception of things by and by. Darwin has brought us a long way toward it. At any rate, the ignorance of the old writers is often more captivating than our exact, but more barren, knowledge.

The old books are full of this dew-scented knowledge—knowledge gathered at first hand in the morning of the world. In our more exact scientific knowledge this pristine quality is generally missing; and hence it is that the results of science are far less available for literature than the results of experience.

Science is probably unfavorable to the growth of literature because it does not throw man back upon himself and concentrate him as the old belief did; it takes him away from himself, away from human relations and emotions, and leads him on and on. We wonder and marvel more, but we fear, dread, love, sympathize less. Unless, indeed, we finally come to see, as we probably shall, that after science has done its best the mystery is as great as ever, and the imagination and the emotions have just as free a field as before.

Science and literature in their aims and methods have but little in common. Demonstrable fact is the province of the one; sentiment is the province of the other. "The more a book brings sentiment into light," says M. Taine, "the more it is a work of literature;" and, we may add, the more it brings the facts and laws of natural things to light, the more it is a work of science. Or, as Emerson says in one of his early essays, "literature affords a platform whence we may command a view of our present life, a purchase by which we may move it." In like manner science affords a platform whence we may view our physical existence, a purchase by which we may move the material world. The value of the one is in its ideality, that of the other in its exact demonstrations. The knowledge which literature most loves and treasures is knowledge of life; while science is intent upon a knowledge of things, not as they are in their relation to the mind and heart of man, but as they are in and of themselves, in their relations to each other and to the human body. Science is a capital or fund perpetually reinvested; it accumulates, rolls up, is carried forward by every new man. Every man of science has all the science before him to go upon, to set himself up in business with. What an enormous sum Darwin availed himself of and reinvested! Not so in literature; to every poet, to every artist, it is still the first day of creation, so far as the essentials of his task are concerned. Literature is not so much a fund to be reinvested, as it is a crop to be ever new grown. Wherein science furthers the eye, sharpens the ear, lengthens the arm, quickens the foot, or extends man farther into nature in the natural bent and direction of his faculties and powers, a service is undoubtedly rendered to literature. But so far as it engenders a habit of peeping and prying into nature, and blinds us to the festive splendor and meaning of the whole, our verdict must be against it.

It cannot be said that literature has kept pace with civilization, though science has; in fact, it may be said without exaggeration that science *is* civilization—the application of the powers of nature to the arts of life. The reason why literature has not kept pace is because so much more than mere knowledge, well-demonstrated facts, goes to the making of it; while little else goes to the making of pure science. Indeed, the kingdom of heaven in literature, as in religion, "cometh not with observation." This felicity is within you as much in the one case as in the other. It is the fruit of the spirit, and not of the diligence of the hands.

Because this is so, because modern achievements in letters are not on a par with our material and scientific triumphs, there are those who predict for literature a permanent decay, and think the field it now occupies is to be entirely usurped by science. But this can never be. Literature will have its period of decadence and of partial eclipse; but the chief interest of mankind in nature or in the universe can never be for any length of time a merely scientific interest—an interest measured by our exact knowledge of these things; though it must undoubtedly be an interest consistent with the scientific view. Think of having one's interest in a flower, a bird, the landscape, the starry skies, dependent upon the stimulus afforded by the text-books, or dependent upon our knowledge of the structure, habits, functions, relations of these objects!

This other and larger interest in natural objects, to which I refer, is an interest as old as the race itself, and which all men, learned and unlearned alike, feel in some degree; an interest born of our relations to these things, of our associations with them. It is the human sentiments they awaken and foster in us, the emotion of love, or admiration, or awe, or fear, they call up; and is, in fact, the interest of literature as distinguished from that of science. The admiration one feels for a flower, for a person, for a fine view, for a noble deed, the pleasure one takes in a spring morning, in a stroll upon the beach, is the admiration and the pleasure literature feels, and art feels; only in them the feeling is freely opened and expanded, which in most minds is usually vague and germinal. Science has its own pleasure in these things; but it is not, as a rule, a pleasure in which the mass of mankind can share, because it is not directly related to the human affections and emotions. In fact, the scientific treatment of nature can no more do away with or supersede the literary treatment of it—the view of it as seen through our sympathies and emotions, and touched by the ideal, such as the poet gives us—than the compound of the laboratory can take the place of the organic compounds found in our food, drink, and air.

Edgar A. Singer, Jr: *A child might have grasped this idea which brought a world to an end.*

Like all very great ideas, this one is of the simplest. It begins with the observation that the flame of a candle grows bigger as we approach it, smaller as we recede from it. Nothing very new in this, you say, nor very imposing. No, it is the next step that was so new in Bruno's day, and of such tremendous destructive and creative power. Yet it is just as simple as the first. What is true of a candle flame must be true of a sun and of a star. Is it

From *Modern Thinkers and Present Problems* (New York: Henry Holt & Co., Inc., 1923), pp. 18–20. Used by permission.

not indeed simple? Yes, but in all the long while the world had lasted it had occurred to no one before Bruno to seize upon this simple idea and to follow whither it led. It led far, wonderfully far. It led Bruno to journey in imagination out and out toward those most distant stars that were then called fixed, and were indeed supposed to be fixed in one great sphere that enclosed all things, beyond which was nothing, and not even nothing, for there was no beyond; space ended where matter ended, at the walls of the world. But Bruno as he journeyed saw this great sun of ours growing smaller and smaller as he receded from it, and yonder star growing larger and larger as he approached it, until the most wonderful thing happened. The sun began to look more and more like a star, and the star more and more like a sun. There was now no escaping the conclusion—the stars that had been called fixed are other suns, our sun but a near-lying star.

A child might have grasped this idea which brought a world to an end.

Frederick J. E. Woodbridge: *Man's history must also be written in terms of aspiration.*

Those who seek to read their destiny from the constellations ascendant at their birth are generally called superstitious; but those who seek to read it from the constitution of matter, or from the mechanism of the physical world, or from the composition of chemical substances, although no less superstitious, are too frequently called scientists. But "dust thou art and unto dust thou shalt return" is an essential truth only about the history of dust; it is only an incidental truth about the history of man. One learns nothing peculiarly characteristic of humanity from it. It affords no measure of the appreciation of poetry, of the constitution of a state, or of the passion for happiness. . . . Human history can

From *The Purpose of History* (New York: Columbia Univ. Press, 1916), pp. 53–57. Used by permission.

not be wholly resolved into physical processes nor the enterprises of men be construed solely as the by-product of material forces. Such resolution of it appears to be unwarranted in view of the conclusions to which a consideration of what history is, leads. The obverse error has long since been sufficiently condemned. We have been warned often enough that water does not *seek* its own level or nature *abhor* a vacuum. Even literary criticism warns us against the pathetic fallacy. But in refusing to anthropomorphize matter, we ought not to be led to materialize man. We should rather be led to recognize that the reasons which condemn anthropomorphic science are precisely the reasons which commend humanistic philosophy. . . .

·   ·   ·   ·   ·

His [man's] history . . . can never be adequately written solely in terms of physics or chemistry, or even of biology; it must be written also in terms of aspiration.

C. Science and Reality

Arthur S. Eddington: *My second table is nearly all empty space.*

I have settled down to the task of writing these lectures and have drawn up my chairs to my two tables. Two tables! Yes; there are duplicates of every object about me—two tables, two chairs, two pens.

. . . . .

One of them has been familiar to me from earliest years. It is a commonplace object of that environment which I call the world. How shall I describe it? It has extension; it is comparatively permanent; it is coloured; above all it is *substantial*. By substantial I do not merely mean that it does not collapse when I lean upon it; I mean that it is constituted of "substance" and by that word I am trying to convey to you some conception of its intrinsic nature. It is a *thing*; not like space, which is a mere negation; nor like time, which is—Heaven knows what! But that will not help you to my meaning because it is the distinctive characteristic of a "thing" to have this substantiality, and I do not think substantiality can be described better than by saying that it is the kind of nature exemplified by an ordinary table. . . .

Table No. 2 is my scientific table. It is a more recent acquaintance and I do not feel so familiar with it. It does not belong to the world previously mentioned—that world which spontaneously appears around me when I open my eyes, though how much of it is objective and how much subjective I do not here consider. It is part of a world which in more devious ways has forced itself on my attention. My scientific table is mostly emptiness. Sparsely

From *The Nature of the Physical World* (New York: Cambridge Univ. Press, 1929), pp. ix–xii. Used by permission.

scattered in that emptiness are numerous electric charges rushing about with great speed; but their combined bulk amounts to less than a billionth of the bulk of the table itself. Notwithstanding its strange construction it turns out to be an entirely efficient table. It supports my writing paper as satisfactorily as table No. 1; for when I lay the paper on it the little electric particles with their headlong speed keep on hitting the underside, so that the paper is maintained in shuttlecock fashion at a nearly steady level. If I lean upon this table I shall not go through; or, to be strictly accurate, the chance of my scientific elbow going through my scientific table is so excessively small that it can be neglected in practical life. Reviewing their properties one by one, there seems to be nothing to choose between the two tables for ordinary purposes; but when abnormal circumstances befall, then my scientific table shows to advantage. If the house catches fire my scientific table will dissolve quite naturally into scientific smoke, whereas my familiar table undergoes a metamorphosis of its substantial nature which I can only regard as miraculous.

There is nothing *substantial* about my second table. It is nearly all empty space . . .

I will not here stress further the non-substantiality of electrons . . . Conceive them as substantially as you will, there is a vast difference between my scientific table with its substance (if any) thinly scattered in specks in a region mostly empty and the table of everyday conception which we regard as the type of solid reality—an incarnate protest against Berkleian subjectivism. It makes all the difference in the world whether the paper before me is poised as it were on a swarm of flies and sustained in shuttlecock fashion by a series of tiny blows from the swarm underneath, or whether it is supported because there is substance below it, it being the intrinsic nature of substance to occupy space to the exclusion of other substance; all the difference in conception at least, but no difference to my practical task of writing on the paper.

I need not tell you that modern physics has by delicate test and remorseless logic assured me that my second scientific table is the only one which is really there—wherever "there" may be. On the other hand I need not tell you that modern physics will never succeed in exorcising that first table—strange compound of external nature, mental imagery and inherited prejudice—which lies visible to my eyes and tangible to my grasp.

T. Percy Nunn: *The philosophy proposed by modern science is believed by nobody.*

It is of high importance to realize what price has been paid for that unity of the physical sciences which can be reached, according to the orthodox, only by the 'elimination of the anthropomorphous'.

. . . the philosophy which . . . has held its own as the guiding principle of scientific studies ever since its birth in the mind of the seventeenth century, the 'century of genius'. And to-day 'it is not only reigning, but it is without a rival'. Nevertheless it is utterly incredible, and in truth is believed by nobody. For the hardest-shelled man of science it is, so to speak, only an official view of the world, maintained without question during business hours for business purposes, but dropped silently, when business is over, for the common instinctive faith that music and laughter, the coloured beauty of living creatures and of sky, sea, mountain, and plain, even in some way the goodly savour of food, wine, and tobacco are realities—not phantasms dwelling only in the mind.

Whitehead has pointed out how deeply the modern mind is troubled by the discordance between the scientific materialism it professes and the attitude of the natural man which it instinctively shares, and there is, I suppose, no one who would not prefer the unsophisticated view of the world if it could be made intellectually respectable.

From *Anthropomorphism and Physics*. A separate publication from the Proceedings of The British Academy, XIII (1926), 9–10. Used by permission of The British Academy.

Arthur S. Eddington: *The whole subject matter of exact science consists of pointer readings and similar indications.*

Let us then examine the kind of knowledge which is handled by exact science. If we search the examination papers in physics and natural philosophy for the more intelligible questions we may come across one beginning something like this: "An elephant slides down a grassy hillside. . . ." The experienced candidate knows that he need not pay much attention to this; it is only put in to give an impression of realism. He reads on: "The mass of the elephant is two tons." Now we are getting down to business; the elephant fades out of the problem and a mass of two tons takes its place. What exactly is this two tons, the real subject-matter of the problem? It refers to some property or condition which we vaguely describe as "ponderosity" occurring in a particular region of the external world. But we shall not get much further that way; the nature of the external world is inscrutable, and we shall only plunge into a quagmire of indescribables. Never mind what two tons *refers* to; what *is* it? How has it actually entered in so definite a way into our experience? Two tons *is* the reading of the pointer when the elephant was placed on a weighing-machine. Let us pass on. "The slope of the hill is 60°." Now the hillside fades out of the problem and an angle of 60° takes its place. What is 60°? There is no need to struggle with mystical conceptions of direction; 60° *is* the reading of a plumb-line against the divisions of a protractor. Similarly for the other data of the problem. The softly yielding turf on which the elephant slid is replaced by a coefficient of friction, which though perhaps not directly a pointer reading is of kindred nature. No doubt there are more roundabout ways used in practice for determining the weights of elephants and the slopes of hills, but these are justified

From *The Nature of the Physical World* (New York: Cambridge Univ. Press, 1929), pp. 251–54. Used by permission.

because it is known that they give the same results as direct pointer readings.

And so we see that the poetry fades out of the problem, and by the time the serious application of exact science begins we are left with only pointer readings. If then only pointer readings or their equivalents are put into the machine of scientific calculation, how can we grind out anything but pointer readings? But that is just what we do grind out. The question presumably was to find the time of descent of the elephant, and the answer is a pointer reading on the seconds' dial of our watch.

The triumph of exact science in the foregoing problem consisted in establishing a numerical connection between the pointer reading of the weighing-machine in one experiment on the elephant and the pointer reading of the watch in another experiment. And when we examine critically other problems of physics we find that this is typical. The whole subject-matter of exact science consists of pointer readings and similar indications. . . . The essential point is that, although we seem to have very definite conceptions of objects in the external world, those conceptions do not enter into exact science and are not in any way confirmed by it. Before exact science can begin to handle the problem they must be replaced by quantities representing the results of physical measurement.

Perhaps you will object that although only the pointer readings enter into the actual calculation it would make nonsense of the problem to leave out all reference to anything else. The problem necessarily involves some kind of connecting background. It was not the pointer reading of the weighing-machine that slid down the hill! And yet from the point of view of exact science the thing that really did descend the hill can only be described as a bundle of pointer readings. (It should be remembered that the hill also has been replaced by pointer readings, and the sliding down is no longer an active adventure but a functional relation of space and time measures.) The word elephant calls up a certain association of mental impressions, but it is clear that mental impressions as such cannot be the subject handled in the physical problem. We have, for example, an impression of bulkiness. To this there is presumably some direct counterpart in the external world, but that counterpart must be of a nature beyond our apprehension, and science can make nothing of it. Bulkiness enters into exact science by yet another substitution; we replace it by a series of readings of a pair of calipers. Similarly the greyish black appearance in our mental impression is replaced in exact science by the readings of a photometer for various wave-lengths of light. And so on until all the characteristics of the elephant are exhausted and it has become reduced to a schedule of measures. There is always the triple correspondence—

(a) a mental image, which is in our minds and not in the external world;

(b) some kind of counterpart in the external world, which is of inscrutable nature;

(c) a set of pointer readings, which exact science can study and connect with other pointer readings.

And so we have our schedule of pointer readings ready to make the descent. And if you still think that this substitution has taken away all reality from the problem, I am not sorry that you should have a foretaste of the difficulty in store for those who hold that exact science is all-sufficient for the description of the universe and that there is nothing in our experience which cannot be brought within its scope.

Irwin Edman: *The voice of a friend is more real than the structure of atoms.*

The sentiments of man are, after all, older and deeper than his reason. The 'really real' elements of a man's world are those features of his experience realized in the intimacy of emotion. Descartes wished to found a philosophy solely on 'clear and distinct ideas.' But it may well be, in the light of modern knowledge, that ideas are not the basic materials out of which to construct a philosophy. The world that we know through our intelligence is

From *Adam, The Baby and the Man from Mars* (Boston: Houghton Mifflin Company, 1929), pp. 199–200. Used by permission.

woven out of the most tenuous and most secondary of abstractions. The color of a sunset or the voice of a friend is metaphysically more real than the structure of atoms or the velocity of light. The first are individual, concrete, and alive; the second are skeletal generalities. All that our minds can give us is a dead abstraction of what comes to us in the tang and pressure of a given moment. What we call emotions or what we dismiss as sentiments is simply inward awareness of the most intensely real outer events in our lives.

The prestige of science has misled us into supposing that there is something more metaphysically respectable about atoms than about ambitions; about diagrams than about moods. But the common man knows better and the scientists are beginning to. Space and time, matter and motion, physical circumstances and economic laws—these are the formulas, not the stuff, of our experience. Many a man feels he has moved from shadow to substance at a flash of poetry or at the birth of love. Neither science nor satire can exhaust 'reality' without taking into account those heightened moments in which reality is intimately touched by living men. In those emotions we have come to despise, when our routine moments are ennobled with 'something far more deeply interfused,' an adequate realism will have to find part of its material. For it is among these emotionally heightened moments that all, save a few mocking spirits, find their most adequate life.

George Santayana: *If we had nothing but physics to think of, the nightmare would soon become intolerable.*

There are books in which the footnotes, or the comments scrawled by some reader's hand in the margin, are more interesting than the text. The world is one of these books. The reciprocal interference of magnetic fields (which I understand is the latest

From *Soliloquies in England* (New York: Charles Scribner's Sons, 1924), pp. 124–25. Used by permission of Daniel Cory.

conception of matter) may compose a marvellous moving pattern; but the chief interest to us of matter lies in its fertility in producing minds and presenting recognizable phenomena to the senses; and the chief interest of any scientific notion of its intrinsic nature lies in the fact that, if not literally true, it may liberate us from more misleading conceptions. Did we have nothing but electrical physics to think of, the nightmare would soon become intolerable. But a hint of that kind, like a hasty glance into the crater of a volcano, sends a wholesome shudder through our nerves; we realize how thin is the crust we build on, how mythical and remote from the minute and gigantic scale of nature are the bright images we seem to move among, all cut out and fitted to our human stature. Yet these bright images are our natural companions, and if we do not worship them idolatrously nor petrify them into substances, forgetting the nimble use of them in mental discourse, which is where they belong, they need not be more misleading to us, even for scientific purposes, than are words or any other symbols.

It is fortunate that the material world, whatever may be its intrinsic structure or substance, falls to our apprehension into such charming units. There is the blue vault of heaven, there are the twinkling constellations, there are the mountains, trees, and rivers, and above all those fascinating unstable unities which we call animals and persons; magnetic fields I am quite ready to believe them, for such in a vast vague way I feel them to be, but individual bodies they will remain to my sensuous imagination, and dramatic personages to my moral sense. They, too, are animate: they, too, compose a running commentary on things and on one another, adding their salacious footnotes to the dull black letter of the world.

Arthur S. Eddington: *The solid substance of things is another illusion.*

One day I happened to be occupied with the subject of "Generation of Waves by Wind". I took down the standard treatise on hydrodynamics, and under that heading I read—

The equations (12) and (13) of the preceding Art. enable us to examine a related question of some interest, viz. the generation and maintenance of waves against viscosity, by suitable forces applied to the surface.

If the external forces p'_{yy}, p'_{xy} be given multiples of e^{ihx+at}, where k and a are prescribed, the equations in question determine A and C, and thence, by (9) the value of η. Thus we find

$$\frac{p'_{yy}}{g\rho\eta} = \frac{(a^2 + 2vk^2a + \sigma^2)\ A - i\ (\sigma^2 + 2vkma)\ C}{gk\ (A - iC)},$$

$$\frac{p'_{xy}}{g\rho\eta} = \frac{a}{gk}\cdot\frac{2ivk^2A + (a + 2vk^2)\ C}{(A - iC)},$$

where σ^2 has been written for $gk + T'\ k^3$ as before. . . .

And so on for two pages. At the end it is made clear that a wind of less than half a mile an hour will leave the surface unruffled. At a mile an hour the surface is covered with minute corrugations due to capillary waves which decay immediately the disturbing cause ceases. At two miles an hour the gravity waves appear. As the author modestly concludes, "Our theoretical investigations give considerable insight into the incipient stages of wave-formation".

From *The Nature of the Physical World* (New York: Cambridge Univ. Press, 1929), pp. 316–19. Used by permission.

On another occasion the same subject of "Generation of Waves by Wind" was in my mind; but this time another book was more appropriate, and I read—

> There are waters blown by changing winds to laughter
> And lit by the rich skies, all day. And after,
>   Frost, with a gesture, stays the waves that dance
> And wandering loveliness. He leaves a white
>   Unbroken glory, a gathered radiance,
> A width, a shining peace, under the night.

The magic words bring back the scene. Again we feel Nature drawing close to us, uniting with us, till we are filled with the gladness of the waves dancing in the sunshine, with the awe of the moonlight on the frozen lake. These were not moments when we fell below ourselves. We do not look back on them and say, "It was disgraceful for a man with six sober senses and a scientific understanding to let himself be deluded in that way. I will take Lamb's *Hydrodynamics* with me next time." It is good that there should be such moments for us. Life would be stunted and narrow if we could feel no significance in the world around us beyond that which can be weighed and measured with the tools of the physicist or described by the metrical symbols of the mathematician.

Of course it was an illusion. We can easily expose the rather clumsy trick that was played on us. Aethereal vibrations of various wave-lengths, reflected at different angles from the disturbed interface between air and water, reached our eyes, and by photo-electric action caused appropriate stimuli to travel along the optic nerves to a brain-centre. Here the mind set to work to weave an impression out of the stimuli. The incoming material was somewhat meagre; but the mind is a great storehouse of associations that could be used to clothe the skeleton. Having woven an impression the mind surveyed all that it had made and decided that it was very good. The critical faculty was lulled. We ceased to analyse and were conscious only of the impression as a whole. The warmth of the air, the scent of the grass, the gentle stir of the breeze, combined with the visual scene in one transcendent impression, around us and within us. Associations emerging from their storehouse grew bolder. Perhaps we recalled the phrase "rippling laughter." Waves—ripples—laughter—gladness—the ideas jostled one another. Quite illogically we were glad; though what there can possibly be to be glad about in a set of aethereal vibrations no sensible person can explain. A mood of quiet joy suffused the whole impression. The gladness in ourselves was in Nature, in the waves, everywhere. That's how it was.

It was an illusion. Then why toy with it longer? These airy fancies which the mind, when we do not keep it severely in order, projects into the external world should be of no concern to the earnest seeker after truth. Get back to the solid substance of things, to the material of the water moving under the pressure of the wind and the force of gravitation in obedience to the laws of hydrodynamics. But the solid substance of things is another illusion. It too is a fancy projected by the mind into the external world. We have chased the solid substance from the continuous liquid to the atom, from the atom to the electron, and there we have lost it. But at least, it will be said, we have reached something real at the end of the chase—the protons and electrons. Or if the new quantum theory condemns these images as too concrete and leaves us with no coherent images at all, at least we have symbolic co-ordinates and momenta and Hamiltonian functions devoting themselves with single-minded purpose to ensuring that $qp-pq$ shall be equal to $ih/2\pi$.

J. Bronowski: *All science is a search for unity in hidden likenesses.*

What is the insight with which the scientist tries to see into nature? Can it indeed be called either imaginative or creative? To the literary man the question may seem merely silly. He has been taught that science is a large collection of facts; and if this

Reprinted by permission of Julian Messner, Inc. from *Science and Human Values*, pp. 19, 23–25. Copyright 1956 by J. Bronowski.

is true, then the only seeing which scientists need do is, he supposes, seeing the facts. He pictures them, the colorless professionals of science, going off to work in the morning into the universe in a neutral, unexposed state. They then expose themselves like a photographic plate. And then in the darkroom or laboratory they develop the image, so that suddenly and startlingly it appears, printed in capital letters, as a new formula for atomic energy.

Men who have read Balzac and Zola are not deceived by the claims of these writers that they do no more than record the facts. The readers of Christopher Isherwood do not take him literally when he writes: "I am a camera." Yet the same readers solemnly carry with them from their school days this foolish picture of the scientist fixing by some mechanical process the facts of nature. . . .

All science is the search for unity in hidden likenesses. The search may be on a grand scale, as in the modern theories which try to link the fields of gravitation and electro-magnetism. But we do not need to be browbeaten by the scale of science. There are discoveries to be made by snatching a small likeness from the air too, if it is bold enough. In 1932 the Japanese physicist Yukawa wrote a paper which can still give heart to a young scientist. He took as his starting point the known fact that waves of light can sometimes behave as if they were separate pellets. From this he reasoned that the forces which hold the nucleus of an atom together might sometimes also be observed as if they were solid pellets. A schoolboy can see how thin Yukawa's analogy is, and his teacher would be severe with it. Yet Yukawa without a blush calculated the mass of the pellet he expected to see, and waited. He was right; his meson was found, and a range of other mesons, neither the existence nor the nature of which had been suspected before. The likeness had borne fruit.

The scientist looks for order in the appearances of nature by exploring such likenesses. For order does not display itself of itself; if it can be said to be there at all, it is not there for the mere looking. There is no way of pointing a finger or a camera at it; order must be discovered and, in a deep sense, it must be created. What we see, as we see it, is mere disorder.

This point has been put trenchantly in a fable by Professor Karl Popper. Suppose that someone wished to give his whole life to science. Suppose that he therefore sat down, pencil in hand, and for the next twenty, thirty, forty years recorded in notebook after notebook everything that he could observe. He may be supposed to leave out nothing: today's humidity, the racing results, the level of cosmic radiation and the stock market prices and the look of Mars, all would be there. He would have compiled the most careful record of nature that has ever been made; and, dying in the calm certainty of a life well spent, he would of course leave his notebooks to the Royal Society. Would the Royal Society thank him for the treasure of a lifetime of observation? It would not. It would refuse to open his notebooks at all, because it would know without looking that they contain only a jumble of disorderly and meaningless items.

Arthur S. Eddington: *We are part of the problem that we have to solve.*

The problem of the scientific world is part of a broader problem—the problem of all experience. Experience may be regarded as a combination of self and environment, it being part of the problem to disentangle these two interacting components. Life, religion, knowledge, truth are all involved in this problem, some relating to the finding of ourselves, some to the finding of our environment from the experience confronting us. All of us in our lives have to make something of this problem; and it is an important condition that we who have to solve the problem are ourselves part of the problem. Looking at the very beginning, the initial fact is the feeling of purpose in ourselves which urges us to embark on the problem. We are meant to fulfil something by our lives. There are faculties with which we are endowed, or which we ought to attain, which must find a status and an outlet

From *The Nature of the Physical World* (New York: Cambridge Univ. Press, 1929), pp. 328–29. Used by permission.

in the solution. It may seem arrogant that we should in this way insist on moulding truth to our own nature; but it is rather that the problem of truth can only spring from a desire for truth which is in our nature.

A rainbow described in the symbolism of physics is a band of aethereal vibrations arranged in systematic order of wavelength from about .000040 cm. to .000072 cm. From one point of view we are paltering with the truth whenever we admire the gorgeous bow of colour, and should strive to reduce our minds to such a state that we receive the same impression from the rainbow as from a table of wave-lengths. But although that is how the rainbow impresses itself on an impersonal spectroscope, we are not giving the whole truth and significance of experience—the starting-point of the problem—if we suppress the factors wherein we ourselves differ from a spectroscope. We cannot say that the rainbow, as part of the world, was meant to convey the vivid effects of colour; but we can perhaps say that the human mind as part of the world was meant to perceive it that way.

Significance and Values. When we think of the sparkling waves as moved with laughter we are evidently attributing a significance to the scene which was not there. The physical elements of the water—the scurrying electric charges—were guiltless of any intention to convey the impression that they were happy. But so also were they guiltless of any intention to convey the impression of substance, of colour, or of geometrical form of the waves. If they can be held to have had any intention at all it was to satisfy certain differential equations—and that was because they are the creatures of the mathematician who has a partiality for differential equations. The physical no less than the mystical significance of the scene is not there; it is *here*—in the mind.

E. N. da C. Andrade: *Science does not deal with the whole of reality.*

Physical science deals with things that can be weighed and measured, but this clearly does not mean the whole of reality. The methods of science imply a choice and an abstraction. As regards choice, the whole history of science has been at every stage governed by what has been selected for measurement and by the decision as to how much time and care should be devoted to perfecting methods of measuring one thing rather than another, and this is a human and personal question. . . . The material world displays an infinite field for experiment and speculation; a drop of water, a grain of sand offer problems that could occupy the greatest brain for a lifetime. What we find, what we think important, is determined by choice. What determines that choice?

Another aspect of this question is what I have called abstraction. Here is a lump of copper. I give it to a physicist and ask him to find out all about it. Probably, after long sessions in the laboratory, he tells me the density, the conductivity for heat and electricity, the specific heat, the elasticity, and many other such properties of the metal of the lump, and if I said that I wanted to know more he might, together with the team he had by now assembled, find out the way in which all these quantities varied with the temperature and the pressure, and investigate the behaviour of the molten metal. . . .

But if I give it to a chemist he will probably first of all supply me with an exact analysis of the metal, giving the impurities which always exist, either as a few parts in a hundred or a few parts in a million. He and his team will study all the salts that can be prepared from it, organic and inorganic. His physical chemical colleagues will measure the electro-chemical potentials, the surface properties of various kinds, the ionic mobilities, and

From *An Approach to Modern Physics* by E. N. da C. Andrade, pp. 244–46. Copyright 1956 by E. N. da C. Andrade. Reprinted by permission of Doubleday & Co., Inc.

what not. All about the copper would now have quite a different aspect. Different again would be the engineer's report, the geologist's report, and so on. Of course, if I asked a business man about it, he would give me the market price, and if I replied that that was not an aspect of reality about the copper, he would doubt my sanity. And it *is* an aspect of reality. It is a figure, a numerical aspect of a reality that to many men, who are also realities, is extremely important.

But let me go further. Suppose I had given the lump of copper to the painter Rembrandt. The play of light on the surface—polarized by reflexion, says the physicist, very truly—slightly oxidized, says the chemist, quite correctly—would probably have been the thing about the copper that interested him, and if he had nothing else to do he might have painted it in a variety of circumstances: against a velvet curtain, at dusk, and who knows how. Is not the play of light on the surface of the copper, as perceived by the artist, a reality? All the properties mentioned, and many others, are aspects of the reality that make up the copper. Science abstracts aspects of the reality that can be measured, but even the scientist leaves a multitude of aspects unmeasured and is always bound to do so. Twenty years ago he could not have measured the behaviour of the copper to radiations of many kinds accessible today: are we to suppose that the next twenty years will reveal no new properties?

Science, then, attempts an accurate description, in terms of current theories which admittedly are makeshifts, of a part of the mechanical side of Nature, a part selected more or less arbitrarily under the influence of the available instruments and methods of experiment and the mental disposition of the great leaders of research.

Morris Kline: *The abstractions are the most significant and most useful facts we have.*

This abstractness [of mathematical thinking] results from the fact that mathematics proper drops the physical meanings originally associated with the undefined terms. Mathematical method is abstract in another sense as well. Out of the medley of experiences proffered by nature, mathematics isolates and concentrates on particular aspects. This is abstraction in the sense of delimiting the phenomenon under investigation. For example, the mathematical straight line has only a few properties compared to those of the straight lines made by the edge of a table or drawn with pencil. The few properties the mathematical line possesses are stated in the axioms; for example, it is determined by two points. The physical lines, in addition to this property, have color and even breadth and depth; moreover, they are built up of molecules each of which has a complicated structure.

It would seem offhand that an attempt to study nature by concentrating on just a few properties of physical objects would fall far short of effectiveness. Yet part of the secret of mathematical power lies in the use of this type of abstraction. By this means we free our minds from burdensome and irrelevant detail and are thereby able to accomplish more than if we had to keep the whole physical picture before us. The success of the process of abstracting particular aspects of nature rests on the divide-and-conquer rule.

In addition to delimiting the problem being studied there are further advantages in concentrating on a few aspects of experience. The experimental scientist, because he deals so directly with physical objects, is usually limited to thinking in terms of objects perceived through the senses. He is chained to the ground. Mathematics, by abstracting concepts and properties from the physical objects, is able to fly on wings of thought beyond the sensible world of sight, sound, and touch. Thus mathematics can 'handle' such 'things' as bundles of energy, which perhaps can never be qualitatively described because they are apparently beyond the realm of sensation. Mathematics can 'explain' gravitation, for example, as a property of a space too vast to visualize. In like manner mathematics can treat and 'know' such mysterious phenomena as electricity, radio waves, and light for which any physical picture is mainly speculative and always inadequate. The abstractions, that is the mathematical formulas, are the most significant and the most useful facts we have about these phenomena.

Morris R. Cohen and Ernest Nagel: *Science analyzes its objects into elements that are related in particular ways.*

Scientific method is largely concerned with the analysis of objects into their constituent elements. Thus the physicist, the chemist, the geologist, and the biologist each seeks to find the constituents of the objects that he studies; psychology, the social sciences, and philosophy try to do the same. It is understandable, therefore, how the misconception arises that science identifies objects with their *elements*. Science, however, does *not* do so, but analyzes its objects into *elements that are related* to each other in certain ways, so that if the same elements were related in different ways they would constitute *other* objects.

This misconception gives rise to two erroneous views: (1) that science denies the reality of the connecting links or relations, and (2) that science is a falsification of reality or the nature of things. Instances of the former are arguments which depend upon regarding, say, scientific books as nothing but words, animate or inanimate nature as nothing but atoms, lines as nothing but points, and society as nothing but individuals—instead of holding

From *An Introduction to Logic and Scientific Method* by Morris R. Cohen and Ernest Nagel, pp. 382–83. Copyright 1934 by Harcourt, Brace and Company, Inc. Reprinted by permission of the publisher.

books, nature, lines, and society to be constituted by words, atoms, points, and individuals, respectively, *connected* in certain ways.

Building on this first mistake, many argue that science is therefore a falsification of reality. The motive for this conclusion appears very naïvely in a dialogue between two popular philosophers, Mutt and Jeff. When the former asks the latter whether he has heard that water is composed (by weight) of eight parts of oxygen to one part of hydrogen, the latter replies, "What! Is there no water in it?" Jeff's difficulty arises from a misapplication of the sound logical principle of identity, that water is water and not something else. What we ordinarily mean by water is a fluid with definite, familiar properties, which are not those of oxygen or hydrogen in isolation; and it seems clear that eight pounds of oxygen and one pound of hydrogen is not the same as nine pounds of water. Nevertheless, not only can water be constituted by or be broken into just such elements in just these proportions, but this fact enables us to understand many of the perceptible properties of water, and has enabled us to discover others which we would not have otherwise suspected. Water *is* hydrogen and oxygen *combined* in a certain way, just as a sentence is a group of words *ordered* in a certain way.

T. Percy Nunn: *The electron's existence is becoming too complicated to be supported.*

We have next to deal with the 'scientific objects' which physics offers us as the reality behind the veil of sensible appearances, the invisible agents of the flux of nature; and the purpose of my argument here is to cast doubt upon their existence. A simple instance of a scientific object is caloric, the fluid whose transference from one body to another was supposed to cause the temperature of the former to fall and of the latter to rise until a state of equilibrium

From *Anthropomorphism and Physics*. A separate publication from the Proceedings of The British Academy, XIII (1926), 18–26. Used by permission of The British Academy.

was attained. The eighteenth century thought of caloric simply
as an invisible, intangible form of matter, subtler than the other
chemical elements, yet belonging to the same order of being: in
Thomas Thomson's classification, it was an 'unconfinable simple
substance'—i.e. one that, unlike gases, it was not possible to retain
in a bottle. Caloric and the 'electric fluid' which appeared in scientific writings in the same epoch were scientific, as distinguished
from natural or physical objects, inasmuch as they were inferred
not observed entities, hypotheses read into the context of physical
phenomena, not things found there. To put the point crudely, no
one ever claimed to have observed either of these fluids, only the
results of their supposed existence and movements. But they were
not scientific objects in the sense that ether was for the nineteenth
century and electrons are for the twentieth. When Oliver Heavi-
side declared that ether and energy were the only physical
realities and that all else was moonshine, he did not think of ether
(as Thomson thought of caloric) as a substance among substances; he thought of it as the primal and ultimate substance from
which all specific forms of materiality are derived. Similarly, electrons and protons, whether conceived as ultimate particles of electricity or as ultimate particles of matter charged with electricity
(whatever the difference may mean) are not regarded by the
physicist as bodies in a world containing other bodies. They are
ultimately the only material bodies that exist, all other bodies, as
we seem to see, hear, smell, taste, feel them, being only the way
in which our perceptive faculties react to gigantic clusters of the
primary particles, in enormously complicated modes of movement. It follows that though we may ascribe size, shape, and
mass to electrons, they have no secondary qualities; they, whose
behaviour is the cause of our sensations of light, colour, fragrance,
and temperature, cannot themselves be luminous or coloured or
odorous or hot or cold.

Now there seem to me to be two strong reasons for disbelieving
in the existence of such scientific objects, one metaphysical, the
other historical. The metaphysical argument . . . appears to me
to be conclusive, but I grant that it derives its force from a general theory which cannot compel universal assent. The second
argument does not suffer from this defect; for it is based upon

facts beyond dispute. It aims at discrediting all scientific objects by showing that in the history of science they have been constantly found out and discarded.

Caloric, to which I have already referred, offers a simple illustration of the thesis. Joseph Black conceived it as a substance capable of quantitative estimation, whose transference from body to body accounted for changes of temperature and such phenomena as the transformation of ice into water. This conception guided him to discoveries of high importance, and so late as 1824 was central in those reflections of Sadi Carnot upon the motive power of heat in which began the science of thermodynamics. Yet investigations prompted by Black's notion of caloric had already led to the knowledge of truths incompatible with it. Count Rumford had shown that heat can be produced in indefinite amount by friction, as in the boring of cannon, and Davy had clinched his argument by proving that two pieces of ice may be melted simply by rubbing them together. In the face of such facts the conception of caloric was at length abandoned . . .

The case of ether is still more illuminating, for the nineteenth century pinned to it a faith which the twentieth has transferred to the electron. An understanding of ether, it was thought, was the key to all the mysteries of the material universe; ether and energy were the only realities, all else was but 'moonshine.' The reality of ether seemed to be very real when confident calculations were made of its elasticity and other properties; and when one considers the magnificent services the idea rendered to science in the hands of the great physicists of the nineteenth century from Fresnel and Maxwell to Larmor and Lorentz, the conviction that it was the fundamental thing in nature is very intelligible. Yet here again history repeated itself. Exploration of the ether theory in the study and the laboratory led to results which made it impossible to hold it in anything like its original simplicity. . . .

Lastly we come to the electron, which is the reigning monarch in physical theory. Is it to be its fate also to be devoured by its children, or is its kingdom secure for ever? When we consider the men who have given their allegiance to it and the magnitude of the conquests they have achieved in its name, it seems impertinent to question the permanence of its rule—until one remembers how great were the votaries of ether, and what triumphs they won under its banner. It is true that experiment seems to have brought us so near to verification of the electron that only an obstinate doctrinaire could resist the evidence for its existence, and there seems here to be a vital difference between this case and those of caloric and of ether. Nevertheless there are not only the metaphysical arguments, whatever they may be worth, but there are also scientific considerations which seem to justify scepticism even in the face of C. T. R. Wilson's and R. A. Millikan's miraculous experiments and measurements. . . .

Even a layman may, without much presumption, go farther and guess that since the electron, which started out, like ether before it, with nothing but straightforward mechanical properties, now finds itself obliged, again like ether, to assume other properties incompatible with these, its ultimate disappearance from physical theory is foreshadowed. Its existence is, in fact, becoming too complicated to be supported.

G. K. Chesterton: *The sun shines because it is bewitched.*

In fairyland we avoid the word "law"; but in the land of science they are singularly fond of it. Thus they will call some interesting conjecture about how forgotten folks pronounced the alphabet, Grimm's Law. But Grimm's Law is far less intellectual than Grimm's Fairy Tales. The tales are, at any rate, certainly tales; while the law is not a law. A law implies that we know the nature of the generalisation and enactment; not merely that we have noticed some of the effects. If there is a law that pick-pockets shall go to prison, it implies that there is an imaginable mental connection between the idea of prison and the idea of picking pockets. And we know what the idea is. We can say why we take liberty from a man who takes liberties. But we cannot say why

From "The Ethics of Elfland," pp. 92–94. Reprinted by permission of Dodd, Mead & Co. and The Bodley Head, Ltd. from *Orthodoxy*. Copyright 1908 by Dodd, Mead & Co.

an egg can turn into a chicken any more than we can say why a bear could turn into a fairy prince. As *ideas*, the egg and the chicken are further off from each other than the bear and the prince; for no egg in itself suggests a chicken, whereas some princes do suggest bears. Granted, then, that certain transformations do happen, it is essential that we should regard them in the philosophic manner of fairy tales, not in the unphilosophic manner of science and the "Laws of Nature." When we are asked why eggs turn to birds or fruits fall in autumn, we must answer exactly as the fairy godmother would answer if Cinderella asked her why mice turned to horses or her clothes fell from her at twelve o'clock. We must answer that it is *magic*. It is not a "law," for we do not understand its general formula. It is not a necessity, for though we can count on it happening practically, we have no right to say that it must always happen. It is no argument for unalterable law (as Huxley fancied) that we count on the ordinary course of things. We do not count on it; we bet on it. We risk the remote possibility of a miracle as we do that of a poisoned pancake or a world-destroying comet. We leave it out of account, not because it is a miracle, and therefore an impossibility, but because it is a miracle, and therefore an exception. All the terms used in the science books, "law," "necessity," "order," "tendency," and so on, are really unintellectual, because they assume an inner synthesis, which we do not possess. The only words that ever satisfied me as describing Nature are the terms used in the fairy books, "charm," "spell," "enchantment." They express the arbitrariness of the fact and its mystery. A tree grows fruit because it is a *magic* tree. Water runs downhill because it is bewitched. The sun shines because it is bewitched.

Joseph Wood Krutch: *The astronomer can tell where the North Star will be ten thousand years hence; the botanist cannot tell where the dandelion will bloom tomorrow.*

No man ever saw a dinosaur. The last of these giant reptiles was dead eons before the most dubious half-man surveyed the world about him. Not even the dinosaurs ever cast their dim eyes upon many of the still earlier creatures which preceded them. Life changes so rapidly that its later phases know nothing of those which preceded them. But the frostflower is older than the dinosaur, older than the protozoan, older no doubt than the enzyme or the ferment. Yet it is precisely what it has always been. Millions of years before there were any eyes to see it, millions of years before any life existed, it grew in its own special way, crystallized along its preordained lines of cleavage, stretched out its pseudo-branches and pseudo-leaves. It was beautiful before beauty itself existed.

We find it difficult to conceive a world except in terms of purpose, of will, or of intention. At the thought of the something without beginning and presumably without end, of something which is, nevertheless, regular though blind, and organized without any end in view, the mind reels. Constituted as we are it is easier to conceive how the slime floating upon the waters might become in time Homo sapiens than it is to imagine how so complex a thing as a crystal could have always been and can always remain just what it is—complicated and perfect but without any meaning, even for itself. How can the lifeless even obey a law?

To a mathematical physicist I once confessed somewhat shame-facedly that I had never been able to understand how inanimate nature managed to follow so invariably and so promptly her own laws. If I flip a coin across a table, it will come to rest at a certain point. But before it stops at just that point, many factors must be taken into consideration. There is the question of the strength of the initial impulse, of the exact amount of resistance offered by the friction of that particular table top, and of the density of the air at the moment. It would take a physicist a long time to work out the problem and he could achieve only an approximation at that. Yet presumably the coin will stop exactly where it should. Some very rapid calculations have to be made before it can do so, and they are, presumably, always accurate.

And then, just as I was blushing at what I supposed he must regard as my folly, the mathematician came to my rescue by informing me that Laplace had been puzzled by exactly the same fact. "Nature laughs at the difficulties of integration," he remarked —and by "integration" he meant, of course, the mathematician's word for the process involved when a man solves one of the differential equations to which he has reduced the laws of motion.

When my Christmas cactus blooms so theatrically a few inches in front of the frost-covered pane, it also is obeying laws but obeying them much less rigidly and in a different way. It blooms at about Christmastime because it has got into the habit of doing so, because, one is tempted to say, it wants to. As a matter of fact it was, this year, not a Christmas cactus but a New Year's cactus, and because of this unpredictability I would like to call it "he," not "it." His flowers assume their accustomed shape and take on their accustomed color. But not as the frostflowers follow their predestined pattern. Like me, the cactus has a history which stretches back over a long past full of changes and developments. He has not always been merely obeying fixed laws. He has resisted and rebelled; he has attempted novelties, passed through many phases. Like all living things he has had a will of his own. He has made laws, not merely obeyed them.

"Life," so the platitudinarian is fond of saying, "is strange." But from our standpoint it is not really so strange as those things which have no life and yet nevertheless move in their predestined orbits and "act" though they do not "behave." At the very least one ought to say that if life is strange there is nothing about it more strange than the fact that it has its being in a universe so astonishingly shared on the one hand by "things" and on the other by "creatures," that man himself is both a "thing" which obeys the laws of chemistry or physics and a "creature" who to some extent defies them. No other contrast, certainly not the contrast between the human being and the animal, or the animal and the plant, or even the spirit and the body, is so tremendous as this contrast between what lives and what does not.

To think of the lifeless as merely inert, to make the contrast merely in terms of a negative, is to miss the real strangeness. Not the shapeless stone which seems to be merely waiting to be acted upon but the snowflake or the frostflower is the true representative of the lifeless universe as opposed to ours. They represent plainly, as the stone does not, the fixed and perfect system of organization which includes the sun and its planets, includes therefore this earth itself, but against which life has set up its seemingly puny opposition. Order and obedience are the primary characteristics of that which is not alive. The snowflake eternally obeys its one and only law: "Be thou six pointed"; the planets their one and only: "Travel thou in an ellipse." The astronomer can tell where the North Star will be ten thousand years hence; the botanist cannot tell where the dandelion will bloom tomorrow.

Life is rebellious and anarchial, always testing the supposed immutability of the rules which the nonliving changelessly accepts. Because the snowflake goes on doing as it was told, its story up to the end of time was finished when it first assumed the form which it has kept ever since. But the story of every living thing is still in the telling. It may hope and it may try. Moreover, though it may succeed or fail, it will certainly change. No form of frostflower ever became extinct. Such, if you like, is its glory. But such also is the fact which makes it alien. It may melt but it cannot die.

If I wanted to contemplate what is to me the deepest of all mysteries, I should choose as my object lesson a snowflake under a lens and an amoeba under the microscope. To a detached observer—if one can possibly imagine any observer who *could* be detached when faced with such an ultimate choice—the snowflake would certainly seem the "higher" of the two. Against its intricate glistening perfection one would have to place a shapeless, slightly turbid glob, perpetually oozing out in this direction or that but not suggesting so strongly as the snowflake does, intelligence and plan. Crystal and colloid, the chemist would call them, but what an inconceivable contrast those neutral terms imply! Like the star, the snowflake seems to declare the glory of God, while the promise of the amoeba, given only perhaps to itself, seems only contemptible. But its jelly holds, nevertheless, not only its promise but ours also, while the snowflake represents some achievement which we cannot possibly share. After the passage of billions of years, one can see and be aware of the other, but the relationship can never be reciprocal. Even after these billions of years no aggregate of colloids can be as beautiful as the crystal always was, but it can know, as the crystal cannot, what beauty is.

E. N. da C. Andrade: *The correct question is, What does electricity?*

From what has been said, it is clear that we must have certain conceptions and laws which we take as fundamental, just as in a game there are certain fundamental rules. If someone asks why it is a fault at lawn tennis if the player's foot is not behind the baseline at the moment of serving, the only possible answer is that that is the way the game is played: the question is a meaningless one if by it the questioner means that he wants an explanation in terms of international law or police regulations. But the question, 'What is electricity?'—so often asked—is just as meaningless, and, to do them justice, the questioners have probably never thought at all about the kind of answer they require. Electricity is one of the fundamental conceptions of physics: it is absurd to expect to be told that it is a kind of liquid, or a known kind of force, when we explain the properties of liquids in terms of electricity, and electric force is perhaps the fundamental con-

From *An Approach to Modern Physics* by E. N. da C. Andrade, pp. 11–12. Copyright 1956 by E. N. da C. Andrade. Reprinted by permission of Doubleday & Co., Inc.

ception of modern physics. The physicist can tell you what he means by an electric charge: he will say that when bodies are in a certain state they repel or attract one another in certain ways, and that then, as a quick way of describing that state, he speaks of the bodies as electrically charged. He can tell you the properties of these charges at rest and in motion: the connection between moving charges and magnetism: the circumstances in which there is a flow of electrical energy: how electrical energy can be converted into other forms of energy: and a thousand such things about electricity. In short, the correct question is, 'What does electricity?' not, 'What is electricity?' The former has a definite meaning, and can be answered: the latter is not a fair question in that the questioner does not really formulate his inquiry in such a way as to convey what he wants to know. If he means 'Can you express what you know about electricity in terms of something more fundamental?' the answer is definitely 'No. We must have in physics something behind which we do not go: if it were not electricity, it would have to be some other conception.'

D. Doubt, Absolute Truth, and Common Sense

Morris R. Cohen: *The feeling of certainty is no guarantee of truth.*

Science, it is generally recognized, is an effort to eliminate baseless opinions and to establish propositions that are supported by evidence or proof. This is commonly expressed by saying that science aims at knowledge that is certain.

The word *certain* in this connection is unfortunate because of the confusion between its logical and psychological senses. Psychologically it denotes a state of feeling, as when we say we are certain that . . . civilization will break down unless our ancient outworn institutions are forthwith abolished. Certainty in this sense is no guarantee of truth, for others feel equally certain of the direct contrary.

So often does our psychologic certainty prevent us from even entering on the pursuit of truth, that it is well to reflect that the *feeling* of certainty is often nothing but our inability to conceive the opposite of what we happen to believe. In this sense there is no certainty as great as the initial one based on complete ignorance of countervailing considerations. Thus men show greater certainty about the complicated and elusive questions of politics and religion than about simpler and more verifiable issues to which they have devoted the prolonged study of the professional expert. The feeling of certainty or conviction is also produced in us by forms of language. Pithy proverbs, the magical utterances of poets, and the sententious remarks of sages or prophets thus

From *Reason and Nature* (2nd ed.; Glencoe, Ill.: The Free Press, 1953), pp. 83–85. Used by permission of Harry N. Rosenfield.

generally carry conviction. But reflection finds that directly opposite views can be expressed just as impressively. . . .

Nor is the feeling of certainty that embodies itself in a con-
sensus of opinion through the ages a guarantee of truth. We need
only think of humanity's certainty about astrology, the existence
of witches, or the impossibility of men walking on the opposite
side of the earth. Neither the extent nor the intensity of the feeling of certainty with which a proposition is held guarantees its
truth.

The certainty which science aims to bring about is not a psychological feeling about a given proposition but a logical ground
on which its claim to truth can be founded. Certainly, if we view
truth not as simply an immediate quality of an assertion in itself,
but as something which has to do with what it means or implies,
doubts about the truth of a given proposition can be met only by
evidence involving its relation to other propositions with which
it is inextricably bound up. In any case we can well say that
science aims to settle doubts or debates between contending
views by showing that a given proposition is the only one logically
tenable or at least that it is better founded than its suggested
alternative. But science does this by the paradoxical or heroic
method of questioning all things that can be questioned, and in
this way it seems to destroy psychologic certainty.

Man's ability to question that which he has from childhood
been taught or accustomed to accept is very limited indeed unless
it is socially cultivated and trained. . . .

The method of science seeks to conquer doubt by cultivating it
and encouraging it to grow until it finds its natural limits and can
go no further.

Ernest Nagel: *It is by recognizing the fallibility of its procedures that science has won its victories.*

And finally, the assumption that there is a superior and more direct way of grasping the secrets of the universe than the painfully slow road of science has been so repeatedly shown to be a romantic illusion, that only those who are unable to profit from the history of the human intellect can seriously maintain it. Certainly, whatever enlightenment we possess about ourselves and the world has been achieved only after the illusion of a "metaphysical wisdom" superior to "mere science" had been abandoned. The methods of science do not guarantee that its conclusions are final and incorrigible by further inquiry; but it is by dropping the pretense of a spurious finality and recognizing the fallibility of its self-corrective procedures that science has won its victories. It may be a comfort to some to learn that in so far as man uses "wisdom" he can aim only at the good; since the most diverse kinds of action—kindly as well as brutal, beneficent as well as costly in human life—are undertaken in the name of wisdom, such a testimonial will doubtless enable everyone engaged in such an undertaking to redouble his zeal without counting the costs. But it is not wisdom but a mark of immaturity to recommend that we simply examine our hearts if we wish to discover the good life; for it is just because men rely so completely and unreflectively on their intuitive insights and passionate impulses that needless sufferings and conflicts occur among them. The point is clear: claims as to what is required by wisdom need to be adjudicated if such claims are to be warranted; and accordingly, objective methods must be instituted, on the basis of which the conditions, the consequences, and the mutual compatibility of different course of action may be established. But if such methods are introduced, we leave the

From *Sovereign Reason* (Glencoe, Ill.: The Free Press, 1954), p. 31. First published in the *Partisan Review*, X, January-February 1943. Reprinted by permission of *Partisan Review* and Mr. Nagel.

miasmal swamps of supra-scientific wisdom, and are brought back again to the firm soil of scientific knowledge.

J. Bronowski: *Dissent is the native activity of the scientist.*

The values of science derive neither from the virtues of its members, nor from the finger-wagging codes of conduct by which every profession reminds itself to be good. They have grown out of the practice of science, because they are the inescapable conditions for its practice.

Science is the creation of concepts and their exploration in the facts. It has no other test of the concept than its empirical truth to fact. Truth is the drive at the center of science; it must have the habit of truth, not as a dogma but as a process. Consider then, step by step, what kind of society scientists have been compelled to form in this single pursuit. If truth is to be found, not given, and if therefore it is to be tested in action, what other conditions (and with them, what other values) grow of themselves from this?

First, of course, comes independence, in observation and thence in thought. I once told an audience of school children that the world would never change if they did not contradict their elders. I was chagrined to find next morning that this axiom outraged their parents. Yet it is the basis of the scientific method. A man must see, do and think things for himself, in the face of those who are sure that they have already been over all that ground. In science, there is no substitute for independence.

It has been a by-product of this that, by degrees, men have come to give a value to the new and the bold in all their work. It was not always so. European thought and art before the Renaissance were happy in the faith that there is nothing new under the sun. . . . Today we find it . . . natural to prize originality . . . Science has bred the love of originality as a mark of independence.

Reprinted by permission of Julian Messner, Inc. from *Science and Human Values*, pp. 77–79. Copyright © 1956 by J. Bronowski.

Independence, originality, and therefore dissent: these words show the progress, they stamp the character of our civilization as once they did that of Athens in flower. . . . the profound movements of history have been begun by unconforming men. Dissent is the native activity of the scientist, and it has got him into a good deal of trouble in the last years. But if that is cut off, what is left will not be a scientist. And I doubt whether it will be a man. For dissent is also native in any society which is still growing. Has there ever been a society which has died of dissent? Several have died of conformity in our lifetime.

Dissent is not itself an end; it is the surface mark of a deeper value. Dissent is the mark of freedom, as originality is the mark of independence of mind. And as originality and independence are private needs for the existence of a science, so dissent and freedom are its public needs. No one can be a scientist, even in private, if he does not have independence of observation and of thought. But if in addition science is to become effective as a public practice, it must go further; it must protect independence. The safeguards which it must offer are patent: free inquiry, free thought, free speech, tolerance. These values are so familiar to us, yawning our way through political perorations, that they seem self-evident. But they are self-evident, that is, they are logical needs, only where men are committed to explore the truth: in a scientific society. These freedoms of tolerance have never been notable in a dogmatic society . . .

Alfred North Whitehead: *A clash of doctrines is an opportunity.*

A clash of doctrines is not a disaster—it is an opportunity. I will explain my meaning by some illustrations from science. The weight of an atom of nitrogen was well known. Also it was an established scientific doctrine that the average weight of such

From *Science and the Modern World* (New York: The Macmillan Co., 1925), pp. 259–60. Used by permission.

atoms in any considerable mass will be always the same. Two experimenters, the late Lord Rayleigh and the late Sir William Ramsay, found that if they obtained nitrogen by two different methods, each equally effective for that purpose, they always observed a persistent slight difference between the average weights of the atoms in the two cases. Now I ask you, would it have been rational of these men to have despaired because of this conflict between chemical theory and scientific observation? Suppose that for some reason the chemical doctrine had been highly prized throughout some district as the foundation of its social order:— would it have been wise, would it have been candid, would it have been moral, to forbid the disclosure of the fact that the experiments produced discordant results? Or, on the other hand, should Sir William Ramsay and Lord Rayleigh have proclaimed that chemical theory was now a detected delusion? We see at once that either of these ways would have been a method of facing the issue in an entirely wrong spirit. What Rayleigh and Ramsay did do was this: They at once perceived that they had hit upon a line of investigation which would disclose some subtlety of chemical theory that had hitherto eluded observation. The discrepancy was not a disaster: it was an opportunity to increase the sweep of chemical knowledge. You all know the end of the story: finally argon was discovered, a new chemical element which had lurked undetected, mixed with the nitrogen. But the story has a sequel which forms my second illustration. This discovery drew attention to the importance of observing accurately minute differences in chemical substances as obtained by different methods. Further researches of the most careful accuracy were undertaken. Finally another physicist, F. W. Aston, working in the Cavendish Laboratory at Cambridge in England, discovered that even the same element might assume two or more distinct forms, termed *isotopes,* and that the law of the constancy of average atomic weight holds for each of these forms, but as between the different isotopes differs slightly. The research has effected a great stride in the power of chemical theory, far transcending in importance the discovery of argon from which it originated. The moral of these stories lies on the surface, and I will leave to you their application to the case of religion and science.

E. N. da C. Andrade: *A scientific theory is true only as long as it is useful.*

Whether the principles [of science] are in the absolute sense true is not a matter on which the man of science, as such, feels called to argue: if their consequences agree with Nature they are true enough to be useful, at any rate. The fundamental principles of science are, therefore, often called *working hypotheses*, since they are devised with the sole purpose of furnishing a basis upon which a system may be built corresponding in appearance with the behaviour of the material world, wherever we are able to make measurements or observations for comparison. We consider that an advance has been made when a wider range of the phenomena which are observed has been brought within the scope of one general principle.

It follows that a scientific theory may be abandoned when it has proved itself insufficient without in any way weakening the general worth of the scientific method. Let us consider for a moment the history of the atomic theory, as an example. Sixty years ago it was generally held that atoms were hard, unbreakable entities, something like exceedingly minute billiard-balls, each element possessing a perfectly definite type of atom, fundamentally different from that of any other element. . . .

Then came the discovery of the electron, which is very much lighter than any atom, and suggested the possibility that the different types of atom might be built up of electrons. . . .

Is the critic, then, justified in reproaching the physicist in this way: *Sixty years ago you told us that atoms were hard, indivisible, and unbreakable, made perfect in the beginning of things, and persisting in unworn perfection ever since. To-day you tell us that atoms are loose structures which can be very easily broken: you speak of radio-active atoms breaking up and changing to simpler*

From *An Approach to Modern Physics* by E. N. da C. Andrade, pp. 2–6. Copyright 1956 by E. N. da C. Andrade. Reprinted by permission of Doubleday & Co., Inc.

atoms, and with your cyclotrons and what not you not only manufacture from one kind of known atom other kinds of known atom,
but even new, hitherto unknown, kinds of atom. You tell us that
the manufacture and breakdown of atoms is an essential part of
the mechanism of the heavens. What are we to believe? Your
accepted theories of one generation are abandoned in the next:
how can I be sure that you are right this time? In my opinion,
the correct answer is that we do not claim any absolute truth for
our theories: we claim, rather, that a theory like our modern
atomic theory has very great merits because most of the phenomena with which we are at present acquainted are just such
as we should expect if it were true.

Nature, in the aspects which the physicist investigates, behaves
as if there were atoms and as if they had the properties which we
now claim for them. The older conception of atoms was good
enough to explain the phenomena then considered, and we can
still use it for certain simpler problems, where introducing the
idea of atomic structure brings in needless complications; but to
explain the facts of atomic change and atomic radiations we must
introduce the newer forms of the atomic theory. We do not claim
any finality for the theory: some new discovery may suddenly
force us to modify our ideas in many particulars, some new discoverer may show that certain complications can be simplified with
advantage, but the successes of the present theory show that we
shall probably have to retain many of its general features. It is an
excellent working hypothesis because it has shown us law where
law was not hitherto discovered, and connections between different phenomena where before we knew of no connection. It has
enabled us to arrange our known facts in a more convenient and
logical way, and has pointed the way to the discovery of very
interesting new facts. It is justified by its works, but it is not final.
Science is a living thing, and living things develop. . . .

On this view, any particular scientific theory is a provisional
tool with which we carve knowledge of the material world out of
the block of Nature. It may at any moment be supplanted by an
improved version or by a completely new theory, but this is only
to say that when we get a better tool, which does all that this one
does and something more as well, we will abandon our present

tool. To refuse to use a tool because some day a better one may be invented is folly: in the same way, not to make use of a theory which has been proved capable of explaining a great many facts, and of suggesting new lines of research, because it has acknowledged flaws, and is incapable of explaining other facts, would be folly. To use another metaphor, the history of science may, as has been said, be full of beautiful theories slain by ugly little facts, but those theories did not die in vain if before their death they had subdued a vast number of jarring facts into a law-abiding populace. Nor do theories generally die a final death: often they are resurrected with some new feature which gets over the old difficulty.

The difference, then, between any religious belief and a scientific theory is that the former has for the believers an element of absolute truth: it is a standard by which they stand or fall, and to abandon it is dishonour and sin. The scientific theory is, however, only true as long as it is useful. The man of science regards even his best theory as a makeshift device to help him on his way, and is always on the lookout for something better and more comprehensive.

Nicholas Murray Butler: *The intellectual life begins when common sense is left behind.*

There are three separate stages or orders of thinking manifested by man. At the first stage, the human mind sees only a world of separate and independent objects. These objects are grouped in certain roughly marked visible and audible ways, or by the pleasure or pain, the comfort or discomfort, that they cause; but their likenesses and unlikenesses and their possible interrelationships are of very subordinate importance. They in no wise limit, alter, or interfere with the separateness of the objects

From "Philosophy" in *Lectures on Science, Philosophy and Art* (New York: Columbia Univ. Press, 1908), pp. 9–12. Used by permission.

themselves or with what is called their reality. Each elm tree
seems a real object, an integer, an independent thing. A falling
apple suggests not a universal law of nature but a means of gratifying an individual appetite. Such relations as one of these separate things appears to have, are looked upon as quite secondary,
even if they are apprehended at all. This is the stage of naïve,
uncritical knowledge. It lies below the horizon of the intellectual
life. It is characteristic of the child and of the countless millions
of unreflecting adults. It has been dignified by the name common
sense. Its proper designation is common ignorance. The intellectual life begins when it is left behind.

At the second stage or order of thinking the world appears as
something quite different. Instead of a world of fixed and definite
objects whose interrelations are unimportant, the mind now sees
that every thing is in relation to every other thing and that relations are of massive significance, indeed that they are controlling.
The elm tree, far from being a simple and single unit, is now
recognized as an organic form of being, a congeries of cells, of
atoms of carbon, of oxygen, of hydrogen, no one of which the
unaided human eye can see, much less the untutored human
mind grasp. A falling apple no longer suggests merely the gratifi-
cation of an appetite; it illustrates the laws which bind the universe into coherent unity. So-called common sense is staggered
by the revelations that this higher form of knowing presses upon
it and insists that it accept, with or without comprehension. It is
now seen that no object is independent. Each depends on every
other, and dependence, relativity, is the controlling principle of
the universe. Under the guidance of Newton, reinforced by the
discoveries of a Helmholtz and a Kelvin, this stage or order of
knowing now goes so far as to say that dependence, relativity, is
so absolute, that if even the slightest of objects be disturbed in
position or altered in mass, the outermost rim of the material universe will be affected thereby; and measurably so, if only our
instruments of precision were able for the task. The point of view,
the method and the results of this second stage or order of knowing are science.

It can now be seen how little truth there is in Huxley's much-
quoted dictum that science is organized common sense. That is

precisely what science is not. Science is a wholly different kind of knowledge from common sense, and it contradicts common sense at almost every point. To common sense, the sun revolves about the earth; to science, the contrary is established fact. To common sense, a plank is still and stable; to science it is a huge group of rapidly revolving centers of energy. To common sense, water is a true element; to science, it is a compound of atoms of the familiar hydrogen and oxygen. To common sense, the Rosetta stone is a bit of rock covered with more or less regular markings, probably for a decorative purpose; to science it is the key to a forgotten language and the open door to the knowledge of a lost civilization. Even when common sense recognizes certain simple relations of dependence, it has no realization of their meaning and it is without the power of analysis needed to climb to the higher plane of science. Here rule the stern laws that scientific knowing has discovered in its objects. The laws of cause and effect, of the persistence of force, of the indestructibility of matter —these and their derivatives bring the known world of relations and related objects under their sway. Anxiously, eagerly, untiringly, one field of intellectual interest after another is added to the domain of science, familiar facts are explained by strange and unfamiliar laws, the obvious and the apparent are traced back to hidden and indeed invisible causes. The human mind, as intelligent, glows with pride at the glad discovery that the nature which invites and tempts it is intelligible, that it is made in the mind's own image.

At the third stage or order of knowing the world or cosmos appears in still another aspect. It is now seen as Totality. When the world is viewed as Totality there is obviously nothing to which it can be related, nothing on which it can be dependent, no source from which its energy can be derived. We pass, therefore, at this stage of knowing, from the plane of interdependence, relativity, to the plane of self-dependence, self-relation, self-activity. Self-active Totality is the source or origin of all the energies and forces and motions which in one manifestation or another are observed in their interrelations and interdependences by the stage or order of knowing which is science. The unrefuted and, I venture to think, the irrefutable arguments of Plato in the Tenth

Book of the *Laws* and of Aristotle in the Eleventh Book of the *Metaphysics*, supported by twenty-five centuries of human experience and the insights of one great thinker, poet and spiritual leader after another, are the foundation on which this third stage or order of knowing rests. Its habit of mind, its standpoint, and its insights are philosophy. Just as science is marked off from common sense and raised above it by analysis and the laws of relativity, so philosophy is marked off from science and raised above it by farther analysis and the laws of self-relation. In proceeding from common sense to science we exchange a chaos of separate units for an ordered whole of interdependent parts; in proceeding from science to philosophy we exchange the working hypotheses of the understanding for the guiding insights of the reason.

SOCIAL DISCIPLINES

A. Reason, Ideals, and Action

William K. Clifford: *It is always wrong to believe any-thing upon insufficient evidence.*

A shipowner was about to send to sea an emigrant-ship. He knew that she was old, and not over-well built at the first; that she had seen many seas and climes, and often had needed repairs. Doubts had been suggested to him that possibly she was not sea-worthy. These doubts preyed upon his mind and made him un-happy; he thought that perhaps he ought to have her thoroughly overhauled and refitted, even though this should put him to great expense. Before the ship sailed, however, he succeeded in over-coming these melancholy reflections. He said to himself that she had gone safely through so many voyages and weathered so many storms that it was idle to suppose she would not come safely home from this trip also. He would put his trust in Providence, which could hardly fail to protect all these unhappy families that were leaving their fatherland to seek for better times elsewhere. He would dismiss from his mind all ungenerous suspicions about the honesty of builders and contractors. In such ways he acquired a sincere and comfortable conviction that his vessel was thoroughly safe and seaworthy; he watched her departure with a light heart, and benevolent wishes for the success of the exiles in their strange new home that was to be; and he got his insurance-money when she went down in mid-ocean and told no tales.

What shall we say of him? Surely this, that he was verily guilty of the death of those men. It is admitted that he did sincerely believe in the soundness of his ship; but the sincerity of his con-viction can in no wise help him, because *he had no right to believe on such evidence as was before him.* He had acquired his belief

From "The Ethics of Belief" available in *Lectures and Essays* (London: Watts & Co., 1918), pp. 95+.

not by honestly earning it in patient investigation, but by stifling his doubts. And although in the end he may have felt so sure about it that he could not think otherwise, yet inasmuch as he had knowingly and willingly worked himself into that frame of mind, he must be held responsible for it.

Let us alter the case a little, and suppose that the ship was not unsound after all; that she made her voyage safely, and many others after it. Will that diminish the guilt of her owner? Not one jot. When an action is once done, it is right or wrong for ever; no accidental failure of its good or evil fruits can possibly alter that. The man would not have been innocent, he would only have been not found out. The question of right or wrong has to do with the origin of his belief, not the matter of it; not what it was, but how he got it; not whether it turned out to be true or false, but whether he had a right to believe on such evidence as was before him. . . .

To sum up: it is wrong always, everywhere, and for any one, to believe anything upon insufficient evidence.

William James: *There are cases where faith in a fact can help create the fact.*

There are two ways of looking at our duty in the matter of opinion,—ways entirely different, and yet ways about whose difference the theory of knowledge seems hitherto to have shown very little concern. *We must know the truth;* and *we must avoid error,*—these are our first and great commandments as would-be knowers; but they are not two ways of stating an identical commandment, they are two separable laws . . . and by choosing between them we may end by coloring differently our whole intellectual life. We may regard the chase for truth as paramount, and the avoidance of error as secondary; or we may, on the other hand, treat the avoidance of error as more imperative, and let

From *The Will to Believe* (New York: Longmans, Green & Co., Inc., 1909), pp. 17–25.

truth take its chance. Clifford . . . exhorts us to the latter course. Believe nothing, he tells us, keep your mind in suspense forever, rather than by closing it on insufficient evidence incur the awful risk of believing lies. You, on the other hand, may think that the risk of being in error is a very small matter when compared with the blessings of real knowledge, and be ready to be duped many times in your investigation rather than postpone indefinitely the chance of guessing true. I myself find it impossible to go with Clifford.

. . . of course, I agree as far as the facts will allow. Wherever the option between losing truth and gaining it is not momentous, we can throw the chance of *gaining truth* away, and at any rate save ourselves from any chance of *believing falsehood*, by not making up our minds at all till objective evidence has come. In scientific questions, this is almost always the case . . . What difference, indeed, does it make to most of us whether we have or have not a theory of the Röntgen rays, whether we believe or not in mind-stuff, or have a conviction about the causality of conscious states? It makes no difference. Such options are not forced on us. On every account it is better not to make them, but still keep weighing reasons *pro et contra* with an indifferent hand.

I speak, of course, here of the purely judging mind. For purposes of discovery such indifference is to be less highly recommended . . . Let us agree, however, that wherever there is no forced option, the dispassionately judicial intellect with no pet hypothesis, saving us, as it does, from dupery at any rate, ought to be our ideal.

The question next arises: Are there not somewhere forced options in our speculative questions, and can we (as men who may be interested at least as much in positively gaining truth as in merely escaping dupery) always wait with impunity till the coercive evidence shall have arrived? It seems *a priori* improbable that the truth should be so nicely adjusted to our needs and powers as that. . . .

Moral questions immediately present themselves as questions whose solution cannot wait for sensible proof. A moral question is a question not of what sensibly exists, but of what is good, or would be good if it did exist. Science can tell us what exists; but to compare the *worths*, both of what exists and of what does not exist, we must consult not science, but what Pascal calls our heart. Science herself consults her heart when she lays it down that the infinite ascertainment of fact and correction of false belief are the supreme goods for man. Challenge the statement, and science can only repeat it oracularly, or else prove it by showing that such ascertainment and correction bring man all sorts of other goods which man's heart in turn declares. The question of having moral beliefs at all or not having them is decided by our will. Are our moral preferences true or false, or are they only odd biological phenomena, making things good or bad for *us*, but in themselves indifferent? How can your pure intellect decide? If your heart does not *want* a world of moral reality, your head will assuredly never make you believe in one. . . .

Turn now from these wide questions of good to a certain class of questions of fact, questions concerning personal relations, states of mind between one man and another. *Do you like me or not?*— for example. Whether you do or not depends, in countless instances, on whether I meet you half-way, am willing to assume that you must like me, and show you trust and expectation. The previous faith on my part in your liking's existence is in such cases what makes your liking come. But if I stand aloof, and refuse to budge an inch until I have objective evidence . . . ten to one your liking never comes. How many women's hearts are vanquished by the mere sanguine insistence of some man that they *must* love him! he will not consent to the hypothesis that they cannot. The desire for a certain kind of truth here brings about that special truth's existence; and so it is in innumerable cases of other sorts. Who gains promotions, boons, appointments, but the man in whose life they are seen to play the part of live hypotheses, who discounts them, sacrifices other things for their sake before they have come, and takes risks for them in advance? His faith acts on the powers above him as a claim, and creates its own verification.

A social organism of any sort whatever, large or small, is what it is because each member proceeds to his own duty with a trust that the other members will simultaneously do theirs. Wherever a desired result is achieved by the co-operation of many independent persons, its existence as a fact is a pure consequence of the precursive faith in one another of those immediately concerned. A government, an army, a commercial system, a ship, a college, an athletic team, all exist on this condition, without which not only is nothing achieved, but nothing is even attempted. A whole train of passengers (individually brave enough) will be looted by a few highwaymen, simply because the latter can count on one another, while each passenger fears that if he makes a movement of resistance, he will be shot before any one else backs him up. If we believed that the whole car-full would rise at once with us, we should each severally rise, and train-robbing would never even be attempted. There are, then, cases where a fact cannot come at all unless a preliminary faith exists in its coming. *And where faith in a fact can help create the fact,* that would be an insane logic which should say that faith running ahead of scientific evidence is the 'lowest kind of immorality' into which a thinking being can fall. Yet such is the logic by which our scientific absolutists pretend to regulate our lives!

Harold Child: *A Utopia begs the question of moral improvement.*

. . . we find certain features common to all. There is no war, except in More's Utopia and in Lytton's, where the happy state of the particular society is protected, when need arises, by a pleasant little war of aggression on peoples less well equipped. There is very little law, since everyone seems agreed that one law leads to another, and that with a little common sense it would be quite easy to get on without them. Government is always carried on in Utopia for the good of the governed by disinterested people who regard office as a bore or, like Mr. Wells's Samurai, as a lofty and exacting duty. There is plenty for everybody,

From "Some English Utopias" in *Essays by Divers Hands* (London: Oxford Univ. Press, 1933), XII, 57–60. Sponsored by the Royal Society of Literature.

whether it comes of itself, as it rather seems to do in Morris's
Nowhere, or is produced by universal and very well organized
labour, using the very best of scientific and mechanical means.
And thus is human life to be brought nearer to perfection. But is
it? Is there not something which nearly all of them have forgotten? Someone is said to have said that you cannot make people
virtuous by Act of Parliament, to which Mr. Bernard Shaw has
somewhere replied to the effect that it is the only way in which
you can make them virtuous. You can, indeed, thus prevent them
acting viciously; but the law always follows, not leads, public
opinion, and new laws are always having to be invented to stop
the holes which human greed and folly are always ingenious
enough to find in the old laws. And there lies the gap, there is the
great gulf fixed between the world that we know and even the
most practical and least ambitious of our Utopias—Mr. Wells's, for
instance. In Hazlitt's words: "Utopia stands where it did—a great
way off indeed". Because in every single one of them the human
heart has already been changed. Reason, good sense, natural virtue, goodwill, inner light, whatever name it is called by, which
we have met in all these Utopias—it is that which causes the improvement; and there are moments when the very wisest of all
our visionaries seems to be old Bishop Godwin in the character
of Domingo Gonsales, the little Spaniard, who roundly says that
his Moon people were perfect, or Graham, who all but destroys
the human race. Hudson had the courage to free his people of
greed and lust and envy, and to accept the next inevitable step,
which was to make them but half alive. "The ending of passion
and strife", said he with a sad wisdom, "is the beginning of decay".
Morris, too, glanced at that in one episode, and looked hurriedly
away. All the others merely improve the conditions of life, and
leave it to be understood that the old reactions have ceased to
follow; but this is no explanation. It is a moral begging of the
question. For in every one of these Utopias there is inequality of
some sort; and where there is inequality, unless the human heart
is changed, there will be greed and envy and possessiveness and
emulation. Again, a little extra pressure of population—without
any feeble neighbour whose country can be absorbed—and your
Outopia will be no *Eutopia!* And not one of our authors will tell

us what we most want to know: how *did* the human heart so change that Man became able to maintain the conditions in which you see him? Well might Milton cry out: "To sequester out of the world into *Atlantic* and *Eutopian* politics, which never can be drawn to use, will not mend our condition; but to ordain wisely as in this world of evil, in the midst whereof God hath placed us unavoidably".

Then, has all their work been wasted? By no means.

Although Utopias may be no use, although they are "a great way off, indeed", although no statesman nor moralist ever thinks of them when he is faced with practical problems, such books as 'Utopia', 'News from Nowhere', 'New Atlantis', 'Erewhon', 'A Crystal Age' are powers. They are literature. They are a means of enlarging, enriching, intensifying the life of each one that reads them.

C. Delisle Burns: *An ideal cannot be understood by mere intellectual analysis.*

The life of every people, in so far as it is not simply formed by circumstances, is governed by their ideals. An ideal is less violent and less unconsidered than a desire or an expectation, and thus it may have less place than passion in moving men to action. But the action to which it moves is progressive, whereas the violence of passion or the inconsiderateness of expectation may destroy almost as often as it urges men forward. An ideal is an emotionally coloured conception of a state of things which would be better than the present. It is, in a sense, intellectual because it is due to a perception of present evils and future possibilities; but it is not a complete programme for action, for a man influenced by an ideal may often stumble over obstacles to its realization because he has not any definite method of attaining what he desires. On the other hand, an ideal must be emotionally appreciated. It is not

From *Greek Ideals* (London: G. Bell & Sons, Ltd., 1919), pp. v–vi. Used by permission.

the kind of reality which can be understood by mere calculation or intellectual analysis. It moves because it is desired. But although ideals of every kind originate in the clear thought or deep emotion of individuals, they are powerful only when many are moved by them. The common experience seems to them to produce a common vision.

Walter Lippmann: *When there is panic in the air, there is no chance for the constructive use of reason.*

Whenever we make an appeal to reason in politics, the difficulty in this parable recurs. For there is an inherent difficulty about using the method of reason to deal with an unreasoning world. Even if you assume with Plato that the true pilot knows what is best for the ship, you have to recall that he is not so easy to recognize, and that this uncertainty leaves a large part of the crew unconvinced. By definition the crew does not know what he knows, and the pilot, fascinated by the stars and winds, does not know how to make the crew realize the importance of what he knows. There is no time during mutiny at sea to make each sailor an expert judge of experts. There is no time for the pilot to consult his crew and find out whether he is really as wise as he thinks he is. For education is a matter of years, the emergency a matter of hours. It would be altogether academic, then, to tell the pilot that the true remedy is, for example, an education that will endow sailors with a better sense of evidence. You can tell that only to shipmasters on dry land. In the crisis, the only advice is to use a gun, or make a speech, utter a stirring slogan, offer a compromise, employ any quick means available to quell the mutiny, the sense of evidence being what it is. It is only on shore where men plan for many voyages, that they can afford to, and must for their own salvation, deal with those causes that take a long time

From *Public Opinion* (New York: The Macmillan Co., 1957), pp. 413–15. Used by permission.

to remove. They will be dealing in years and generations, not in emergencies alone. And nothing will put a greater strain upon their wisdom than the necessity of distinguishing false crises from real ones. For when there is panic in the air, with one crisis tripping over the heels of another, actual dangers mixed with imaginary scares, there is no chance at all for the constructive use of reason, and any order soon seems preferable to any disorder.

It is only on the premise of a certain stability over a long run of time that men can hope to follow the method of reason. This is not because mankind is inept, or because the appeal to reason is visionary, but because the evolution of reason on political subjects is only in its beginnings. Our rational ideas in politics are still large, thin generalities, much too abstract and unrefined for practical guidance, except where the aggregates are large enough to cancel out individual peculiarity and exhibit large uniformities. Reason in politics is especially immature in predicting the behavior of individual men, because in human conduct the smallest initial variation often works out into the most elaborate differences. That, perhaps, is why when we try to insist solely upon an appeal to reason in dealing with sudden situations, we are broken and drowned in laughter.

P. W. Bridgman: *Social scientists lack a disinterested point of view.*

The first observation I want to venture from the outside is the difference in general atmosphere between the physical and the social disciplines. It seems to me that in the social sciences there is lacking, to such a large extent as to make a difference in the general atmosphere, that disinterested point of view which in the physical sciences we associate with so-called pure science as distinguished from applied science. There has been much discussion as to the difference between pure and applied science, and some

From "The Strategy of the Social Sciences" in *Reflections of a Physicist* (New York: Philosophical Library, 1955), pp. 442–43. Used by permission.

people even do not recognize a difference at all. I think that although for some purposes it may be a mistake to try to make the distinction, nevertheless one who has worked in the subject can recognize differences which, for some purposes at least, it is profitable to emphasize. A pure scientist is primarily interested in understanding phenomena which confront him, without any regard for their practical application. I realize that even the pure scientist has a mixture of attitudes; but in as far as he is a "pure" scientist there is a large component of sheer intellectual curiosity. Standing on the outside, and I may be entirely wrong in this, it seems to me that the social sciences do not include very many men who have this disinterested attitude. The reason is easy enough to see. All the social sciences have practical applications, and the need of solving the problems of the present is so desperate that it is almost inevitable that the demand for immediate application should obscure purely intellectual interest. That seems to me a statement of fact.

What you can do about it I do not know, but I think it must be recognized as one of the handicaps that social scientists have to struggle against. I think it is a fact of human nature, proved by experience, that for the long view the best way to get things done, the surest way to make progress into new domains, is to start from the point of view of purely intellectual curiosity without immediate regard for practical application. Seldom in history is it that a successful solution of a complicated problem has come by direct frontal attack. The other things came first, and the solution which was eventually found came more or less incidentally.

George Stuart Fullerton: *Man lives first and thinks afterwards.*

When William James published his lecture on the "Will to Believe," that declaration of the Rights of Man . . . the bold assertion of the right to permit faith to rise to a height unattainable

From *The World We Live In* (New York: The Macmillan Co., 1912), pp. 262–63. Used by permission.

by indubitable evidence seemed to strengthen a claim very dear
to the heart, and which mankind has urged from time immemorial.
Men have always guided their lives in accordance with the principle; here they find themselves justified.

What men have done, and what men do, we have only to open
our eyes to see for ourselves. In the gradual evolution of a social
order which has resulted in making the life of man something
different from the existence of the brute, conscious reasoning has
undoubtedly played its part. No one would dream of denying
that. Nor, I suppose, would any one care to deny that it is desirable that men should see clearly, and should be capable of regarding critically their own lives and the social order in which they
are imbedded. But to suppose that there ever has been a time in
which the social, political, and ethical faiths which have animated
men's actions have been based wholly upon marshaled evidence,
and have been given their distinctive outlines as a result of explicit reasonings, is to betray an ignorance of man that seems little
excusable. Man lives first and thinks afterwards; he desires, and
he then becomes partially conscious of what it is that he desires;
he wills, and it is only with effort that he attains to a clear realization of what it is that he wills. All is not in the foreground of the
picture, all lines are not sharp and hard; there are mysterious
depths and shadowy outlines which he feels rather than sees, but
which cannot be left out of account by one who would appreciate
justly the significance of the whole.

Take men as they are. How many men are in a position to give
explicit reasons for the implicitly accepted maxims which guide
their daily lives? for the exceptions which they make in the applications of such? for their likes and dislikes? for their approval of
certain innovations? for the instinct which warns them that certain
others will result in loss and not in gain? When they are asked to
justify their attitude, they usually adduce reasons which really
have very little to do with motives which actually impel them—
superficial reasons, plausible reasons, reasons which sound well in
discussion, but are of little actual significance. The complicated
system of forces, the total outcome of which is the social order
which embraces us and supports us, does not lie wholly in the
light of day. To throw light upon it, so far as we can, is a manifest

duty; to ignore all that is not brightly illuminated, and to reason consequently upon such a basis, argues a keen but a narrow and unsympathetic mind, and a courage not easy to differentiate from obstinacy.

George Santayana: *Importance springs from the cry of life, not from reason.*

. . . reason, taken psychologically, is an old inherited passion like any other, the passion for consistency and order; and it is just as prone as the other passions to overstep the modesty of nature and to regard its own aims as alone important. But this is ridiculous; because importance springs from the stress of nature, from the cry of life, not from reason and its pale prescriptions. Reason cannot stand alone; brute habit and blind play are at the bottom of art and morals, and unless irrational impulses and fancies are kept alive, the life of reason collapses for sheer emptiness. What tragedy could there be, or what sublime harmonies rising out of tragedy, if there were no spontaneous passions to create the issue, no wild voices to be reduced to harmony? Moralists have habitually aimed at suppression, wisely perhaps at first, when they were preaching to men of spirit; but why continue to harp on propriety and unselfishness and labour, when we are little but labour-machines already, and have hardly any self or any passions left to indulge? Perhaps the time has come to suspend those exhortations, and to encourage us to be sometimes a little lively, and see if we can invent something worth saying or doing. We should then be living in the spirit of comedy, and the world would grow young. Every occasion would don its comic mask, and make its bold grimace at the world for a moment. . . .

Objections to the comic mask—to the irresponsible, complete, extreme expression of each moment—cut at the roots of all expression. Pursue this path, and at once you do away with gesture: we

From *Soliloquies in England* (New York: Charles Scribner's Sons, 1924), pp. 137–39. Used by permission of Daniel Cory.

must not point, we must not pout, we must not cry, we must not laugh aloud; we must not only avoid attracting attention, but our attention must not be obviously attracted; it is silly to gaze, says the nursery-governess, and rude to stare. Presently words, too, will be reduced to a telegraphic code. A man in his own country will talk like the laconic tourist abroad; his whole vocabulary will be *Où? Combien? All right! Dear me!* Conversation in the quiet home will dispense even with these phrases; nothing will be required but a few pragmatic grunts and signals for action. Where the spirit of comedy has departed, company becomes constraint, reserve eats up the spirit, and people fall into a penurious melancholy in their scruple to be always exact, sane, and reasonable, never to mourn, never to glow, never to betray a passion or a weakness, nor venture to utter a thought they might not wish to harbour for ever. . . .

What, on the contrary, could be more splendidly sincere than the impulse to play in real life, to rise on the rising wave of every feeling and let it burst, if it will, into the foam of exaggeration? Life is not a means, the mind is not a slave nor a photograph: it has a right to enact a pose, to assume a *panache*, and to create what prodigious allegories it will for the mere sport and glory of it. . . . To embroider upon experience is not to bear false witness against one's neighbour, but to bear true witness to oneself. Fancy is playful and may be misleading to those who try to take it for literal fact; but literalness is impossible in any utterance of spirit, and if it were possible it would be deadly. Why should we quarrel with human nature, with metaphor, with myth, with impersonation? The foolishness of the simple is delightful; only the foolishness of the wise is exasperating.

L. T. Hobhouse: *The psychologist descends upon the mother with the intellectualist fallacy.*

The further we go into questions of origin and development the less we shall be disposed to admit the abstract and absolute separation of the worlds of thought and feeling. On the contrary, the evidence goes to show that intelligence takes its rise within the sphere of impulse, and has for its first function to define the direction of impulse, and shape it to a foreseen End. Impulse, informed by a definite idea of an End, becomes Purpose, and Purpose is at least the beginning of rationality in action. . . . The significance of the act to the agent may then be only a very small part of its significance as understood by the psychologist who traces it to causes of which the agent is unaware and knows that it performs a function which the agent does not grasp. At this point the psychologist is tempted to maintain that the act is irrational unless the reasons which he sees for it are also those which the agent sees. But this is an arbitrary requirement. The truer inference is that the sphere of intelligence—we will not here say "reason"—in action varies in extent as the bearing and significance of the act is more or less clearly and fully understood. It is fallacious to attribute to every agent a full understanding of all the logical implications of all that he does. It is equally fallacious to maintain that he understands nothing on the ground that he does not understand everything.

To take a simple instance. A mother nurses her querulous baby to sleep. The plain man regards her action as purposive and intelligent. She loves the child, cannot bear to see it fret, knows how to quiet it, and does so. The ease of the child is her direct purpose, and so she herself would say. The psychologist descends upon the plain man, and the mother alike with the intellectualist fallacy. For him her action is instinctive and emotional. It is the impulsive outcome of the maternal feeling nourished through ages

From *The Rational Good* (London: George Allen & Unwin, Ltd., 1921), pp. 30–32. Used by permission.

of selection as a means of securing maternal care for the helpless young. It is rooted in a hereditary mechanism. The embraces and caresses by which it is effected are the instinctive, almost reflex, responses fixed by the inherited machine, and its significance is seen in the importance of maternal care to the life of the species. Of all this the mother, as mother, recks nothing. She is thinking only of the child and its immediate comfort. She is acting, then, not from reason, but from impulse. But this account is really the intellectualist fallacy itself, turned inside out. The mother is not concerned with all the causes that have made her what she is, nor with all the effects which will flow from her actions. But those causes have made her an intelligent being with a certain area of purpose, within which she consciously adopts whatever means she finds best suited within that area. If it is an intellectualist fallacy to say that she acts from a conscious sense of the functions of motherhood, it is another form of the same fallacy—since it assumes that what is rational in action must be deduced from abstract principles, independent of impulse-feeling—to maintain that, unless she does so, she is acting by pure impulse. The simple truth in that case lies with the "plain man." The mother acts intelligently for the purpose that she has in view, not on the theory which psychologists may frame about the origin or signification of such purposes.

Crane Brinton: *Those who think ideals are of no use are very much mistaken.*

How do ideas work in this world? Any answer must take into account the fact that often *ideas* are really *ideals*—expressions of hopes and aspirations, goals of human desire and effort. We say, for instance, that "all men are created equal," or, with the poet Keats,

> "Beauty is truth, truth beauty,"—that is all
> Ye know on earth, and all ye need to know.

From *Ideas and Men: The Story of Western Thought* (Englewood Cliffs, N. J.: Prentice-Hall, Inc., 1950), pp. 15–17. Used by permission.

What can statements like these mean? If you assert that a heavy weight and a lighter weight will drop through the air at different rates, you can drop them from a height and see. Galileo did this, though not, we now know, from the Leaning Tower of Pisa. Witnesses can also see, and should agree after they have checked what they saw. But you cannot possibly test the assertion of human equality or the identity of truth and beauty in any such fashion, and you can be very sure that after argument on such propositions, a random sample of human beings will not in fact agree about them.

In a general way, the kind of knowledge we have called cumulative, that is, scientific knowledge, is subject to the kind of test that makes it possible for all sane, properly trained men to agree upon its truth or falsehood; and the kind of knowledge we have called non-cumulative is not subject to such a test, nor capable of producing such an agreement. Hence, as stated earlier, some have concluded that non-cumulative knowledge is of no use, is not really knowledge, has no meaning, and, above all, has no real effect on human behavior. These people often fancy themselves as hard-boiled realists, as sensible people who know what the world really is like. They are actually very mistaken people, as narrow-minded as the most innocent of the idealists they condemn.

For, at the very least, a proposition like "all men are created equal" means that somebody *wants* all men to be equal in some respects. In the form "all men ought to be equal" the proposition would be frankly what we call an ideal. This confusion of "ought" and "is" turns out for the intellectual historian to be another of the abiding habits of men thinking. Moreover, he will realize that "ought" and "is" influence one another mutually, are parts of a whole process, not independent, and not—at least not often— mutually contradictory. Indeed, he will know that the effort to close the gap between ideal and real, between "ought" and "is," supplies one of the main interests of intellectual history. The gap has never been closed, certainly not by idealists who deny the "is," nor by realists who deny the "ought." Men do not consistently act in logical (rational) accordance with their professed ideals; here the realist scores. But their professed ideals are not meaning-

less, and thinking about ideals is not a silly and ineffective activity
that has no effect on their lives. Ideals, as well as appetites, push
men into action; here the idealist scores.

Irwin Edman: *To be effective, moral standards must have emotional support.*

Reflection upon morals, even when it goes beyond the stage of
criticism and proceeds to the reconstruction of habits and customs
upon a more reasonable basis, is yet inadequate. However logically convincing a code of morals may be, it is not efficacious
simply as logic. . . .

Moral standards, in order to be effective, must have emotional
support and be constantly applied. Men must be in love with the
good, if good is to be their habitual practice. And only when the
good is an habitual practice, can men be said to be living a moral
life instead of merely subscribing verbally to a set of moral ideals.
Justice, honesty, charity, mercy, benevolence, these are names for
types of behavior, and are real in so far as they do describe men's
actions. . . . The virtues are not static or frozen; they are names
we give to varieties of action, and are exhibited, as they exist,
only in action.

The mere preaching of virtue will thus not produce its practice.
Those standards which reflection discovers, however useful in the
guidance of life, are not sufficient to improve human conduct.
They must, as noted above, be emotionally sanctioned to become
habitual . . . Great thinkers upon morals have not been content to
work out interesting systems which were logically conclusive,
abstract methods of attaining happiness. They have worked out
their ethical systems as genuinely preferred ways of life, they
have offered them as solutions of the difficulties men experience
in controlling their own passions and in adapting their desires to
the conditions which limit their fulfillment.

From *Human Traits and Their Social Significance* (Boston: Houghton
Mifflin Company, 1920), pp. 435–38. Used by permission.

. . . the greatest ethical reformers have not been those who have convinced men through the impeccability of their logic. They have been rather the supreme seers, the Hebrew prophets, Christ, Saint Francis, who have won followers not so much by the conclusiveness of their demonstration as through the persuasive fervor and splendor of their vision.

Leo Tolstoy: *Every human action is conceived by us as a combination of free will and necessity.*

Whatever presentation of the activity of one man or of several persons we examine, we always regard it as the product partly of that man or men's free will, partly of the laws of necessity.

Whether we are discussing the migrations of peoples and the inroads of barbarians, or the government of Napoleon III, or the action of some man an hour ago in selecting one direction for his walk out of several, we see nothing contradictory in it. The proportion of freedom and necessity guiding the actions of those men is clearly defined for us.

Very often our conception of a greater or less degree of freedom differs according to the different points of view from which we regard the phenomenon.

But every human action is always alike conceived by us as a certain combination of free will and necessity.

In every action we investigate, we see a certain proportion of freedom and a certain proportion of necessity. And whatever action we investigate, the more necessity we see, the less freedom, and the more freedom, the less necessity.

The proportion of freedom to necessity is decreased or increased, according to the point of view from which the act is regarded; but there always remains an inverse ratio between them.

A drowning man clutching at another and drowning him, or a hungry mother starved by suckling her baby and stealing food,

From *War and Peace.* Available in Modern Library edition (New York: Random House), p. 1136.

or a man trained to discipline who at the word of command kills a defenceless man, all seem less guilty—that is, less free and more subject to the law of necessity to one who knows the circumstances in which they are placed, and more free to one who did not know that the man was himself drowning, that the mother was starving, that the soldier was on duty, and so on. In the same way a man who has twenty years ago committed a murder and afterwards has gone on living calmly and innocently in society seems less guilty, and his acts seem more subject to the law of necessity, to one who looks at his act after the lapse of twenty years than to one looking at the same act the day after it was perpetrated. And just in the same way the act of a madman, a drunkard, or a man labouring under violent excitement seems less free and more inevitable to one who knows the mental condition of the man who performed the action, and more free and less inevitable to one who does not know it. In all such cases the conception of freedom is increased or diminished, and that of necessity correspondingly diminished or increased, according to the point of view from which the action is regarded. So that the more necessity is seen in it the less freedom. And *vice versa*.

F. Ernest Johnson: *Facts may get in the way of truth.*

I suggest that truth gets its meaning not from correspondence to a preconceived arrangement of the "facts" in the subject matter field, but from what the proposition in question does to the value structure to which it is relevant. A factual narrative leaves the situation as it was. Finding the truth involves restructuring the field of our awareness of the situation. It is reconstructive, often ethically redemptive. Thus the saintly Bishop Bienvenu in Victor Hugo's great novel coolly fabricates a story to save a thief from arrest, and says to him, "Jean Valjean, my brother, you belong no longer to evil, but to good. It is your soul that I am buying

From "Fact, Fiction, and Reality" in *Conflict of Loyalties*, ed. R. M. MacIver (New York: Harper & Bros., 1952), pp. 27–28.

for you. I withdraw it from dark thoughts and from the spirit of perdition and I give it to God." The virtue of truth is somehow related to justice and equity. From this viewpoint, facts may actually get in the way of truth.

It is related that a British contemporary of Lloyd George was once asked what sort of man the celebrated Welshman was. "Well," he answered, "I'll tell you. He's the sort of man that won't stand any nonsense from some damn fact." Admittedly that pithy remark is susceptible of more than one interpretation. Yet, it does point to an important aspect of life: that meaning and significance are never found in factual fragments isolated from the context of human experience in which they occur.

It would be an egregious error, however, to suppose that this approach to the problem of truth and truthfulness simplifies the business of ethical living. Quite the contrary. To be sure, escape from bondage to brute fact saves one often from embarrassment. But we noted at the outset that the bias toward exactness in utterance has an authentic quality, in principle. Manipulating facts does put a burden of proof on the manipulator. When violence is done to the letter a strain is put upon the spirit. I once heard a famous woman preacher explaining her views on the merits of "telling the truth" in a situation where the reputation of an indubitably upright person was at stake—where the "literal truth" would do irreparable damage to one who in the distant past had committed a serious fault. Asked pointblank what she would do if required to say yes or no as to the correctness of the accusation she said unequivocally, "I would tell the lie." But when a troubled hearer asked, "Would it not do violence to something within you?" she replied with quick firmness, "Yes! That is the price we pay for living in this world." If truth is understood as bound up with goodness, justice, fairness, the pursuit of truth is no easy matter, but it is endlessly rewarding.

William E. H. Lecky: *Reasoning which in one age would make no impression whatever, in the next age is received with enthusiastic applause.*

The pressure of the general intellectual influences of the time determines the predispositions which ultimately regulate the details of belief; and though all men do not yield to that pressure with the same facility, all large bodies are at last controlled. A change of speculative opinions does not imply an increase of the data upon which those opinions rest, but a change of the habits of thought and mind which they reflect. Definite arguments are the symptoms and pretexts, but seldom the causes of the change. Their chief merit is to accelerate the inevitable crisis. They derive their force and efficacy from their conformity with the mental habits of those to whom they are addressed. Reasoning which in one age would make no impression whatever, in the next age is received with enthusiastic applause. It is one thing to understand its nature, but quite another to appreciate its force.

And this standard of belief, this tone and habit of thought, which is the supreme arbiter of the opinions of successive periods, is created, not by the influences arising out of any one department of intellect, but by the combination of all the intellectual and even social tendencies of the age. Those who contribute most largely to its formation are, I believe, the philosophers. Men like Bacon, Descartes, and Locke have probably done more than any others to set the current of their age. They have formed a certain cast and tone of mind. They have introduced peculiar habits of thought, new modes of reasoning, new tendencies of enquiry. The impulse they have given to the higher literature, has been by that literature communicated to the more popular writers; and the impress of these master-minds is clearly visible in the writings of multitudes who are totally unacquainted with their works. But

From *History of the Rise and Influence of the Spirit of Rationalism in Europe* (London: Longman, Roberts, & Green, 1865), I, vii–ix.

philosophical methods, great and unquestionable as is their power, form but one of the many influences that contribute to the mental habits of society. Thus the discoveries of physical science, entrenching upon the domain of the anomalous and the incomprehensible, enlarging our conceptions of the range of law, and revealing the connection of phenomena that had formerly appeared altogether isolated, form a habit of mind which is carried far beyond the limits of physics. Thus the astronomical discovery, that our world is not the centre and axis of the material universe, but is an inconsiderable planet occupying to all appearance an altogether insignificant and subordinate position, and revolving with many others around a sun which is itself but an infinitesimal point in creation, in as far as it is realised by the imagination, has a vast and palpable influence upon our theological conceptions. Thus the commercial or municipal spirit exhibits certain habits of thought, certain modes of reasoning, certain repugnances and attractions, which make it invariably tend to one class of opinions. To encourage the occupations that produce this spirit, is to encourage the opinions that are most congenial to it. It is impossible to lay down a railway without creating an intellectual influence.

James Bryce: *There is little individual thinking in political opinion.*

In examining the process by which opinion is formed, we cannot fail to note how small a part of the view which the average man entertains when he goes to vote is really of his own making. Although he supposes his view to be his own, he holds it rather because his acquaintances, his newspapers, his party leaders all hold it. His acquaintances do the like. Each man believes and repeats certain phrases, because he thinks that everybody else on his own side believes them, and of what each believes only a small part is his own original impression, the far larger part being

From *The American Commonwealth* (3rd ed.; New York: The Macmillan Co., 1920), II, 253–54. Used by permission.

the result of the commingling and mutual action and reaction of
the impressions of a multitude of individuals, in which the element of pure personal conviction, based on individual thinking,
is but small.

Every one is of course predisposed to see things in some one
particular light by his previous education, habits of mind, accepted dogmas, religious or social affinities, notions of his own
personal interest. No event, no speech or article, ever falls upon
a perfectly virgin soil: the reader or listener is always more or
less biased already. When some important event happens, which
calls for the formation of a view, these pre-existing habits, dogmas, affinities, help to determine the impression which each man
experiences, and so far are factors in the view he forms. But they
operate chiefly in determining the first impression, and they
operate over many minds at once. They do not produce variety
and independence: they are soon overlaid by the influences which
each man derives from his fellows, from his leaders, from the
press.

Orthodox democratic theory assumes that every citizen has, or
ought to have, thought out for himself certain opinions, i.e., ought
to have a definite view, defensible by arguments, of what the
country needs, of what principles ought to be applied in governing it, of the men to whose hands the government ought to be
entrusted. There are persons who talk, though certainly very few
who act, as if they believed this theory . . . But one need only try
the experiment of talking to that representative of public opinion
whom the Americans call "the man in the cars," to realize how
uniform opinion is among all classes of people, how little there
is in the ideas of each individual of that individuality which they
would have if he had formed them for himself, how little solidity
and substance there is in the political or social beliefs of nineteen
persons out of every twenty. These beliefs, when examined, mostly
resolve themselves into two or three prejudices and aversions,
two or three prepossessions for a particular leader or party or section of a party, two or three phrases or catchwords suggesting or
embodying arguments which the man who repeats them has not
analyzed. It is not that these nineteen persons are incapable of
appreciating good arguments, or are unwilling to receive them.

On the contrary, and this is especially true of the working classes, an audience is pleased when solid arguments are addressed to it, and men read with most relish the articles or leaflets, supposing them to be smartly written, which contain the most carefully sifted facts and the most exact thought. But to the great mass of mankind in all places, public questions come in the third or fourth rank among the interests of life, and obtain less than a third or a fourth of the leisure available for thinking. It is therefore rather sentiment than thought that the mass can contribute, a sentiment grounded on a few broad considerations and simple trains of reasoning; and the soundness and elevation of their sentiment will have more to do with their taking their stand on the side of justice, honor, and peace, than any reasoning they can apply to the sifting of the multifarious facts thrown before them, and to the drawing of the legitimate inferences therefrom.

Frank L. Lucas: *Language has often mastered mankind.*

But men not only underestimate the difficulty of language; they often underestimate also its appalling power. True, the literary (for very human reasons) are sometimes tempted, on the contrary, to exaggerate it. We may well smile at writers who too confidently claim that the pen is mightier than the sword. Fletcher of Saltoun's exaltation of the songs of a people as more important than its laws, Shelley's glorification of poets as the unacknowledged legislators of mankind, Tennyson's poet whose word shakes the world, O'Shaughnessy's three men who trample down empires with the lilt of a new song—these, I feel, are somewhat too complacent half-truths. With all his powers of speech, Demosthenes could not save Greece; nor Cicero the Roman Republic; nor Milton the English Commonwealth. Yet it does seem rational to say

From *Style* (London: Cassell & Co. Ltd., 1955), pp. 18–20. Available from The Macmillan Co., New York. Reprinted by permission of The Macmillan Co. and Cassell & Co., Ltd.

that Voltaire and Burke became, in a sense, European powers; that Rousseau's *Contrat Social* left a permanent mark on the history of Europe, and Paine's *Common Sense* on that of America. This, if we brush away the blur of familiarity, remains astonishing enough. And these men, I think, won their triumphs not more (if so much) by force of thought than by force of style. Nor let us forget the influence of the English Bible.

How different, too, might have been the history of our own time if the written and spoken style of Adolf Hitler, detestable in itself, had been less potent to intoxicate the German people; or if the German people had had enough sense of style to reject that repellent claptrap; or again if Winston Churchill had not possessed a gift of phrase to voice and fortify the feelings of his countrymen in their darkest and their finest hour! Even the curious mind of Communism does not reject style as a bauble of the bourgeoisie. 'It is the business', we have been told, 'of the linguist and the critic to study the style of Stalin.' 'Learn to write as Stalin writes.' In such fulsome hyperboles there is at least a sense of the importance of style; if little sense of any other kind.

Some years ago, indeed, a distinguished scientist, enraged by the airs of the literary, protested impatiently that in this, 'the hydro-electric age', men's worship of mere verbiage was out of date—for 'the spark-gap is mightier than the pen'. Seemingly it escaped him that the rhetoric of the Führer had already reduced the scientists of the Third Reich into docile slaves, who demonstrated at his bidding the virtues of a non-existent Aryan race, or forged the weapons that were to force his infernal gospel on the world. Similarly in the Soviet Union we have seen biologists compelled to bow to 'Marxism' and to find once more, like Galileo, orthodoxy mightier than science. . . .

Our grandfathers hopefully chanted 'Great is the truth, and shall prevail'; they knew little of propaganda. Mankind has not yet mastered language; often it has mastered *them*—scientists and all. Few of them realize this. And that only makes it worse.

B. Leaders, Reformers, and Ordinary Citizens

Woodrow Wilson: *Nations are renewed from the bottom, not from the top.*

When I look back on the processes of history, when I survey the genesis of America, I see this written over every page: that the nations are renewed from the bottom, not from the top; that the genius which springs up from the ranks of unknown men is the genius which renews the youth and energy of the people. Everything I know about history, every bit of experience and observation that has contributed to my thought, has confirmed me in the conviction that the real wisdom of human life is compounded out of the experiences of ordinary men. The utility, the vitality, the fruitage of life does not come from the top to the bottom; it comes, like the natural growth of a great tree, from the soil, up through the trunk into the branches to the foliage and the fruit. The great struggling unknown masses of the men who are at the base of everything are the dynamic force that is lifting the levels of society. A nation is as great, and only as great, as her rank and file.

So the first and chief need of this nation of ours to-day is to include in the partnership of government all those great bodies of unnamed men who are going to produce our future leaders and renew the future energies of America. And as I confess that, as I confess my belief in the common man, I know what I am saying. The man who is swimming against the stream knows the strength of it. The man who is in the mêlée knows what blows

From "Life Comes from the Soil" in *The New Freedom* (1918), pp. 79–80, 86. Used by permission of Edith Bolling Wilson.

are being struck and what blood is being drawn. The man who is on the make is the judge of what is happening in America, not the man who has made good; not the man who has emerged from the flood; not the man who is standing on the bank looking on, but the man who is struggling for his life and for the lives of those who are dearer to him than himself. That is the man whose judgment will tell you what is going on in America; that is the man by whose judgment I, for one, wish to be guided.

. . . . .

The only way that government is kept pure is by keeping these channels open, so that nobody may deem himself so humble as not to constitute a part of the body politic, so that there will constantly be coming new blood into the veins of the body politic; so that no man is so obscure that he may not break the crust of any class he may belong to, may not spring up to higher levels and be counted among the leaders of the state.

William Bennett Munro: *It must follow that if you differ from the reformer, you are wrong.*

The reformers who bulk large in the public eye are, for the most part, men and women of unconventional personality. A reform movement is conceived in a spirit of protest; it draws into its ranks those who are protestants by natural reaction and can easily be roused to an intensity of feeling. But the very trait which renders these men and women susceptible to the call of reform makes them also impatient of leadership and discipline. The individual whose habits of mental independence make it impossible for him to maintain allegiance to any of the regular party organizations is not likely to prove a tractable soldier in a new crusade. Amenability to discipline does not come easy to him. He finds it

From *Personality in Politics* (New York: The Macmillan Co., 1924), pp. 4–6. Used by permission of Caroline S. G. Munro.

hard to reconcile himself to the idea that other men may be intellectually honest and yet hold opinions which differ widely from his own. For that reason there is usually (and unhappily) a larger measure of intolerance among reformers than among the general run of men and women.

The mental process which the average reformer uses is simple enough. He begins by taking it for granted that he is right. Then it must follow, as the night the day, that if you differ from him you are wrong. That is the sum and substance of his premises and logic. And if you are wrong there can be no compromise with you, for truth cannot enter into any compromise with error. The reformer, when he runs true to type, is not open to argument concerning the validity of his convictions. He will not barter away "his principles." The half loaf, to his way of thinking, is worse than no bread. He will not arbitrate an issue of righteousness. As well ask him to dicker on the Golden Rule or the Ten Commandments.

This inclination toward a categorical stand has often led reformers to extreme and indefensible positions. There is such a thing as being too logical in politics. It is not well to carry everything to its inevitable conclusion. Politics is not an exact science, like physics or mathematics. Two and two would make four in politics as in arithmetic, to be sure; but in politics you do not deal with anything so definite as two and two,—you deal altogether with variable and unknown quantities. That is why political prognostications are so baffling even to the thoroughly initiated. Multiplying one unknown factor by another merely gives you an unknown result. An Oxford don once said of logic that it is neither a science nor an art, but only a dodge. And a strict conformance to the rules of logic in forging a chain of political reasoning betrays the neophyte in politics.

Frederick J. E. Woodbridge: *Those doing the work of the world do not like to be told how to do it by others who are not doing that work.*

This last contrast [between the doer and the reformer] cuts deeper into the social body than any other. It creates a moral distinction which makes of reformers the superior class and of doers the inferior. There is something peculiarly irritating in being put into the class of those who need to be reformed, and often something meanly subservient in accepting that position voluntarily. There is also something very egotistical in undertaking the reformation of others as a profession, especially when one thereby makes a living or becomes socially prominent and featured. Those who are being reformed and those who are doing the reforming are rarely bound together in the ordinary ties of human fellowship, sympathy, and esteem. People may actually wish to be improved in the sense of being helped to become better-off in their social, economic, or intellectual status where they may reap the fruits of a fuller life, but they do not like to be improved by a class of professional improvers who see in them, not fellow-human beings subject to the common exigencies of existence, but beings to be made over before they can have any respectable status at all. Those who are doing the work of the world do not like to be told how to do it by others who are not doing that work and have no responsibility for the consequences of doing it. And the reason is simple. Those who have not done that work do not know what it is and what it involves. They have a tendency to conceive it in terms of moral categories which are clear-cut, when it operates in terms of interests, adjustments, and compromise. A man who has worked hard to bring discordant and conflicting forces into harmony and coöperation, is annoyed when asked if he

From *The Son of Apollo* (Boston: Houghton Mifflin Co., 1929), pp. 260–62. Used by permission.

has really done right. Cephalus, in the 'Republic,' could meet the question, What is justice? with a smile. Others might meet it with a cup of hemlock. When the question has reached a point where certain things must either be allowed to go on or be stopped, the answer is not a discussion or a definition; it is an act.

Sidney Hook: *Politics is a messy business, and life is short.*

If everyone, or even many, were candidates for political leadership, social life would be far more disturbed than it is. We would not need to be fearful of this disturbance if mechanisms of selection were evolved that would give us highly qualified leaders responsive to the needs and wishes of an informed and politically active electorate. But this is a long way off, and we are discussing what has been and is. A survey of political history shows that aspirants for leadership constitute, comparatively speaking, a mere handful in every community. The truth seems to be that the overwhelming majority of people have little desire to assume positions of power and responsibility.

Conditions of political leadership, of course, change, but politics pursued as a professional career has been and always will be a risky game. Sometimes reluctance to serve as political leader has been so strong that elections have been conducted by lot as in the Greek cities. Even in modern times individuals have often been "drafted" from plow or workshop or office to fill offices. The point is, not that there is ever really lacking a sufficient number of persons willing, and even eager, to assume leadership, but rather that the ease with which such persons usually acquire and keep power, and the manifold ways by which they expand the authority originally delegated to them, would be impossible unless there were comparatively so few others interested in competing for the posts of leadership. So long as they are permitted to grumble,

From *The Hero in History* (New York: The John Day Co., 1943), pp. 23–26. Copyright 1943 by Sidney Hook. Used by permission.

most people are gratefully relieved to find someone to do their chores, whether they are household chores or political chores. Politics is a messy business, and life is short. We put up with a great many evils in order to avoid the trouble of abolishing them.

· · · · ·

Yet it is an old story that when we refuse to upset our "normal life" by plunging into the political maelstrom, and entrust power to others, we awake someday to find that those to whom we entrusted it are well on their way to destroying "the normal life" we feared to interrupt. This is not only an old story but an ever-recurrent one. It will repeat itself until it is widely realized that political decisions must be made in any event; that responsibilities cannot be avoided by inaction or escape, for these have consequences; and that, considered even in its lowest terms, political effort and its attendant risks and troubles are a form of social insurance.

. . . To the extent that these elementary truths are disregarded, every aspirant to leadership—even to dictatorship—can count to an appreciable degree upon the indifference of the population. They will yield him homage after he has succeeded. Whether they do or don't, if *he* cares enough about it, he has the means today to make them pay homage to him.

James Bryce: *Why are great men not chosen as Presidents?*

Europeans often ask, and Americans do not always explain, how it happens that this great office, the greatest in the world, unless we except the Papacy, to which any one can rise by his own merits, is not more frequently filled by great and striking men. In America, which is beyond all other countries the country of a "career open to talents," a country, moreover, in which politi-

From *The American Commonwealth* (New York: The Macmillan Co., 1934), abridged ed., pp. 58–61. Used by permission.

cal life is unusually keen and political ambition widely diffused, it might be expected that the highest place would always be won by a man of brilliant gifts. . . .

Several reasons may be suggested for the fact, which Americans are themselves the first to admit.

One is that the proportion of first-rate ability drawn into politics is smaller in America than in most European countries. . . .

Another is that the methods and habits of Congress, and indeed of political life generally, give fewer opportunities for personal distinction, fewer modes in which a man may commend himself to his countrymen by eminent capacity in thought, in speech, or in administration, than is the case in the free countries of Europe. . . .

A third reason is that eminent men make more enemies, and give those enemies more assailable points, than obscure men do. They are therefore in so far less desirable candidates. . . . The famous man has probably attacked some leaders in his own party, has supplanted others, has expressed his dislike to the crotchet of some active section, has perhaps committed errors which are capable of being magnified into offences. . . . Hence, when the choice lies between a brilliant man and a safe man, the safe man is preferred. . . . The safe candidate may not draw in quite so many votes from the moderate men of the other side as the brilliant one would, but he will not lose nearly so many from his own ranks. Even those who admit his mediocrity will vote straight when the moment for voting comes. Besides, the ordinary American voter does not object to mediocrity. He has a lower conception of the qualities requisite to make a statesman than those who direct public opinion in Europe have. He likes his candidate to be sensible, vigorous, and, above all, what he calls "magnetic," and does not value, because he sees no need for, originality or profundity, a fine culture or a wide knowledge . . .

After all, too, a President need not be a man of brilliant intellectual gifts.

Charles W. Eliot: *In a democracy, public offices are not the places of greatest influence.*

It is often assumed that the educated classes become impotent in a democracy, because the representatives of those classes are not exclusively chosen to public office. This argument is a very fallacious one. It assumes that the public offices are the places of greatest influence; whereas, in the United States, at least, that is conspicuously not the case. In a democracy, it is important to discriminate influence from authority. Rulers and magistrates may or may not be persons of influence; but many persons of influence never become rulers, magistrates, or representatives in parliaments or legislatures. The complex industries of a modern state, and its innumerable corporation services, offer great fields for administrative talent which were entirely unknown to preceding generations; and these new activities attract many ambitious and capable men more strongly than the public service. These men are not on that account lost to their country or to society. The present generation has wholly escaped from the conditions of earlier centuries, when able men who were not great land-owners had but three outlets for their ambition—the army, the church, or the national civil service. The national service, whether in an empire, a limited monarchy, or a republic, is now only one of many fields which offer to able and patriotic men an honorable and successful career. Indeed, legislation and public administration necessarily have a very secondhand quality; and more and more legislators and administrators become dependent on the researches of scholars, men of science, and historians, and follow in the footsteps of inventors, economists, and political philosophers. Political leaders are very seldom leaders of thought; they are generally trying to induce masses of men to act on principles thought out long before. Their skill is in the selection of practicable approximations to the ideal; their arts are arts of exposition

From *American Contributions to Civilization and Other Essays and Addresses* (New York: Appleton-Century-Crofts, Inc., 1897), pp. 26–27.

and persuasion; their honor comes from fidelity under trying circumstances to familiar principles of public duty. The real leaders of American thought in this century have been preachers, teachers, jurists, seers, and poets. While it is of the highest importance, under any form of government, that the public servants should be men of intelligence, education, and honor, it is no objection to any given form, that under it large numbers of educated and honorable citizens have no connection with the public service.

Sydney Smith: *Our ancestors are younger than we are.*

This mischievous and absurd fallacy [Wisdom of our Ancestors] springs from the grossest perversion of the meaning of words. Experience is certainly the mother of wisdom, and the old have, of course, a greater experience than the young; but the question is, who are the old? and who are the young? Of *individuals* living at the same period, the oldest has, of course, the greatest experience; but among *generations* of men the reverse of this is true. Those who come first (our ancestors) are the young people, and have the least experience. We have added to their experience the experience of many centuries; and, therefore, as far as experience goes, are wiser, and more capable of forming an opinion than they were. The real feeling should be, *not*, can we be so presumptuous as to put our opinions in opposition to those of our ancestors? but can such young, ignorant, inexperienced persons as our ancestors necessarily were, be expected to have understood a subject as well as those who have seen so much more, lived so much longer, and enjoyed the experience of so many centuries? All this cant, then, about our ancestors is merely an abuse of words, by transferring phrases true of contemporary men to succeeding ages. . . .

From a review of Jeremy Bentham's *Book of Fallacies. Works of Sydney Smith.* London, 1840. II, 106–7.

We cannot of course be supposed to maintain that our ancestors wanted wisdom, or that they were necessarily mistaken in their institutions, because their means of information were more limited than ours. But we do confidently maintain that when we find it expedient to change any thing which our ancestors have enacted, we are the experienced persons, and not they. The quantity of talent is always varying in any great nation. To say that we are more or less able than our ancestors is an assertion that requires to be explained. All the able men of all ages, who have ever lived in England, probably possessed, if taken altogether, more intellect than all the able men now in England can boast of. But if authority must be resorted to rather than reason, the question is, What was the wisdom of that single age which enacted the law, compared with the wisdom of the age which proposes to alter it? What are the eminent men of one and the other period? If you say that our ancestors were wiser than us, mention your date and year. If the splendour of names is equal, are the circumstances the same? If the circumstances are the same, we have a superiority of experience, of which the difference between the two periods is the measure.

Viscount Haldane: *Leadership always depends on personality.*

There is always some kind of uniqueness in the men whom the world distinguishes as leaders, something that appeals to the imagination. No man is great merely because he preaches a particular doctrine. Whether it be in his deeds or in his words or in his writing, what moves those who follow him is what is beyond his mere doctrine, that in him which fires the imagination and makes others feel that in him there is what cannot be adequately described or forecast. He is for them an individual marked out from the others around him by a quality that cannot be exhausted

From *The Philosophy of Humanism* (New Haven: Yale Univ. Press, 1922), pp. 86–87. Used by permission.

in any phrases. It suggests what is not capable of being included in any abstract description. . . . We feel that in his way, if we recognise him as leader, we shall not look on just the like of this man again. . . . The great man stands for the transforming man. If he be an administrator of genius he will compel those around him to do his will by the inspiring power he brings to bear on them. If he be of the first order in literature or science he will create a school of disciples, inspired by faith, by the sense of what is unseen, and not merely by notional agreement with what he lays down. To exercise such power and to bring its might to fruition may in some cases require time, while in others the result comes quickly. The variety of such personalities is infinite, as the history of action and thought shows. But the lesson we learn is always that leadership depends on personality in some form . . . A great leader is no mere book to read. It is because the study of him is inexhaustible, and involves the appeal to the imaginative and pictorial, that he lays hold of the mind of the man in the street. The approach to what is purely particular in character is here as elsewhere elusive, for it is asymptotic and incapable of definition. He may be very human, very finite. He may often be wrong. But if his knowledge or his power of action is dynamic and can compel the imaginations of men, his shortcomings, very real perhaps to the few that are sufficiently equipped to estimate them, will not destroy his power over the multitude who are drawn after his banner.

Sidney Hook: A democracy must be suspicious of great men.

Great men, then, may be good men. And still a democracy must be suspicious of them! For essential to democracy is the participation of the governed in determining their own welfare. This participation is coupled with the *hope* that the governed

From *The Hero in History* (New York: The John Day Co., 1943), pp. 230–39. Copyright 1943 by Sidney Hook. Used by permission.

will select and elect their governors wisely, that is, in such a way as to gratify as many of their needs and wants as the situation permits. But more important than this hope, which is sometimes sadly at variance with the facts, is the belief that it is more worthy of men to decide their own fate than to let others decide it for them.

The hero in a democratic community—the potentially event-making man—may sincerely believe that he accepts its underlying philosophy. But sooner or later he finds himself straining against two features of the democratic process. The first is the principle of majority rule, especially when he is convinced that the majority is wrong on a matter of great import. The second is the slowness of its operation even when he believes the majority is right.

· · · · ·

The "potential hero" in a democracy sees what others do not. His will to action is stronger. His knowledge of what must be done to realize what he sees is surer. For these reasons, he finds himself, more likely than not, in a minority. His sense of his vocation impels him to fight for his insight. His loyalty to the democratic ideal compels him to make this insight the common faith of the majority. If the latter remain stubbornly intractable, his chances of heroic action, as a democrat, are lost. The hero fades into history as a "village Hamden."

Superior talent and strong vision, however, press for expression. So far as the hero does not renounce politics as a sphere of activity, his task becomes to get himself accepted by a majority. For, as a democrat, he does not dare to admit to himself or to others that he wants to make himself independent of the majority. In pursuit of a majority, he may seek to win it, broadly speaking, by the patient methods of education, relying upon the inherent reasonableness of his vision to make its way.

Insofar as he does this, and only so far, democracy is safe from the hero. This means that he courts failure. But the hero may master the arts of the demagogue and use the very instruments of democracy to debase its quality. Yet as long as democratic controls are not abolished, the hero as demagogue must still build up, cajole, and cater to the majority. He acquires a contempt for the group he leads by virtue of the methods by which he corrupts them. In the process, if his own will and insight grow uncertain and cloudy, he becomes just another politician. He is a hero who has missed his chance. But where his will and insight remain firm, the hero as demagogue must "fool" his following into accepting them. He must develop a public platform, on the basis of which he solicits confidence, and a secret program in whose behalf he uses the confidence so won. He becomes a threat to democracy. The greater his faith in himself, the more disinterested his intentions, the more fateful the issue to which his heroic vision drives him, the more insidious is the menace to the whole rationale of democracy. Particularly so if the hero or potential event-making character believes himself to be the indispensable instrument of his vision.

Arthur M. Schlesinger, Jr.: Why should our age be without great men?

Ours is an age without heroes—and, when we say this, we suddenly realize how spectacularly the world has changed in a generation. Most of us grew up in a time of towering personalities. For better or for worse, great men seemed to dominate our lives and shape our destiny. In the United States we had Theodore Roosevelt, Woodrow Wilson, Franklin Roosevelt. In Great Britain, there were Lloyd George and Winston Churchill. In other lands, there were Lenin, Stalin, Hitler, Mussolini, Clemenceau, Gandhi, Kemal, Sun Yat-sen. Outside of politics there were Einstein, Freud, Keynes. Some of these great men influenced the world for good, others for evil; but, whether for good or for evil, the fact that each had not died at birth made a difference, one believed, to everyone who lived after them.

Today no one bestrides our narrow world like a colossus: we have no giants who play roles which one can imagine no one else

From "The Decline of Greatness" in *The Saturday Evening Post*, November 1, 1958, p. 25. Used by permission of the author.

playing in their stead. There are a few figures on the margin of uniqueness, perhaps: Adenauer, Nehru, Tito, De Gaulle, Chiang Kai-shek, Mao Tse-tung. But there seem to be none in the epic style of those mighty figures of our recent past who seized history with both hands and gave it an imprint, even a direction, which it otherwise might not have had. As De Gaulle himself remarked on hearing of Stalin's death, "The age of giants is over." Whatever one thought, whether one admired or detested Roosevelt or Churchill, Stalin or Hitler, one nevertheless felt the sheer weight of such personalities on one's own existence. We feel no comparable pressures today. . . .

Why have giants vanished from our midst? One must never neglect the role of accident in history; and accident no doubt plays a part here. But too many accidents of the same sort cease to be wholly accidental. One must inquire further. Why should our age not only be without great men but even seem actively hostile to them? Surely one reason we have so few heroes now is precisely that we had so many a generation ago. Greatness is hard for common humanity to bear. As Emerson said, "Heroism means difficulty, postponement of praise, postponement of ease, introduction of the world into the private apartment, introduction of eternity into the hours measured by the sitting-room clock." A world of heroes keeps people from living their own private lives.

Moreover, great men live dangerously. They introduce extremes into existence—extremes of good, extremes of evil—and ordinary men after a time flinch from the ultimates and yearn for undemanding security. The Second World War was the climax of an epoch of living dangerously. It is no surprise that it precipitated a universal revulsion against greatness. The war itself destroyed Hitler and Mussolini. And the architects of victory were hardly longer-lived. After the war, the British repudiated Churchill, and the Americans (with the adoption of the 22nd Amendment), Roosevelt. In due course, the French repudiated De Gaulle (they later repented, but it took the threat of civil war to bring him back); the Chinese, Chiang Kai-shek; and the Russians, Stalin. Khrushchev, in toppling Stalin from his pedestal, pronounced the general verdict against the uncommon man: the modern world, he said, had no use for the "cult of the individual." And, indeed carried to the excesses to which the worshipers of Hitler and Stalin carried it, even to the much milder degree to which admirers of Roosevelt and Churchill sometimes carried it, the cult of the individual was dangerous. No man is infallible, and every man needs to be reminded of this on occasion. Still, our age has gone further than this—it objects not just to hero worship but to heroes. The century of the common man has come into its own.

R. M. MacIver: *Democracy is not to the disadvantage of the elite.*

Whenever men separate themselves from the bulk of their fellow men, especially when they think that their higher culture entitles them to think meanly of the average citizen, they are apt to nourish the aristocratic fallacy. The fallacy lies not in their claim to be "aristocrats"—that claim may or may not be justified —but in the doctrine they on that account entertain concerning the nature of government and especially concerning the significance of democracy.

Democracy, they say, is the rule of the incompetent. It puts the average man on the throne. The average man is opaque to new ideas, blind to new needs, obfuscated, routinized, uncomprehending—in short, unfit to rule. All quality, all achievement, all advance, comes from the few, the elite. Apart from them mankind would still be living in the mud huts of the primaeval savage. When the elite are bereft of power and the masses, contrary to the first law of existence, are exalted over them, everything is reduced "to a dead level of incapacity."

Democracy is not the rule of "the masses" nor is it something for "the masses" only. Democracy is not the enthronement of mediocrity, to the disadvantage of the elite, the enlightened, the cultivated. Democracy is the political liberation of *all* men from the chains of power. Democracy in origin and in action is a system

From *The Ramparts We Guard* (New York: The Macmillan Co., 1950), pp. 41–42. Used by permission.

devised to break the primal source of all tyranny, which is the coercive power of group over group, or of the few over the many. It is not the "common man" alone who has suffered from the irresponsibility of power, from "the oppressor's wrong, the proud man's contumely," from "the insolence of office, and the spurns that patient merit of the unworthy takes," from the worst insolence of all, which says in effect: "I have power over you, therefore what I believe about man and God, about science and art, about life and society, about right and wrong, you *must* believe." Those who suffer most from this oppression, who find it most intolerable, are the true elite among men, the thinkers, the artists, the men of deep faith, the men of generous heart and of free spirit, the creators of all that has enriched and ennobled mankind, those who search beneath the appearance of things, those who wrestle with the unknown, those who dream and those who aspire. Unmitigated power has most of the time sought to crush and tame them, to enslave them, and when it has failed it has consigned them to the dungeon, the scaffold, the stake, and the cross. And often enough the indoctrinated masses have cried out, "Crucify him," taking sides with power.

Democracy provides the way of liberation alike from mass intolerance and from the ruthlessness and corruption of power.

Carl J. Friedrich: *The common man is "safer" than the uncommon man.*

In spite of modern psychology and industrial technology, the belief in the common man is not only vital to the democratic creed but quite tenable. But it is tenable only if we state it in terms quite different from those which have come down to us from the visionary prophets of the democratic age. Naught but ill results from the thoughtless repetition of outworn formulas. The almost incredible faith in the omnicompetence and rationality of

From *The New Image of the Common Man* (Boston: Beacon Press, 1950), pp. 40–42. Used by permission.

the common man, of you and me, must be replaced by a tempered yet firm conviction of the common man's *political* capacity. We need to insist, first of all, upon this *limited* competence, indeed upon the fallibility of every man, be he ever so uncommon. Whether there be an ultimate right or wrong, good or bad, no man knows what it is. In the absence of such absolute standards, communal policies depend upon calculations of probability. The common man, even in the aggregate, is not infallible; far from it. But he perceives more readily than the expert the general impact of proposed policies. The judgment of the common man in which we believe is a collective, not an individual, judgment. Therefore, judgments involving discriminating evaluation of exceptional achievement are altogether outside the sphere of these judgments of the common man in which we can trust. The common man is trustworthy because he is, in the aggregate, a man of character rather than of intellect—consistent, and averse to highfalutin deviations. He is "safer" than the uncommon man.

While a tempered belief in the common man is basic for democracy, a limitless belief in him results in the "revolt of the masses" and is part and parcel of totalitarian dictatorship. Here a popularly acclaimed "leader" is the final judge of everything. Hitler is the common man run amuck. He poses as the incarnation of Rousseau's "general will," the builder of a "real" democracy. It is belief turned into superstition. Limitless and without real content, the belief in the common man destroys rather than maintains constitutionalism and democracy.

But if, as a result of such superstitions, we allow ourselves to be frightened into abandoning the belief in the common man altogether, if we become despondent and lose faith in ourselves, our plight is worse. What we need is a balanced confidence in our power to operate a community of common men by common judgments upon matters of common concern. Exceptional men, if truly exceptional, will devote themselves to the exceptional tasks. The mass of common men will gratefully acknowledge the achievements of such uncommon men by the time they have become common property—part of the life of common man.

Matthew Arnold: *It is not well for proctors to tell the large class of men what it wants.*

If experience has established any one thing in this world, it has established this: that it is well for any great class or description of men in society to be able to say for itself what it wants, and not to have other classes, the so-called educated and intelligent classes, acting for it as its proctors, and supposed to understand its wants and to provide for them. They do not really understand its wants, they do not really provide for them. A class of men may often itself not either fully understand its own wants or adequately express them; but it has a nearer interest and a more sure diligence in the matter than any of its proctors, and therefore a better chance of success.

From "The Future of Liberalism" in *Mixed Essays, Irish Essays and Others* (New York: Macmillan and Co., 1879), p. 383.

P. W. Bridgman: *The glorification of the common man is one of the hardest things to understand.*

To me the glorification of the common man and the interest in him merely because he is common is one of the hardest things to understand about this country, for there is no gainsaying that common man is also mediocre man. I had supposed that the most important thing for the long range progress of a society was the way it treats its exceptional men, and I can understand a passionate admiration of supreme ability. It is easy for me to understand how mediocre man can fight for his own exaltation at the

From "Democracy and the Forgotten Physicist" in *Reflections of a Physicist* (New York: Philosophical Library, 1955), pp. 520–22. Used by permission.

expense of his superior fellow, and I can understand how in the
past he has been to a certain extent justified in his fight by the
abuses of economic power by those who possessed it. But it seems
to me that the evils of this situation have by now been obviously
over corrected, and I can understand how the superior man can
continue to welcome the triumph of mediocrity only by supposing him the victim of a short sighted sentimentalism. Is mediocrity really admirable, or can you admire the sort of thing
mediocrity is on its way to turning this country into now that it
has received the green light? Is it admirable for a man to be willing to be guaranteed a minimum wage whether or not he is
capable of earning it? Is it admirable for a labor union to compel
its ablest members to limit their output to that of the poorest,
thus essentially making a public enemy out of the exceptional
man? Is it admirable for a man to be willing to sponge on his
neighbors to compensate him for deficiencies in the abilities with
which nature furnished him? The slogan "To everyone according
to his need, from everyone according to his abilities," when associated with the Marxist social philosophy, is not usually regarded
in this country as admirable or consistent with self respect, but
this is exactly what is involved in the philosophy which justifies
our graded income tax. If the mediocre man had imagination,
how would he expect the superior man to react to the claim of
mediocrity that it has a right to exact from superiority more than
its proportionate contribution, or how would the superior man
react to this claim if he had guts and self respect? The economic
philosophy which has seriously supported the proposition that no
individual should be allowed to keep more than $25,000 a year for
his services, to me constitutes as keen an affront to my self respect
as ever a militant suffragette smarted under, denied the right to
vote simply because of her sex. Whichever way you look at this
proposition it is equally bad. The thesis either has to be that no
individual is able to make a contribution to the community worth
more than $25,000 a year, whereas I know that no limit can be
put on the value of the contribution that unusual ability is able
to make. Or else the community has to declare that it will not pay
more than $25,000 for any contribution, no matter how much
more it may be worth, and this bespeaks a churlishness and jeal-

ousy toward the fortunate individual possessing exceptional ability which makes me blush to be in any way a partner to such an
enterprise.

Joseph Wood Krutch: *From defending the common man we pass on to exalting him.*

This . . . is the Age of the Common Man. But we as well as he
[the European] are not quite certain what we mean by that.
In so far as we mean only the age of universal opportunity, what
was once called simply "the career open to talents," nothing but
good could seem to come of it. But many people do, sometimes
without being entirely aware of it, mean something more. When
we make ourselves the champion of any particular group we
almost inevitably begin to idealize that group. From defending
the common man we pass on to exalting him, and we find ourselves beginning to imply, not merely that he is as good as anybody else, but that he is actually better. Instead of demanding
only that the common man be given an opportunity to become as
uncommon as possible, we make his commonness a virtue and,
even in the case of candidates for high office, we sometimes praise
them for being nearly indistinguishable from the average man in
the street. Secretly, no doubt, we hope that they are somehow
superior, but we feel at the same time that a kind of decency
requires them to conceal the fact as completely as possible.

The logical extreme of this opinion would be the conviction
that any deviation in either direction from the statistical average
is unadmirable; even, to take a concrete example, that the ideal
man or woman could best be represented, not by an artist's dream,
but by a composite photograph of the entire population. And
though few would explicitly acknowledge their acceptance of this

From "Is Our Common Man Too Common?" in *Saturday Review*, January 10, 1953, p. 9+. Used by permission of Joseph Wood Krutch and the
Saturday Review.

extreme position, there is a very strong tendency to emphasize quantitative rather than qualitative standards in estimating achievement. We are, for instance, more inclined to boast how many Americans go to college than to ask how much the average college education amounts to; how many people read books rather than how good the books are; how many listen to the radio rather than how good what they hear from it really is.

· · · · ·

One might sum up the situation in a series of propositions. (1) The Age of the Common Man has begun. (2) Despite all the gains that it may legitimately claim, they are threatened by those confusions which arise when the common denominator is consciously or unconsciously allowed to function as a standard of excellence. (3) The dominance of mass media almost exclusively under the control of those who are little concerned with anything except immediate financial gain does tend to debase taste. (4) Ultimate responsibility for the future rests with the thinkers and the educators whose most important social task at the moment is to define democratic culture in some fashion which will both reserve a place for uncommon excellence and, even in connection with the largest masses, emphasize the highest rather than the lowest common denominator.

C. A Way of Life: Aspects and Attitudes

Irwin Edman: *There is probably no other country in the world where idleness is one of the deadly sins.*

The best test of the quality of a civilization is the quality of its leisure. Not what the citizens of a commonwealth do when they are obliged to do something by necessity, but what they do when they can do anything by choice, is the criterion of a people's life. One can tell much about a man by noting the objects and pastimes to which he spontaneously turns for joy. The same may be said of a nation. It was a suggestive comment of Maxim Gorky's on visiting Coney Island, 'What an unhappy people it must be that turns for happiness here.' The most serious criticism leveled against American civilization is not that its work is standardized and its business engulfing, but that its pleasures are mechanical and its leisure slavish. It is not that we have not time. Foreign observers are repeatedly astonished at the number of hours an ever-increasing number of Americans have to themselves. It is not time that we lack, but leisure.

Leisure is indeed an affair of mood and atmosphere rather than simply of the clock. It is not a chronological occurrence but a spiritual state. It is unhurried pleasurable living among one's native enthusiasms. Leisure consists of those pauses in our lives when experience is a fusion of stimulation and repose. Genuine leisure yields at once a feeling of vividness and a sense of peace. It consists of moments so clear and pleasant in themselves that one might wish they were eternal.

. . . . .

From *Adam, The Baby and the Man from Mars* (Boston: Houghton Mifflin Co., 1929), pp. 3–7. Used by permission.

... for Americans the word 'leisure' has distinctively Old World associations. That is partly because some Americans have there known it best. Cut off from the pressure and compulsions of their normal occupations at home, they have moved with freedom amid the grace of a leisurely tradition. But there is a deeper reason which lies in the contrast between that European tradition and our own. The quality of leisure in Europe is partly the heritage of a long leisure-class tradition, partly the patience of peoples that have the sense of age and are not obsessed with hastening toward the new and building the possible in a hurry. In our own civilization, originally and in spirit partly pioneer, there is a working- rather than a leisure-class tradition, and the impress and atmosphere of work have come to control our lives even when we are not working. To be busy has been with us a primary virtue, and even our play has had to find a place for itself as a kind of business.

... we carry the morals and ideals of an essentially industrial, essentially business civilization over into our play. Leisure—a quiet and emancipated absorption in things and doings for their own sake—has always seemed to us effeminate and exotic. We wish leisure for relief, for release, for escape; for instruction, enlightenment, or advancement. There is something immoral about moments that are good in themselves. There is probably no other country in the world where idleness is one of the deadly sins.

Lewis Mumford: *The segregation of the spiritual life from the practical life is a curse.*

Human culture, plainly, cannot be sustained unless values enter into every activity. Otherwise we are cursed with a Sunday morality, in which decency and brotherhood and justice are flouted for six days and then piously reinstated on the seventh: a system under which our deeds never by any accident coincide with our professions.

From *Faith for Living.* Copyright 1940 by Lewis Mumford, pp. 214–217. Reprinted by permission of Harcourt, Brace & Co., Inc.

The Athenians were right in believing that the ultimate goods of life could be enjoyed only by free men; they meant by this that they can not be fully enjoyed if they are offered to people who are forced to spend their days in some spiritually deadening or physically exhausting task, whether in the market, the mine, or the workshop. Human development requires both periods of activity and periods of leisure, in which the results of this activity may be meditated upon, absorbed, digested. One of the reasons that country folk, with limited experience, are nevertheless so much better companions for an artist or a thinker than city people of the same class, is that the former have always kept for themselves a little free time to sit still and brood, whittling wood around a winter fire, or bent impassively over a fishing pole, watching the trout's canny flirtations. The city worker may be better read; but the countryman is more reflective: such experience as he has encountered he has salted down.

But it is equally true—and the intellectual tends always to forget this—that spiritual life suffers by complete divorce from the vivid experiences and the salutary restraints of practical activity. The Athenians, fortunately, before they became engrossed in imperialist ambitions, managed to retain in some measure their hold upon the fundamental manual and operative realities of sport and war. They had tough muscles and well-tempered bodies and eyes quick to note how the grapes were ripening or how the potter molded his clay on the wheel. That sense distinguished Plato from every philosopher down to Descartes. So it is possibly no accident that the most original mind among the Athenians was a stonecutter by trade and the son of a midwife, or that perhaps the greatest tragic dramatist was also a general. Nor was it an accident, in our own American Golden Day, that Henry Thoreau was a pencil maker and a surveyor, that Herman Melville was a sailor, that Walt Whitman was a carpenter and a printer good enough to set up his own "Leaves of Grass"; or that Abe Lincoln was a rail-splitter who retained to the end of his life a solid confidence in himself that was based on his sure axmanship and shoulders that could carry a heavier burden than his neighbor's.

The segregation of the spiritual life from the practical life is a curse that falls impartially upon both sides of our existence. A society that gives to one class all the opportunities for leisure, and to another all the burdens of work, dooms both classes to spiritual sterility. The first will make busy work for itself: games, fox hunts, parties, organized inanities; while the other will make work itself empty, and even go the forces that make it empty one better, by reducing work to "as little as you can get away with"— only to lose self-respect as well as craftsmanlike pleasure in that very act. One of the main tasks of a purposive intelligence is to keep the inner world and the outer, the spiritual and the practical, the personal and the mechanical or automatic, in constant interaction. They form a dynamic unity.

The moral to be drawn from this is that servile labor—even if it produces social necessities—should be minimized to the utmost. The problem is not entirely solved by the invention of automatic machines; because, if pushed too far, the routine of mechanized production robs those engaged in it, and even more those displaced by it, of the opportunities for educative, person-satisfying activities. Such work as remains servile or dangerous in our society—whether on the assembly line or on the battlefield—should be shared by the entire adult community.

In short, justice demands either equality of life-sustenance and leisure, in times of plenty and peace, or equality of sacrifice in times of hardship and war. The principle is the same in both cases; and if we introduce the element of sacrifice into our economic system now, where it will affect principally the middle classes and those above them, we may as a country have some guarantee for fruitful and refined leisure—for the good life itself— when at long last we emerge from this murky period.

Henry David Thoreau: *Every walk is a sort of crusade.*

I wish to speak a word for Nature, for absolute freedom and wildness, as contrasted with a freedom and culture merely civil,— to regard man as an inhabitant, or a part and parcel of Nature,

From "Walking" in *Excursions* (Boston: Ticknor & Fields, 1863), pp. 160–63, 206–7.

rather than a member of society. I wish to make an extreme statement, if so I may make an emphatic one, for there are enough
champions of civilization: the minister and the school-committee
and every one of you will take care of that.

I have met with but one or two persons in the course of my
life who understood the art of Walking, that is, of taking walks,—
who had a genius, so to speak, for *sauntering:* which word is beautifully derived "from idle people who roved about the country,
in the Middle Ages, and asked charity, under pretense of going
à la Sainte Terre," to the Holy Land, till the children exclaimed,
"There goes a *Sainte-Terrer,*" a Saunterer, a Holy-Lander. They
who never go to the Holy Land in their walks, as they pretend,
are indeed mere idlers and vagabonds; but they who do go there
are saunterers in the good sense, such as I mean. Some, however,
would derive the word from *sans terre*, without land or a home,
which, therefore, in the good sense, will mean, having no particular home, but equally at home everywhere. For this is the secret
of successful sauntering. He who sits still in a house all the time
may be the greatest vagrant of all; but the saunterer, in the good
sense, is no more vagrant than the meandering river, which is all
the while sedulously seeking the shortest course to the sea. But I
prefer the first, which, indeed, is the most probable derivation.
For every walk is a sort of crusade, preached by some Peter the
Hermit in us, to go forth and reconquer this Holy Land from the
hands of the Infidels.

It is true, we are but faint-hearted crusaders, even the walkers,
nowadays, who undertake no persevering, never-ending enterprises. Our expeditions are but tours, and come round again at
evening to the old hearth-side from which we set out. Half the
walk is but retracing our steps. We should go forth on the shortest
walk, perchance, in the spirit of undying adventure, never to return,—prepared to send back our embalmed hearts only as relics
to our desolate kingdoms. If you are ready to leave father and
mother, and brother and sister, and wife and child and friends,
and never see them again,—if you have paid your debts, and made
your will, and settled all your affairs, and are a free man, then you
are ready for a walk. . . .

While almost all men feel an attraction drawing them to society, few are attracted strongly to Nature. In their reaction to Nature men appear to me for the most part, notwithstanding their arts, lower than the animals. It is not often a beautiful relation, as in the case of the animals. How little appreciation of the beauty of the landscape there is among us! We have to be told that the Greeks called the world Κόσμος, Beauty, or Order, but we do not see clearly why they did so, and we esteem it at best only a curious philological fact.

For my part, I feel that with regard to Nature I live a sort of border life, on the confines of a world into which I make occasional and transient forays only, and my patriotism and allegiance to the State into whose territories I seem to retreat are those of a moss-trooper. Unto a life which I call natural I would gladly follow even a will-o'-the-wisp through bogs and sloughs unimaginable, but no moon nor firefly has shown me the causeway to it. Nature is a personality so vast and universal that we have never seen one of her features. The walker in the familiar fields which stretch around my native town sometimes finds himself in another land than is described in their owners' deeds, as it were in some far-away field on the confines of the actual Concord, where her jurisdiction ceases, and the idea which the word Concord suggests ceases to be suggested. These farms which I have myself surveyed, these bounds which I have set up, appear dimly still as through a mist; but they have no chemistry to fix them; they fade from the surface of the glass; and the picture which the painter painted stands out dimly from beneath. The world with which we are commonly acquainted leaves no trace, and it will have no anniversary.

David G. Ritchie: *Positive liberty depends on the existence of a strong and stable government.*

Negative liberty means simply "being let alone." Whether that is a good or a bad thing in itself is a perfectly useless question to discuss. It is (to adapt an illustration of Sir James Stephen's) just like asking whether a hole is a good thing in itself. All depends on what the hole is made *in*, and on what you want to put into the hole. A hole in my coat is useful, if it is a buttonhole or the place my arm has to go through; but a hole in the wrong place is not desirable. And so it is with liberty in the merely negative sense of non-interference. We must know who or what is being left alone, on what occasions, in what places, and who it is that is leaving any one alone, before we can profitably discuss the good or evil of freedom. To give a baby its freedom on the verge of a precipice and to attempt to supervise every act of grown men are both foolish and culpable proceedings. When people praise liberty, it may simply be a way of expressing their strong detestation of some particular form of restraint; but more often, there is implied also in the praise the ideal of some *positive* powers of doing something which they consider worth doing. Positive or real liberty, as we might call it, to distinguish it from the negative or merely formal liberty of being let alone, means the opportunity or capacity of doing something. Such liberty is, in its turn, good or bad according as the things which can be done are good or bad. . . .

But this positive and qualified meaning of liberty has not always been recognised as clearly distinguished from the mere negative sense of being let alone; nor is it always realised how very much any real positive liberty depends upon the existence of elaborate social arrangements, and on a strong and stable gov-

From *Natural Rights* (New York: The Macmillan Co., 1895), pp. 138–40. Used by permission of the Macmillan Co. and George Allen & Unwin, Ltd.

ernment. In this country no one is hindered by law from reading
all the works of Mr. Herbert Spencer. That is negative liberty.
But if a man cannot read at all, or if he can read but has not any
money to spare for the purpose of buying so many volumes, or if
he has no access to any public library, or if the managers of any
library to which he has access refuse to permit such works on
their shelves, or if, having access to them, he has no leisure in
which to read them, or if he has not had such an education as
enables him to understand what he reads, he cannot be said to get
much good out of the fact that the law of the land does not pro-
hibit him from reading Mr. Spencer's works. Thus, in order that
the great mass of the inhabitants of this country should really
enjoy the privilege of appreciating the philosophical basis on
which Mr. Spencer founds his objections to State education, State
libraries, and all such forms of interference with individual liberty,
it is necessary that such forms of State interference with individual liberty—and a good many others—should be in active operation; at least experience has not yet shown us any instance in
which opportunities of culture have been accessible to all, or
nearly all, the inhabitants of densely populated countries without
some such interference with the liberty of being ignorant, the liberty of keeping children ignorant, the liberty of working for excessive hours, and other individual liberties of that kind.

Thus, liberty in the sense of positive opportunity for self-de-
velopment, is the creation of law, and not something that could
exist apart from the action of the State.

Edmund Burke: *Liberty is power.*

When I see the spirit of liberty in action, I see a strong principle at work; and this, for a while, is all I can possibly know of
it. The wild *gas*, the fixed air, is plainly broke loose: but we ought
to suspend our judgment until the first effervescence is a little sub-

From *Reflections on the Revolution and Other Essays.* Available in the
edition published by J. M. Dent & Sons, Ltd., 1916, pp. 6–7.

sided, till the liquor is cleared, and until we see something deeper than the agitation of a troubled and frothy surface. I must be tolerably sure, before I venture publicly to congratulate men upon a blessing, that they have really received one. Flattery corrupts both the receiver and the giver; and adulation is not of more service to the people than to kings. I should therefore suspend my congratulations on the new liberty of France, until I was informed how it had been combined with government; with public force; with the discipline and obedience of armies; with the collection of an effective and well-distributed revenue; with morality and religion; with the solidity of property; with peace and order; with civil and social manners. All these (in their way) are good things too; and, without them, liberty is not a benefit whilst it lasts, and is not likely to continue long. The effect of liberty to individuals is, that they may do what they please: we ought to see what it will please them to do, before we risk congratulations, which may be soon turned into complaints. Prudence would dictate this in the case of separate, insulated, private men; but liberty, when men act in bodies, is *power*. Considerate people, before they declare themselves, will observe the use which is made of *power;* and particularly of so trying a thing as *new* power in *new* persons, of whose principles, tempers, and dispositions they have little or no experience, and in situations, where those who appear the most stirring in the scene may possibly not be the real movers.

David G. Ritchie: *Labor in a civilized society is social and not individual.*

In a complicated society there is no such thing as individual labour, unless a person were purposely to isolate himself and live like a savage; and even then it would only be by the recognised law and custom of the society that he could maintain his isolation

From *Natural Rights* (New York: The Macmillan Co., 1895), pp. 268–69. Used by permission of the Macmillan Co. and George Allen & Unwin, Ltd.

unmolested. Mr. Edward Carpenter, in his polemic against civilisation, calls the policeman a "parasite." In a crowded country the
policeman is only a part of the orderly organisation which makes
it possible for the peaceable citizen to abuse civilisation at his
ease. Locke, in propounding his theory of property, recognises
fully that to the making of a loaf of bread in a civilised community there go an immense number of industries besides that of
the baker; but he does not recognise, as he should have done, that
those who keep the peace within the society, those who defend it
from attack from without, and those who in any way advance the
orderliness and the intelligence of the society and its power over
nature, all contribute their share to the making even of a loaf of
bread. So that when we come to consider fairly the question,
"Whose is the loaf?" not merely the miller, the farmer, the iron-
worker, the miner may put in their claim for a portion, but the
magistrate, the policeman, the soldier, the man of science, the
schoolmaster. All labour in a civilised society is social and not individual labour; and therefore no law of nature helps us to determine *a priori* how the produce of labour ought to be distributed.

To some persons, indeed, a great part of the highly paid work
of the world, the work of the lawyer or the merchant, for instance,
or the work of the general and of the officials of the War Office,
may seem useless or even mischievous work, while the work of the
"labouring man" seems honest in comparison. To this it need only
be answered that the mere fact of work being manual does not
make it socially beneficial. The enterprising capitalist who puts
adulterated or deleterious goods in the market may be more
morally blameworthy than the workmen he employs to execute his
nefarious plot upon the community; but it cannot be pretended
that these workmen are conferring any benefit upon society. And,
if they deserve credit simply because they are busy—no matter at
what—the same plea must serve for many of those whom the "labourer," or the labourer's advocate, calls "parasites."

Sidney Hook: *It would be the height of foolishness to rely on pacifism to prevent war.*

In a world where the engines of human destruction are becoming more and more deadly, the problem of preventing war must be met before modern civilization goes down into shambles. Few people profess to enjoy war, everyone deplores its costs, and although the different sides lose unequally in a war, it is questionable whether any long war is economically profitable to anybody. Why then should not the universal acceptance of an absolute pacifism like Tolstoy's be the solution to the problem? Let us grant that if everyone, or almost everyone, actually adopted the Tolstoyian or Gandhian position, war would be impossible. We shall consider the proposal only from the point of view of its efficacy in bringing about the desired results.

It is logically not inconceivable that enough human beings may be converted to pacifist doctrine to prevent wars in the future. But there are so many "laws" of social behavior that would have to be suspended for the doctrine to spread, that the prospect of its adoption must be dismissed as Utopian. Some men will risk their lives because of the intrinsic nobility of an ideal or the truth of a doctrine. But the vast majority of individuals, past and present, have fought for ideals in order to further interests of a more concrete kind, like security, a longer life, or a materially better one. It is not absolutely excluded that in time the vast majority of men might be won to the position of Tolstoy that to be holy is better than to be, and that to forgive one's enemies is better than to insist on justice from them. But long before enough have been converted, the situation will enable some unpacific men to further their existing interests by profiting from the nonresisting behavior of those who practice absolute pacifism. The latter will not fight for their own lives and possessions or for the lives and possessions of friends, children, and countrymen. In that case, others, perhaps from countries and regions in which the ideals of pacifism

From *The Hero in History* (New York: John Day Co., 1943), pp. 255–57. Copyright 1943 by Sidney Hook. Used by permission.

are held in scorn, will discover that it is truly to their interest to be aggressively militant and to cut down and enslave the pacifists. The pacifist argument that it pays everyone not to have wars runs up against the fact that it would pay some people, in a world where others were pacifist, to make war on the pacifists. Consequently, *for the pacifist position to be truly effective the vast majority of mankind would have to adopt it at once in order to achieve its universal benefits.* For until it is adopted by everyone, it pays those who are not pacifists to reject it. The only kind of war that is always profitable is a war against pacifists.

What is the chance that everyone, or almost everyone, would adopt the pacifist position at once? So small that it would be the height of foolishness to rely upon it in order to prevent war. The more want, the more boredom, the more fear there is in the world, the smaller the chance. We must therefore declare that, as a practical means of preventing war, absolute pacifism is bound to fail, barring a miraculous change in the natures of men in present-day society. It is significant that every absolute pacifist, although he hopes that the propagation of his philosophy will prevent war, will never surrender his philosophy even if he is compelled by the evidence to admit that it cannot be successful. In other words, the ground on which he holds it, ultimately, has nothing to do with its instrumental efficacy in preventing war.

Does this mean that we must accept a law to the effect that there will always be wars between nations and classes in world society? Yes, *if* we accept the major institutions, economic, educational, ethnic, political, that have so far existed in history as permanent features of the social scene. No, *if* we believe that we can use our knowledge of other laws of human behavior to modify these institutions, to experiment and devise new ones, and to correct them in the light of their consequences. *The frequency and intensity of wars can be diminished in a world society in which through peaceful social processes men can actually get at a lesser cost the things they believe—often mistakenly—that war can win for them.* It is not a matter of fate that men must war on one another. Nor are men altogether free not to fight when conflicts of basic interests cannot be resolved to their mutual satisfaction through means other than war.

Bertrand Russell: *All tolerated injustice has two bad sides.*

Wherever unjust inequalities exist, a man who profits by them tends to protect himself from a sense of guilt by theories suggesting that he is some way better than those who are less fortunate. These theories involve a limitation of sympathy, and opposition to justice, and a tendency to defend the *status quo*. They thus make the more fortunate members of the community into opponents of all progress; fear invades their souls, and they shrink timidly from all doctrines that they suspect of having a subversive tendency, and of being therefore a threat to their own comfort. On the other hand, the less fortunate members of the community must either suffer such intellectual atrophy that they do not perceive the injustice of which they are the victims, and such moral loss of self-respect that they are willing to bow down before men intrinsically no better than themselves; or they must be filled with anger and resentment, protesting indignantly, feeling a continual sense of grievance, and gradually coming to view the world through the jaundiced eyes of the victim of persecution mania. All tolerated injustice has thus two bad sides: one as regards the fortunate, and the other as regards the unfortunate. It is for these reasons rather than from any abstract excellence in justice for its own sake, that unjust social systems are evil. In a community based upon injustice, the ethical side of education can never be what it should be. Emotions of resentment which, considered in themselves, are bad, may be a very necessary motive force in eliminating injustice, whether between classes, nations, or sexes. But they do not cease to be intrinsically undesirable by being politically necessary. And it should be a touch-stone of the good society that, in it, the useful emotions will be those that are kindly, friendly, and constructive, rather than those that are angry and destructive. This consideration, if followed out, will lead us very far.

Reprinted from *Education and the Modern World* by Bertrand Russell. By permission of W. W. Norton & Company, Inc. and George Allen & Unwin, Ltd. Copyright 1932 by Bertrand Russell, pp. 152–54.

John Stuart Mill: *Collision with error heightens truth.*

If all mankind minus one, were of one opinion, and only one person were of the contrary opinion, mankind would be no more justified in silencing that one person, than he, if he had the power, would be justified in silencing mankind. Were an opinion a personal possession of no value except to the owner; if to be obstructed in the enjoyment of it were simply a private injury, it would make some difference whether the injury was inflicted only on a few persons or on many. But the peculiar evil of silencing the expression of an opinion is, that it is robbing the human race; posterity as well as the existing generation; those who dissent from the opinion, still more than those who hold it. If the opinion is right, they are deprived of the opportunity of exchanging error for truth: if wrong, they lose, what is almost as great a benefit, the clearer perception and livelier impression of truth, produced by its collision with error.

From *On Liberty* (New York: Henry Holt & Co., 1882), p. 35.

Gilbert Murray: *The best traditions make the best rebels.*

Every man who possesses real vitality can be seen as the resultant of two forces. He is first the child of a particular age, society, convention; of what we may call in one word a tradition. He is secondly, in one degree or another, a rebel against that tradition. And the best traditions make the best rebels. Euripides is the child of a strong and splendid tradition and is, together with Plato, the fiercest of all rebels against it.

There is nothing paradoxical in this. No tradition is perfect. The best brings only a passing period of peace or triumph or

From *Euripides and His Age.* One of the volumes in the Home University Library Series (New York: Oxford University Press), pp. 14–15.

stable equilibrium; humanity rests for a moment, but knows that it must travel further; to rest for ever would be to die. The most thorough conformists are probably at their best when forced to fight for their ideal against forces that would destroy it. And a tradition itself is generally at its best, not when it is universally accepted, but when it is being attacked and broken. It is then that it learns to search its own heart and live up to its full meaning. And in a sense the greatest triumph that any tradition can accomplish is to rear noble and worthy rebels. The Greek tradition of the fifth century B.C., the great age of Athens, not only achieved extraordinary advances in most departments of human life, but it trained an extraordinary band of critical or rebellious children. Many a reader of Plato's most splendid satires against democratic Athens will feel within him the conclusive answer: "No place but Athens could ever have reared such a man as this, and taught him to see these faults or conceive these ideals."

D. Philosophical Insights

George Santayana: *The later we come down in the history of philosophy, the less important philosophy becomes.*

What true progress is, and how it is usually qualified by all sorts of backsliding and by incompatible movements in contrary directions, is well illustrated by the history of philosophy. There has been progress in it; if we start with the first birth of intelligence and assume that the end pursued is to understand the world, the progress has been immense. We do not understand the world yet; but we have formed many hypotheses about it corroborated by experience, we are in possession of many arts which involve true knowledge, and we have collated and criticized—especially during the last century—a great number of speculations which, though unverified or unverifiable, reveal the problems and the possibilities in the case; so that I think a philosopher in our day has no excuse for being so utterly deceived in various important matters as the best philosophers formerly were through no fault of theirs, because they were misled by a local tradition, and inevitably cut off from the traditions of other ages and races. Nevertheless the progress of philosophy has not been of such a sort that the latest philosophers are the best: it is quite the other way. Philosophy in this respect is like poetry. There is progress in that new poets arise with new gifts, and the fund of transmitted poetry is enriched; but Homer, the first poet amongst the Greeks, was also the best, and so Dante in Italy, and Shakespeare in England. When a civilization and a language take shape they have a wonderful vitality, and their first-fruits are some love-child, some incomparable creature in whom the whole genius of the young race bursts forth uncontaminated and untrammelled. What fol-

From *Soliloquies in England* (New York: Charles Scribner's Sons, 1924), pp. 208–9. Used by permission of Daniel Cory.

lows is more valuable in this respect or in that; it renders fitly the partial feelings and varying fashions of a long decadence; but nothing, so long as that language and that tradition last, can ever equal their first exuberance. Philosophy is not so tightly bound as poetry is to language and to local inspiration, but it has largely shared the same vicissitudes; and in each school of philosophy only the inventors and founders are of any consequence; the rest are hacks. Moreover, if we take each school as a whole, and compare it with the others, I think we may repeat the same observation: the first are the best. Those following have made very real improvements; they have discovered truths and methods before unknown; but instead of adding these (as they might have done) to the essential wisdom of their predecessors, they have proceeded like poets, each a new-born child in a magic world, abandoned to his fancy and his personal experience. Bent on some specific reform or wrapped up in some favourite notion, they have denied the obvious because other people had pointed it out; and the later we come down in the history of philosophy the less important philosophy becomes, and the less true in fundamental matters.

Arthur James Balfour: *A community that spent its time in hunting for first principles is a community that would starve.*

Can anyone doubt that in our creed of common knowledge are many beliefs of crucial importance, which no competent thinker would call self-evident, but which, proved or unproved, it is in practice impossible for us to abandon? Do we not, for example, believe ourselves to live in a world of men and things; a world extended and enduring; a world where, within limits, we are free to act; a world where at least some degree of regularity prevails; where memory supplies some knowledge of the past, and probability offers some guidance for the future? So far, if no further,

From *Theism and Thought* (New York: Harper & Bros., 1924), pp. 211, 213–15. Reprinted by permission.

the whole human race is compelled to travel in company; the wise with the foolish, the learned with the ignorant, the latest product of the schools with the most primitive and ignorant of barbarians. . . .

Facts like these suggest some curious speculations. We are apt to dwell on the variety of opinions which divide mankind, on their passionate disputations over trifles, on the multiplicity of their superstitions about the unseen, on their fantastic explanations of things constantly before their eyes. But are not their agreements stranger than their differences? . . . We must remember that in ordinary life any answer is treated as sufficient which successfully appeals to facts and principles accepted by all the parties to the discussion. And this is as it should be. In no other way could the business of the world be carried on. A community that spent its time in hunting for first principles is a community that would certainly starve. But what is sufficient for daily life is quite insufficient for philosophy—even for a philosophy of the familiar. . . .

It seems therefore that the remarkable agreement which prevails with regard to our familiar beliefs has little to do with reasoning. This is curious. But not less curious is the disagreement which immediately declares itself when reasoning is used either to establish these familiar beliefs or to transcend them. . . . About the foundations of knowledge (assuming that they can be found), about the higher realities (assuming that they exist) there has never been agreement. It is only on the uncritical level of ordinary practice that anything resembling harmony can be said to exist.

G. E. Moore: *It is by no means easy to avoid mistaking bad reasons for good.*

But I may perhaps remind you that this question, "How do we know so and so?" "What reason have we for believing it?" is one of which philosophy is full; and one to which the most various

From *Philosophical Studies* (Reprint ed.; New York: Humanities Press, Inc., 1951), pp. 38–39. Used by permission of Humanities Press and Routledge & Kegan Paul, Ltd.

answers have been given. Philosophy largely consists in giving reasons; and the question what are good reasons for a particular conclusion and what are bad, is one upon which philosophers have disagreed as much as on any other question. For one and the same conclusion different philosophers have given not only different, but incompatible, reasons; and conversely different philosophers have maintained that one and the same fact is a reason for incompatible conclusions. We are apt, I think, sometimes to pay too little attention to this fact. When we have taken, perhaps, no little pains to assure ourselves that our own reasoning is correct, and especially when we know that a great many other philosophers agree with us, we are apt to assume that the arguments of those philosophers, who have come to a contradictory conclusion, are scarcely worthy of serious consideration. And yet, I think, there is scarcely a single reasoned conclusion in philosophy, as to which we shall not find that some other philosopher, who has, so far as we know, bestowed equal pains on his reasoning, and with equal ability, has reached a conclusion incompatible with ours. We may be satisfied that we are right, and we may, in fact, be so; but it is certain that *both* cannot be right: either our opponent or we must have mistaken bad reasons for good. And this being so, however satisfied we may be that it is not we who have done so, I think we should at least draw the conclusion that it is by no means easy to avoid mistaking bad reasons for good; and that no process, however laborious, which is in the least likely to help us in avoiding this should be evaded.

Richard Falckenberg: *One view of the world cannot be refuted by another.*

In speaking above of the worth of the philosophical doctrines of the past as defying time, and as comparable to the standard character of finished works of art, the special reference was to those elements in speculation which proceed less from abstract

From *History of Modern Philosophy* (New York: Henry Holt & Co., Inc., 1897), pp. 3–4. Used by permission.

thinking than from the fancy, the heart, and the character of the individual, and even more directly from the disposition of the people; and which to a certain degree may be divorced from logical reasoning and the scientific treatment of particular questions. These may be summed up under the phrase, views of the world. The necessity for constant reconsideration of them is from this standpoint at once evident. . . . The views of the world which proceed from the spirits of different ages, as products of the general development of culture, are not so much thoughts as rhythms in thinking, not theories but modes of intuition saturated with feelings of worth. We may dispute about them, it is true; we may argue against them or in their defense; but they can neither be established nor overthrown by cogent proofs. . . . Even though they operate with the instruments of thought, they remain in the last analysis matters of faith, of feeling, and of resolution. . . . One view of the world is forced to yield its pre-eminence to another, which it has itself helped to produce by its own one-sidedness; only to reconquer its opponent later, when it has learned from her, when it has been purified, corrected, and deepened by the struggle. But the elder contestant is no more confuted by the younger than the drama of Sophocles by the drama of Shakspere, than youth by age or spring by autumn.

C. Delisle Burns: *Today philosophy means a special form of study, and not a "way of life."*

In our time the philosopher often belongs to a small and exclusive class of "wise" men. Their controversies leave the average man cold, even when he hears of their existence. Their conclusions have no immediate effects upon ordinary life, and the average man is hardly aware of the names of those who teach or study philosophy. On the other hand the philosopher in modern times is

From *Greek Ideals* (London: G. Bell & Sons, Ltd., 1919), pp. 192–95. Used by permission.

hardly at all influenced by the current habits of thought or action. Perhaps he does not even meet men of the poorer classes, and he seldom condescends to speak of his subject with the ordinary educated man. His ethics and his metaphysics are not immediately affected by the religious practice or conventional beliefs of his time.

This segregate position is due not to any deficiency of modern philosophers or the modern man in the street but to the increasing segmentation of modern society in respect of "interests," and it is partly for this reason that philosophy means now a special form of study and not a "way of life" as it did for Plato and Aristotle. Whereas in former times men were separated chiefly by geographical obstacles and distances, now that these have been almost overcome, we tend to be separated by differences of occupation. A common dwelling-place now does not necessarily bring the inhabitants into contact, each with the other. In the great city-regions no one knows his neighbours. And it is more and more possible for men to meet only those who are interested in the same segment of life, however far-off those others may dwell. Geographical or linguistic divisions are still sufficiently important, but the tendency of modern life seems to be in the direction of separating and uniting men in reference to occupation or interest; so that the modern man, in a society actually more complex, may be in touch with fewer differences of view than the ancient Athenian.

By contrast, in Athens of the fifth and fourth centuries the philosopher was compelled to be in contact with men who were interested in many different aspects of life. It was impossible for Plato or Aristotle to avoid conversation with shoemakers and merchants and politicians and "men about town." The philosopher walked in processions or at least attended popular fêtes. He was affected at every moment by what quite unphilosophic men were thinking and doing; and therefore his evidence for social life was perhaps more complex and was certainly more personal than the evidence of the modern members of the "thinking" caste. He knew men and did not read statistics. On the other hand . . . the influence of current life is not as acutely felt by thinkers as it was in Athens. Much as we may have gained, therefore, since the days of Plato and Aristotle, they had evidence for social and ethical facts of a peculiarly valuable kind. Athens was always before them; and their ideals were Athenian even when they went beyond the average man in desiring consistent thought or intellectual insight. It is clear, then, that we may speak of Plato and Aristotle as Athenian in a sense in which we could not speak of a modern philosopher as representing the atmosphere or expressing the ideals of his city.

Charles S. Peirce: A few clear ideas are worth more than many confused ones.

The very first lesson that we have a right to demand that logic shall teach us is, how to make our ideas clear; and a most important one it is, depreciated only by minds who stand in need of it. To know what we think, to be masters of our own meaning, will make a solid foundation for great and weighty thought. It is most easily learned by those whose ideas are meagre and restricted; and far happier they than such as wallow helplessly in a rich mud of conceptions. A nation, it is true, may, in the course of generations, overcome the disadvantage of an excessive wealth of language and its natural concomitant, a vast, unfathomable deep of ideas. We may see it in history, slowly perfecting its literary forms, sloughing at length its metaphysics, and, by virtue of the untirable patience which is often a compensation, attaining great excellence in every branch of mental acquirement. The page of history is not yet unrolled which is to tell us whether such a people will or will not in the long run prevail over one whose ideas (like the words of their language) are few, but which possesses a wonderful mastery over those which it has. For an individual, however, there can be no question that a few clear ideas are worth more than many confused ones. A young man would hardly be persuaded to sacrifice the greater part of his thoughts

From *Chance, Love, and Logic* by Charles S. Peirce. Copyright 1923. Pp. 36–37. Reprinted by permission of Harcourt, Brace & Co., Inc., and Routledge & Kegan Paul, Ltd.

to save the rest; and the muddled head is the least apt to see the necessity of such a sacrifice. Him we can usually only commiserate, as a person with a congenital defect. Time will help him, but intellectual maturity with regard to clearness comes rather late, an unfortunate arrangement of Nature, inasmuch as clearness is of less use to a man settled in life, whose errors have in great measure had their effect, than it would be to one whose path lies before him. It is terrible to see how a single unclear idea, a single formula without meaning, lurking in a young man's head, will sometimes act like an obstruction of inert matter in an artery, hindering the nutrition of the brain, and condemning its victim to pine away in the fullness of his intellectual vigor and in the midst of intellectual plenty. Many a man has cherished for years as his hobby some vague shadow of an idea, too meaningless to be positively false; he has, nevertheless, passionately loved it, has made it his companion by day and by night, and has given to it his strength and his life, leaving all other occupations for its sake, and in short has lived with it and for it, until it has become, as it were, flesh of his flesh and bone of his bone; and then he has waked up some bright morning to find it gone, clean vanished away like the beautiful Melusina of the fable, and the essence of his life gone with it. I have myself known such a man; and who can tell how many histories of circle-squarers, metaphysicians, astrologers, and what not, may not be told in the old German story?

George Stuart Fullerton: *The philosopher is, as a rule, a man influenced by his emotions.*

Were the philosopher really so independent and unprejudiced a creature as we are sometimes given to understand that he is . . . System would not rise out of system as it manifestly does. There

From *The World We Live In* (New York: The Macmillan Co., 1912), pp. 264–65. Used by permission.

would be no schools in philosophy. That there are such cannot be attributed to the fact that a philosopher leaves behind him a basis of indubitable truth upon which his successor, if he is to build at all, must perforce stand. Men of equal intelligence embrace widely diverging doctrines, and there is no unquestionably objective control, no irrefutable verification, which can coerce them into agreement. Here again let us look at the actual facts. Why is one man a scholastic, another a Hegelian, a third a positivist, a fourth a Spencerian, a fifth a pragmatist? He knows the philosophers little who supposes that each is an impersonal mouthpiece through which the passionless voice of reason communicates to us its colorless utterances.

That the philosopher is a man, and like other men, is swayed by the impulse to believe even where there is not present such evidence as men generally would admit to be scientifically coercive, appears to be a patent fact. That he *tries* to be objective, so far as he can, let us freely admit. But let us recognize that he is a man. And he is, as a rule, a man influenced by his emotions, and in need of some satisfying outlook upon life.

The philosopher has, in his day, bowed down to gods many and to lords many. He is still to be found on his knees before a variety of shrines. Think of the "One's," the "Absolute's," the "Ultimate Reality's," the "Unknowable's," the "Over-soul's," the "Super-individual Ego's," the "Nature's," the "Cosmic Will's," that have compelled his adoration! . . .

When those who have not been schooled by him in their youth come to examine his account of the object of his worship, they are sometimes filled with admiration of his speculative genius, and often with wonder at the transparent emptiness of the Abstraction upon the altar. They ask themselves how it is possible that a man of such clear vision has found it possible to balance himself upon his bridge of a single hair, and, nevertheless, to persuade himself that his feet have never left the solid ground.

Herbert J. Muller: *The tragic sense is the profoundest sense of our common humanity.*

. . . I am pleased to believe—out of faith, hope, and charity, as out of respect for truth and for mystery—that history finally solves and settles nothing: that it yields no more certain meaning than Unamuno's call 'to live, seeing that we all have to die; to live, because life is an end in itself.' Such progress as man has made has not been a measurable advance in the pursuit of happiness, toward any demonstrable prospect of a heaven on earth. It has consisted rather in the very faith in progress, the awareness of finer possibilities and further goals, the sense of freedom and the open road—the happiness of pursuit. As Horace Kallen has said, 'The going is the goal.' To keep going we can still hope for the best, and must; but we cannot hope for final solutions, and must not. Because history 'shows' nothing so simple and certain as both progressives and conservatives are wont to make out, it may show something more valuable for our living purposes. It is perhaps the best means to a full consciousness of both necessity and freedom, permanence and change—of the always difficult but honorable terms of mortality, on which man has repeatedly failed, and in failure has created deathless values. In this consciousness we may know more freedom amid our necessities, more rest amid change.

· · · · ·

Today, I suppose, the most apparent use of the 'tragic' view of history is the melancholy one of helping to prepare us for the worst. It gives us vast and eminent company in our misery; for if we feel that our society is damned and doomed, we can add that all the great societies were sufficiently damned and were certainly doomed. We might also remember what written history too seldom shows, that ordinary men have always had to suffer the history their leaders were making. Yet the tragic sense is the pro-

From *The Uses of the Past: Profiles of Former Societies* by Herbert J. Muller. Copyright 1952 by Oxford Univ. Press, Inc., pp. 373–74. Reprinted by permission.

foundest sense of our common humanity, and may therefore be a positive inspiration. If all the great societies have died, none is really dead. Their peoples have vanished, as all men must, but first they enriched the great tradition of high, enduring values. Like Burckhardt we might be heartened as well as sobered by the thought that we shall vanish into the same darkness, and live on in the same tradition. We might be freed from the vanity of grandiose hopes, as of petty concerns. We might learn that 'ripeness is all,' and that it is enough.

René Descartes: *There is not a single matter in philosophy that is not still in dispute.*

Of Philosophy I will say nothing, except that when I saw that it had been cultivated for many ages by the most distinguished men, and that yet there is not a single matter within its sphere which is not still in dispute, and nothing, therefore, which is above doubt, I did not presume to anticipate that my success would be greater in it than that of others; and further, when I considered the number of conflicting opinions touching a single matter that may be upheld by learned men, while there can be but one true, I reckoned as well-nigh false all that was only probable.

As to the other Sciences, inasmuch as these borrow their principles from Philosophy, I judged that no solid superstructures could be reared on foundations so infirm; and neither the honour nor the gain held out by them was sufficient to determine me to their cultivation: for I was not, thank heaven, in a condition which compelled me to make merchandise of Science for the bettering of my fortune; and though I might not profess to scorn glory as a Cynic, I yet made very slight account of that honour which I hoped to acquire only through fictitious titles. And, in fine, of false Sciences I thought I knew the worth sufficiently to escape

From *A Discourse on Method: Meditations on the First Philosophy; and Principles of Philosophy*, Everyman's Library edition, pp. 8–10. Reprinted by permission of E. P. Dutton & Co., Inc. and J. M. Dent & Sons, Ltd.

being deceived by the professions of an alchemist, the predictions of an astrologer, the impostures of a magician, or by the artifices and boasting of any of those who profess to know things of which they are ignorant.

For these reasons, as soon as my age permitted me to pass from under the control of my instructors, I entirely abandoned the study of letters, and resolved no longer to seek any other science than the knowledge of myself, or of the great book of the world. I spent the remainder of my youth in travelling, in visiting courts and armies, in holding intercourse with men of different dispositions and ranks, in collecting varied experience, in proving myself in the different situations into which fortune threw me, and, above all, in making such reflection on the matter of my experience as to secure my improvement. For it occurred to me that I should find much more truth in the reasonings of each individual with reference to the affairs in which he is personally interested, and the issue of which must presently punish him if he has judged amiss, than in those conducted by a man of letters in his study, regarding speculative matters that are of no practical moment, and followed by no consequences to himself, farther, perhaps, than that they foster his vanity the better the more remote they are from common sense; requiring, as they must in this case, the exercise of greater ingenuity and art to render them probable. In addition, I had always a most earnest desire to know how to distinguish the true from the false, in order that I might be able clearly to discriminate the right path in life, and proceed in it with confidence.

It is true that, while busied only in considering the manners of other men, I found here, too, scarce any ground for settled conviction, and remarked hardly less contradiction among them than in the opinions of the philosophers. So that the greatest advantage I derived from the study consisted in this, that, observing many things which, however extravagant and ridiculous to our apprehension, are yet by common consent received and approved by other great nations, I learned to entertain too decided a belief in regard to nothing of the truth of which I had been persuaded merely by example and custom: and thus I gradually extricated myself from many errors powerful enough to darken our Natural

Intelligence, and incapacitate us in great measure from listening
to Reason. But after I had been occupied several years in thus
studying the book of the world, and in essaying to gather some
experience, I at length resolved to make myself an object of study,
and to employ all the powers of my mind in choosing the paths I
ought to follow; an undertaking which was accompanied with
greater success than it would have been had I never quitted my
country or my books.

William F. Ogburn: *Not too much should be expected from social science in solving value conflicts.*

The high development of a science of society, which I hold to
be greatly desired, would nevertheless not solve all our social
problems. The existence of a body of knowledge is not a guarantee that it will be used, or that it will be used rightly. For instance
an employer may not care to have knowledge about the low
standard of living and the hazards of life for his employees nor
to use it for the purpose of raising their wages. As an executive
he may be much more responsive to the pressures of his stock-
holders for profits. So also the government of South Africa, when
dealing with the large number of Negroes, may not use the knowledge which anthropology furnishes about racial equality. It may
be primarily interested in maintaining white dominance. Thus if
knowledge is an obstacle to power it may not be used.

Knowledge may also be misused. We have some knowledge
about the influence of propaganda and of how to persuade individuals to act. Herr Goebbels, the minister of propaganda under
the Nazi regime, possessed such knowledge and great skill in
using it. Yet who shall say that he used such knowledge for the

From "Science and Society" in *Science and Civilization*, ed. Robert C.
Stauffer. (Madison, Wis.: The Univ. of Wisconsin Press, 1949), pp. 208–9.
Reprinted with permission of the copyright owners, the Regents of The Uni-
versity of Wisconsin.

good of society? Knowledge is sometimes like an invention—for instance, a knife which may be used for good or for bad.

It is not clear that scientific knowledge will solve the social problems that arise from the abuse of power. Those in power can use scientific knowledge to remain in power as truly as those who suffer from the abuse of power may use scientific knowledge to improve their position and to control power. Even if we should ever acquire the knowledge to prevent power and selfishness, or even to lessen them, and did so, society might be the loser, for the love of power and selfishness are great driving forces.

However, it seems to me that a large accumulation of scientific knowledge about society should help somewhat the resolution of difficulties that arise because of different value systems. In class and race prejudice, knowledge of the distribution of inherited ability lessens the power of the subjective factor in building rationalizations to support prejudice, but not too much should be expected from social science in solving value conflicts. Even though knowledge reduces the freedom to rationalize emotion, it must be observed that the educated seem to rationalize about as easily as the illiterate.

These remarks are made to suggest cautions in our expectations from social science. The achievements of science have been most spectacular in physics, chemistry, astronomy, and biology—so much so that our hopes are that similar scientific marvels may be achieved in all walks of life. To many of us science has been oversold. Men live emotionally rather than scientifically or even rationally much of the time. A large part of our life is taken up in acquiring, playing, worshiping, loving, praising and receiving praise, adventuring, seeking sociability, and trying to forget. Social science knowledge is more likely to affect the materials and milieu of these activities than the nature of them or the time put in on them.

E. Thoughts on History

R. G. Collingwood: *When a historian tries to reopen an old question, he finds that the question has changed.*

What is this thing called evidence, and what is its relation to the finished historical work?

We already know what evidence is not. It is not ready-made historical knowledge, to be swallowed and regurgitated by the historian's mind. Everything is evidence which the historian can use as evidence. But what can he so use? It must be something here and now perceptible to him: this written page, this spoken utterance, this building, this finger-print. And of all the things perceptible to him there is not one which he might not conceivably use as evidence on some question, if he came to it with the right question in mind. The enlargement of historical knowledge comes about mainly through finding how to use as evidence this or that kind of perceived fact which historians have hitherto thought useless to them.

The whole perceptible world, then, is potentially and in principle evidence to the historian. It becomes actual evidence in so far as he can use it. And he cannot use it unless he comes to it with the right kind of historical knowledge. The more historical knowledge we have, the more we can learn from any given piece of evidence; if we had none, we could learn nothing. Evidence is evidence only when some one contemplates it historically. Otherwise it is merely perceived fact, historically dumb. It follows that historical knowledge can only grow out of historical knowledge; . . . In principle the aim . . . is to use the entire perceptible here-and-now as evidence for the entire past through whose process it

From *The Idea of History* (Oxford, England: The Clarendon Press, 1949), pp. 246–48. Used by permission.

has come into being. In practice, this aim can never be achieved. The perceptible here-and-now can never be perceived, still less interpreted, in its entirety; and the infinite process of past time can never be envisaged as a whole. But this separation between what is attempted in principle and what is achieved in practice is the lot of mankind, not a peculiarity of historical thinking. The fact that it is found there only shows that herein history is like art, science, philosophy, the pursuit of virtue, and the search for happiness.

It is for the same reason that in history, as in all serious matters, no achievement is final. The evidence available for solving any given problem changes with every change of historical method and with every variation in the competence of historians. The principles by which this evidence is interpreted change too; since the interpreting of evidence is a task to which a man must bring everything he knows: historical knowledge, knowledge of nature and man, mathematical knowledge, philosophical knowledge; and not knowledge only, but mental habits and possessions of every kind: and none of these is unchanging. Because of these changes, which never cease, however slow they may appear to observers who take a short view, every new generation must rewrite history in its own way; every new historian, not content with giving new answers to old questions, must revise the questions themselves; and—since historical thought is a river into which none can step twice—even a single historian, working at a single subject for a certain length of time, finds when he tries to reopen an old question that the question has changed.

Frederick J. E. Woodbridge: *The historian may write in either of two ways.*

The writer of history may, consequently, attain his purpose within the limits of the practical and moral difficulties which beset it in either of two ways. He may give us the contemporane-

From *The Purpose of History* (New York: Columbia Univ. Press, 1916), pp. 24–25. Used by permission.

ous understanding of what has happened in terms of the outlook and perspective of his own day, giving us a vision of what has gone before as an enlightened mind of his time might see it. His history might then be that of ancient peoples beheld in the new perspective into which they have now been placed. Could he, by miracle, recall the ancients back to life, they would doubtless fail to recognize their own history, truthful as it might be. But comprehension might dawn upon them as they read, and they might exclaim: "These were the things we were really doing, but we did not know it at the time; we have discovered what we were; our history has revealed to us ourselves." Or the historian, by the restrained exercise of his imagination, may give us what has happened in the perspective of the time in which it happened, or in a perspective anterior to his own day. He may seek to recover the sense, so to speak, of past contemporaneity, transplanting us in imagination to days no longer ours and to ways of feeling and acting no longer presently familiar. Such a history would be less comprehensive and complete than the former. It would also be more difficult to write, because historical imagination of this kind is rare and also because it is not easy to divest the past of its present estimate. Yet the imagination has that power and enables us to live again in retrospect what others have lived before us. But in both cases the history would be an active conservation of events in time; it would reveal their truth, their meaning, and their purpose.

Richard McKeon: *The facts with which historians deal are not possessed of fixed characteristics.*

The problems of method in history, notwithstanding the natural tendency to distinguish facts from their interpretation, are problems of relevance as well as of fact. The problems of historical

From "Evidence in History" in *Freedom and Reason*, ed. Salo Baron, Ernest Nagel and Kopfel S. Pinson (New York: Conference on Jewish Relations, 1951), pp. 201–3. Reprinted by permission of Jewish Social Studies.

evidence which bear on discovering and demonstrating what took place cannot be separated wholly from the problems of historical interpretation which bear on reconstructing in argument how or why it took place. If problems of method are restricted to problems of fact, historical method may be thought to be conditioned only by a subject matter which the historian, in guise of scientist, must investigate objectively. The facts with which historians deal, however, are not atomic entities possessed of proper and fixed characteristics. . . . The arguments and reasons which bind the facts into plausible account are inseparable from the discoveries and demonstrations which establish the facts, . . .

The calculation of evidence available and the balance of its probabilities implies some determination of what constitutes evidence and relevance. Once his subject matter has been delimited, whether by tacit preconception or explicit definition, the historian may use "scientific methods" for the collection of data, for induction and generalization, for the estimation of probabilities, or even for the formulation of principles. He may state his basic laws or assume them as common truths in no need of explicit formulation or adapt them from one or more of the sciences, from economics, sociology, anthropology, politics, psychology, physics, biology, geology, or cosmology. His treatment of evidence, thereafter, may resemble the statistical interpretation of curves and tendencies, the social, biological or psychopathic diagnoses of symptoms, or the philosophic reconstruction of causes of events, tempers of ages, or cycles of birth and destruction. The historian who treats happenings and times in one fashion, however, is faced not only with the problems involved in his data but also those presented by the opposed methods and different data of historians who approach the same period and related occurrences on other assumptions. The economic historian must find at least a problem in the data and methods of the historian who delineates the morphology and physiognomy of ages or the historian who traces the causal influences of political actions or, if such data and methods seem too far removed, at least in those of the economic historian of another persuasion, classical or Marxist. The problem of evidence is involved not merely in the interpretation of commonly accepted data, but in the correlation of apparently irreducible differences of data found in different interpretations and thought acceptable on different grounds and in the estimation of incommensurate weights of importance and cogency assigned to them. In the treatment of the latter problems, methods of inquiry and proof, in which history is similar to science, are subordinated to methods of persuasion or dissuasion, edification, or even exhortation and imprecation in the interests of utility or salvation, in which history, continuing an old tradition, is a branch of rhetoric, or literature, or politics, or theology.

Ernest R. May: *Ghost writing builds an impenetrable thicket around the truth.*

There are, however, some valid objections to ghost writing. An obvious one is that the voter may get from ghost-written speeches or letters a false impression of a candidate or public officer. But an extension of this, and an objection not so obvious, is that the same false impressions may pass into history; and if history is made up of many such false impressions, the lessons it teaches to future generations are likely to be misleading.

History is written from the testimony of firsthand observers— from their diaries, letters, speeches and autobiographies. Historical truth cannot depend on secondhand interpretation any more than justice can depend on hearsay. And a ghost-written diary, letter, speech or autobiography is secondhand testimony, the ghost writer's interpretation of what his employer said or thought. . . .

. . . . .

To use speeches, letters and memoirs of this kind for the reconstruction of a man's thoughts is impossible unless the man's own contribution can be winnowed from what his ghost writer added. The choice and order of words in Jefferson's writings enabled Adrienne Koch and others to rebuild and portray his pattern of thinking, but for contemporary public figures similar analysis is

From "Ghost Writing and History" in *The American Scholar*, Autumn 1953, pp. 459–61. Used by permission of author and publisher.

practically impossible. If, on the basis of letters and speeches, a scholar should try to analyze Franklin Roosevelt's mind, he would emerge with a figure made up of Roosevelt and the fragments of Roosevelt's ghosts—Rosenman, Sherwood, Michelson, Grace Tully, Missy Le Hand, even the sprightly apparition of Harold Ickes. The only dependable keys to Roosevelt himself would have to be the documents which the President wrote by hand, for any typewritten text would automatically be open to immediate question.

Examples could be taken from any era to show how ghost-written sources have built an impenetrable thicket around the truth. . . . Between the Quarantine Address of 1938 and the Yalta Declaration, one wanders through a maze of undecided questions concerning Roosevelt's foreign policies.

But to use as an example a point that is not enmeshed in either academic or newspaper controversy, take Ray Stannard Baker's interpretation of Woodrow Wilson's "neutrality in thought" proclamation of August 18, 1914. In his biography of Wilson, Baker takes several pages to analyze the motives behind this proclamation, and he uses it as a key document for the interpretation of Wilson's World War attitudes. With the proclamation as his only source, Baker wrote: "The President . . . saw that neutrality might easily degenerate into mechanical and external observances, cynically challenged by partisans of both sides. What he desired was a sincere neutrality, a genuine suspension of judgment, in the hope that the United States might serve as first friend in the interest of peace."

A later exploration of the State Department archives, however, turned up the original draft of this proclamation in the handwriting of Robert Lansing, with changes and notations by Secretary of State William Jennings Bryan. All the words and phrases of the proclamation, save one sentence relating to America's desire to mediate the war, were written by Lansing and Bryan. Therefore, if any character is revealed in the words of this proclamation, it is that of Lansing or perhaps that of Bryan. Certainly it is doubtful that Wilson's innermost thoughts appeared in words which he merely approved.

C. G. Crump: *Great historians have tried to write objectively and have failed.*

Now it is often suggested that the student should . . . endeavour to . . . become that impartial spectator of the past who alone has the right to call himself an historian. No one will dispute the magnificence of the ideal, but it is permissible to doubt whether even those who praise it most eloquently ever attain to it, or even know how much the impartial man must forfeit in his pursuit of that splendid virtue. . . .

One thing is at least clear. Even those who believe that impartiality and objectivity are duties incumbent upon historians must admit that they are not easy duties. Minds capable of this task are few; only those can work in those high places who can endure solitude. Only those can attain to them who have been fortified by long study and strengthened by participation in great events. For minds not so equipped the pursuit of these qualities is an adventure too high. Let anyone who doubts this make a list of those historians to whom he would allow these merits without qualification. No such list will be attempted here. But it is easy to mention names which have no claim to be placed in it; Gibbon, Voltaire, Michelet, Macaulay, Carlyle, Mommsen, Treitschke. All are great names, and many more could be added. Nor would it be difficult to give a list of great historians who have tried the adventure and failed, or only succeeded by writing history without considering the passions of the men who lived among the events of which they write. Yet these men too have written great works. But it is the men in the first list who command the attention of their readers and their words still live. Yet if any of them had tried to write impartially or objectively, that very effort would have silenced them. The very fact that they have a definite point of view to maintain inspired them and attracts the reader whether he agrees with them or is provoked to dissent.

From *History and Historical Research* (London: Routledge & Kegan Paul, Ltd., 1928), pp. 6, 9–10. Used by permission.

R. G. Collingwood: *As works of imagination, the historian's work and the novelist's do not differ.*

Each of them [the historian and the novelist] makes it his business to construct a picture which is partly a narrative of events, partly a description of situations, exhibition of motives, analysis of characters. Each aims at making his picture a coherent whole, where every character and every situation is so bound up with the rest that this character in this situation cannot but act in this way, and we cannot imagine him as acting otherwise. The novel and the history must both of them make sense; nothing is admissible in either except what is necessary, and the judge of this necessity is in both cases the imagination. Both the novel and the history are self-explanatory, self-justifying, the product of an autonomous or self-authorizing activity; and in both cases this activity is the *a priori* imagination.

As works of imagination, the historian's work and the novelist's do not differ. Where they do differ is that the historian's picture is meant to be true. The novelist has a single task only: to construct a coherent picture, one that makes sense. The historian has a double task: he has both to do this, and to construct a picture of things as they really were and of events as they really happened. This further necessity imposes upon him obedience to three rules of method, from which the novelist or artist in general is free.

First, his picture must be localized in space and time. The artist's need not; essentially, the things that he imagines are imagined as happening at no place and at no date. Of *Wuthering Heights* it has been well said that the scene is laid in Hell, though the place-names are English. . . .

Secondly, all history must be consistent with itself. Purely imaginary worlds cannot clash and need not agree; each is a world

From *The Idea of History* (Oxford, England: The Clarendon Press, 1949), pp. 245–46. Used by permission.

to itself. But there is only one historical world, and everything in it must stand in some relation to everything else, even if that relation is only topographical and chronological.

Thirdly, and most important, the historian's picture stands in a peculiar relation to something called evidence. The only way in which the historian or any one else can judge, even tentatively, of its truth is by considering this relation; and, in practice, what we mean by asking whether an historical statement is true is whether it can be justified by an appeal to the evidence: for a truth unable to be so justified is to the historian a thing of no interest.

Hugh Ross Williamson: *The fictional version is surely the truer history.*

What there is no room for in history is any genuinely creative imagination. It is imaginative fiction—yes; but imaginative fiction of a low order. Even where the historian has grasped the truth that genuine history is the interaction of character, not the invention of myths, he is circumscribed by the extent of his discoveries. He cannot invent speeches and thoughts for his actors; he can only record what he can prove, by the citation of documents, they actually said or thought. To take an example. After James II's stormy interview with the seven bishops who refused to acknowledge the royal power and read the Declaration of Indulgence, the King said to them 'in conclusion borrowing the phraseology of the Puritans but conveying little meaning: "I tell you there are seven thousand men, and of the Church of England too, that have not bowed the knee to Baal".' 'Conveying little meaning.' The sentence I have quoted is the recording of the scene by James's most recent biographer. He has had to confine himself to the actual record of James's words and he finds—as others have—that they seem to lack logic.

From "History and the Writer" in *Essays by Divers Hands* (London: Oxford Univ. Press, 1955), XXVII, 132. Sponsored by Royal Society of Literature. Used by permission of Hugh Ross Williamson.

But an historical novelist, re-creating the scene, cannot avail himself of such a comment—or such an excuse. He must solve the meaning. And in doing so he may write: 'James dismissed the Bishops with: "There are seven of you. But I tell you there are seven thousand—and of the Church of England too—that have not bowed their knees to the Baal of rebellion."'

Immediately, you see, we have risen to historical reconstruction of an altogether higher order than the academic. The fictional version is surely the truer history.

Thomas Babington Macaulay: *A historian may, by showing nothing but the truth, produce all the effect of the grossest falsehood.*

Diversity, it is said, implies error: truth is one, and admits of no degrees. We answer, that this principle holds good only in abstract reasonings. When we talk of the truth of imitation in the fine arts, we mean an imperfect and a graduated truth. No picture is exactly like the original; nor is a picture good in proportion as it is like the original. When Sir Thomas Lawrence paints a handsome peeress, he does not contemplate her through a powerful microscope, and transfer to the canvas the pores of the skin, the blood-vessels of the eye, and all the other beauties which Gulliver discovered in the Brobdignaggian maids of honor. If he were to do this, the effect would not merely be unpleasant, but, unless the scale of the picture were proportionably enlarged, would be absolutely *false*. And, after all, a microscope of greater power than that which he had employed would convict him of innumerable omissions. The same may be said of history. Perfectly and absolutely true it cannot be: for, to be perfectly and absolutely true, it ought to record *all* the slightest particulars of the

From "History" in *Critical, Historical and Miscellaneous Essays and Poems* (New York: A. L. Burt, n. d.), I, 277–78.

slightest transactions—all the things done and all the words uttered during the time of which it treats. The omission of any circumstance, however insignificant, would be a defect. If history were written thus, the Bodleian library would not contain the occurrences of a week. What is told in the fullest and most accurate annals bears an infinitely small proportion to what is suppressed. . . .

No picture, then, and no history, can present us with the whole truth; but those are the best pictures and the best histories which exhibit such parts of the truth as most nearly produce the effect of the whole. He who is deficient in the art of selection may, by showing nothing but the truth, produce all the effect of the grossest falsehood. It perpetually happens that one writer tells less truth than another, merely because he tells more truths. In the imitative arts we constantly see this. There are lines in the human face, and objects in landscape, which stand in such relations to each other, that they ought either to be all introduced into a painting together or all omitted together. A sketch into which none of them enters may be excellent; but, if some are given and others left out, though there are more points of likeness, there is less likeness. An outline scrawled with a pen, which seizes the marked features of a countenance, will give a much stronger idea of it than a bad painting in oils. Yet the worst painting in oils that ever hung at Somerset House resembles the original in many more particulars. A bust of white marble may give an excellent idea of a blooming face. Color the lips and cheeks of the bust, leaving the hair and eyes unaltered, and the similarity, instead of being more striking, will be less so.

History has its foreground and its background: and it is principally in the management of its perspective that one artist differs from another. Some events must be represented on a large scale, others diminished; the great majority will be lost in the dimness of the horizon; and a general idea of their joint effect will be given by a few slight touches.

James Harvey Robinson: *The specialist in history and the general historian correct each other.*

Since all departments of knowledge have now become historical, what need is there of history in general? If politics, war, art,
law, religion, science, literature, be dealt with genetically, will
not history tend inevitably to disintegrate into its organic elements? . . .

Let us assume that historical specialization has done its perfect
work, that every distinct phase of man's past, every institution,
sentiment, conception, discovery, achievement or defeat which is
recorded has found its place in the historical treatment of the particular branch of research to which it has been assigned according
to the prevailing classification of the sciences. This process of
specialization would serve to rectify history in a thousand ways,
and to broaden and deepen its operations, but, instead, of destroying it, it would rather tend, on the contrary, to demonstrate with
perfect clearness its absolute indispensability. Human affairs and
human change do not lend themselves to an exhaustive treatment
through a series of monographs upon the ecclesiastical or military
organization of particular societies, their legal procedure, agrarian
system, their art, domestic habits or views on higher education.
Many vital matters would prove highly recalcitrant when one
attempted to force them into a neat scientific cubby-hole. Physical, moral and intellectual phenomena are mysteriously interacting in that process of life and change which it falls to the historian
to study and describe.

Man is far more than the sum of his scientifically classifiable
operations. Water is composed of hydrogen and oxygen, but it is
not like either of them. Nothing could be more artificial than the
scientific separation of man's religious, aesthetic, economic, political, intellectual and bellicose properties. These may be studied,

From "History" in *"Lectures on Science, Philosophy and Art* (New York:
Columbia Univ. Press, 1908), pp. 27–28. Used by permission.

each by itself, with advantage, but specialization would lead to the most absurd results if there were not someone to study the process as a whole; and that someone is the historian. Imagine the devotees of the various social sciences each engaged in describing his particular interest in the Crusades or the Protestant Revolt or the French Revolution. When they had finished would not the historian have to retell the story in his way, utilizing all that they had accomplished, including what they had all omitted, and rectifying the errors into which each of the specialists had fallen on account of his ignorance of the general situation?

Frederick J. E. Woodbridge: *The history of nothing is complete.*

No historical fact can ever have its history fully written: and this, not because the adequate data, the wise and unbiased mind, and the moderate supply of genius are lacking, but because it is itself the producer of new history the more it is historically understood. It grows, it changes, it expands the more adequately we apparently grasp it. We seem never to be at the end of its career and we must stop abruptly with its history still unfinished. Others may take up our task, but they will end as we have ended. The history of nothing is complete.

To understand is not simply difficult, it is also endless. But this fact does not make it hopeless. The understanding of history grows by what it feeds on, enlarges itself with every fresh success, constantly reveals more to be understood. Our illustrations may serve us again. From the accessible records of the battle of Marathon we can understand with tolerable success the immediate antecedents and consequents of that great event. But in calling the event great we do not simply eulogize its participants. We indicate, rather, that its antecedents and consequents have been far-reaching and momentous. Greece, we say, was saved. But what are we

From *The Purpose of History* (New York: Columbia Univ. Press, 1916), pp. 14, 19, 22–24. Used by permission.

to understand by that salvation? To answer we must write and rewrite her own history, the history of what she has been and is; and with every fresh writing the battle of Marathon becomes better understood. It becomes a different battle with a different truth. And more than this: with every rewriting we understand better what went before and what followed after until the battle itself becomes but the symptom of deeper things. . . .

It seems clear, therefore, that historical truth, if we do not mean by that simply the truth of the records with which we deal, is something which can not be ascertained once for all. It is a living and dynamic truth. It is genuinely progressive. We may say that it is like something being worked out in the course of time, and something which the sequence of events progressively exposes or makes clear. If, therefore, we declare that Herodotus, or any other historian, has not told the truth, and do not mean thereby that he has uttered falsehoods, we mean only that the truth has grown beyond him and his time. For his time it might well be that he told the truth sufficiently. Ancient Greece may then have been precisely what he said it was. To blame him for not telling us what ancient Greece is now, is to blame him irrationally. In the light of historical truth, the Father of History and all his children have been, not simply historians of times old and new, but also contributors to that truth and progressive revealers of it. . . . A book of history differs radically from a museum of antiquities. In the museum, the past is preserved, but it is a dead past, the flotsam and jetsam of the stream of time. It may afford material for history, and then it is quickened into life. In a book of history, the past lives. It is in a very genuine sense progressive. It grows and expands with every fresh study of it, because every fresh study of it puts it into a larger, a more comprehensive, and a new perspective, and makes its meaning ever clearer. . . . History is, therefore, a career in time. That is why no historical item can be so placed and dated that the full truth of it is definitely prescribed and limited to that place and date. Conformably with the calendar and with geography we may be able to affirm that a given event was or is taking place, but to tell what that event is in a manner which ensures understanding of it, is to write the history of its career in time as comprehensively as it can be written. It is to conserve that event, not as an isolated and detached specimen of historical fact, but as something alive which, as it continues to live, reveals more and more its connections in the ceaseless flow of history itself.

F. Reflections on Education:
Objectives

Bertrand Russell: *No plan could be so suitable as rival propagandists in every school.*

Although it is scarcely probable that governments will adopt the expedient of exposing the young to propaganda from opposite sides on important vexed questions, I have no doubt that this would be the best plan if it could be introduced. To demand of a teacher that he shall abstain altogether from expressing controversial opinions is to demand that he shall be dull and shall suppress half his personality. There are those, it is true, who have no party feelings, but they seldom make inspiring teachers. Nor is it desirable that education should artificially avoid all the questions upon which contemporary events turn. Young people should be encouraged to think about such questions by hearing them discussed from every point of view. . . . This would be a real preparation for taking part in a democracy, and would teach the difficult art of extracting the truth from an *ex parte* statement. It is not propaganda as such that is at fault, but one-sided propaganda. To be critical of propaganda, to have what is called in America "sales resistance," is highly desirable, and is not to be achieved by remoteness from propaganda, any more than immunity from measles is achieved by remoteness from measles. It is achieved by experiencing propaganda and discovering that it is often misleading. For this purpose, no plan could be so suitable as rival propagandists in every school, for which broadcasting supplies the mechanism.

. . . . .

Reprinted from *Education and the Modern World*, pp. 218–21. By permission of W. W. Norton & Company, Inc. and George Allen & Unwin, Ltd. Copyright 1932 by Bertrand Russell.

One of the most important parts of education, and one of the most neglected, is that which teaches how to reach true conclusions on insufficient data. As a logician I am conscious of uttering what is, in strict logic, mere nonsense when I say this; nevertheless all success in practical life depends upon ability to perform this apparently impossible feat. The successful general is the one who guesses correctly what his opponent will do; the successful organiser is the one who can choose good subordinates after brief interviews. Even the successful man of science makes a guess which afterwards is verified. In politics, the data are hardly ever sufficient to enable a rational man to reach a reasoned conclusion, but they are often such as to enable a man who is both rational and shrewd to reach a sagacious conclusion. To do this requires the scientific absence of bias and power of hypothetical thought, but it requires also something else, that quality which is vaguely called "judgment." This is a quality which is greatly improved in any given direction by experience of the appropriate material. Young people ought, at some stage in their education, to be taught political judgment, by listening to eloquence known in advance to be misleading, by reading partisan statements about past events and trying to infer what really happened, and so on. All this is the opposite of propaganda; it is the technique for rendering men immune to propaganda.

Thomas H. Huxley: *Suppose your life, one day or other, depended upon your winning or losing a game at chess.*

Suppose it were perfectly certain that the life and fortune of every one of us would, one day or other, depend upon his winning or losing a game at chess. Don't you think that we should all consider it to be a primary duty to learn at least the names and the moves of the pieces; to have a notion of a gambit, and a keen

From *Lay Sermons, Addresses, and Reviews* (New York: Appleton-Century-Crofts, Inc., 1903), pp. 31–35. Used by permission.

eye for all the means of giving and getting out of check? Do you not think that we should look with a disapprobation amounting to scorn, upon the father who allowed his son, or the state which allowed its members, to grow up without knowing a pawn from a knight?

Yet it is a very plain and elementary truth, that the life, the fortune, and the happiness of every one of us, and, more or less, of those who are connected with us, do depend upon our knowing something of the rules of a game infinitely more difficult and complicated than chess. It is a game which has been played for untold ages, every man and woman of us being one of the two players in a game of his or her own. The chess-board is the world, the pieces are the phenomena of the universe, the rules of the game are what we call the laws of Nature. The player on the other side is hidden from us. We know that his play is always fair, just, and patient. But also we know, to our cost, that he never overlooks a mistake, or makes the smallest allowance for ignorance. To the man who plays well, the highest stakes are paid, with that sort of overflowing generosity with which the strong shows delight in strength. And one who plays ill is checkmated—without haste, but without remorse.

. . . . .

Well, what I mean by Education is learning the rules of this mighty game. In other words, education is the instruction of the intellect in the laws of Nature, under which name I include not merely things and their forces, but men and their ways; and the fashioning of the affections and of the will into an earnest and loving desire to move in harmony with those laws. For me, education means neither more nor less than this. Anything which professes to call itself education must be tried by this standard, and if it fails to stand the test, I will not call it education, whatever may be the force of authority, or of numbers, upon the other side.

It is important to remember that, in strictness, there is no such thing as an uneducated man. Take an extreme case. Suppose that an adult man, in the full vigour of his faculties, could be suddenly placed in the world, as Adam is said to have been, and then left to do as he best might. How long would he be left uneducated? Not five minutes. Nature would begin to teach him, through the eye, the ear, the touch, the properties of objects. Pain and pleasure would be at his elbow telling him to do this and avoid that; and by slow degrees the man would receive an education, which, if narrow, would be thorough, real, and adequate to his circumstances, though there would be no extras and very few accomplishments.

And if to this solitary man entered a second Adam, or, better still, an Eve, a new and greater world, that of social and moral phenomena, would be revealed. Joys and woes, compared with which all others might seem but faint shadows, would spring from the new relations. Happiness and sorrow would take the place of the coarser monitors, pleasure and pain; but conduct would still be shaped by the observation of the natural consequences of actions; or, in other words, by the laws of the nature of man.

To every one of us the world was once as fresh and new as to Adam. And then, long before we were susceptible of any other mode of instruction, Nature took us in hand, and every minute of waking life brought its educational influence, shaping our actions into rough accordance with Nature's laws, so that we might not be ended untimely by too gross disobedience. Nor should I speak of this process of education as past, for any one, be he as old as he may. For every man, the world is as fresh as it was at the first day, and as full of untold novelties for him who has the eyes to see them. And Nature is still continuing her patient education of us in that great university, the universe, of which we are all members . . .

Those who take honours in Nature's university, who learn the laws which govern men and things and obey them, are the really great and successful men in this world. The great mass of mankind are the "Poll," who pick up just enough to get through without much discredit. Those who won't learn at all are plucked; and then you can't come up again. Nature's pluck means extermination.

Thus the question of compulsory education is settled so far as Nature is concerned. Her bill on that question was framed and passed long ago. But, like all compulsory legislation, that of Nature is harsh and wasteful in its operation. Ignorance is visited as sharply as wilful disobedience—incapacity meets with the same punishment as crime. Nature's discipline is not even a word and a blow, and the blow first; but the blow without the word. It is left to you to find out why your ears are boxed.

The object of what we commonly call education—that education in which man intervenes and which I shall distinguish as artificial education—is to make good these defects in Nature's methods; to prepare the child to receive Nature's education, neither incapably nor ignorantly, nor with wilful disobedience; and to understand the preliminary symptoms of her displeasure, without waiting for the box on the ear. In short, all artificial education ought to be an anticipation of natural education. And a liberal education is an artificial education, which has not only prepared a man to escape the great evils of disobedience to natural laws, but has trained him to appreciate and to seize upon the rewards, which Nature scatters with as free a hand as her penalties.

That man, I think, has had a liberal education, who has been so trained in youth that his body is the ready servant of his will, and does with ease and pleasure all the work that, as a mechanism, it is capable of; whose intellect is a clear, cold, logic engine, with all its parts of equal strength, and in smooth working order; ready, like a steam engine, to be turned to any kind of work, and spin the gossamers as well as forge the anchors of the mind; whose mind is stored with a knowledge of the great and fundamental truths of Nature and of the laws of her operations; one who, no stunted ascetic, is full of life and fire, but whose passions are trained to come to heel by a vigorous will, the servant of a tender conscience; who has learned to love all beauty, whether of Nature or of art, to hate all vileness, and to respect others as himself.

Such an one and no other, I conceive, has had a liberal education; for he is, as completely as a man can be, in harmony with Nature. He will make the best of her, and she of him. They will get on together rarely; she as his ever beneficent mother; he as her mouth-piece, her conscious self, her minister and interpreter.

Archibald MacLeish: *What is required is not a differ-*
ent kind of education, but a
better education of our own
kind.

[Woodrow Wilson] recognized the fact that his university was
American, and that its educational policies would either be derived from the character of the American community—"Men do
not live in ruts in America"—or be educationally meaningless—or
worse.

What our frightened friends who wish us to emulate the Russians and mass-produce little physicists and little engineers forget
is precisely that fact. Science is universal; its laws are theoretically
the same in every corner of the earth. Technology is universal; its
adepts can practice their skills in any country. But education is
not universal. It is a function—far and away the most important
function—of the community in which it exists, and a radical
change in educational policy cannot be ordered as an automobile
manufacturer orders a new model. When it comes it will come
out of a change in the community's conception of itself. And no
one, no matter how frightened he may be by Soviet statistics or
nuclear horrors, can hope that the American conception of the
American future will ever express itself in terms of the specialized
man.

The present indictment of American education is in fact a new
form of an old charge. It was often said in Hitler's time that free
institutions cannot compete with totalitarian states. The fears
were not justified in the event then, and I should think it doubtful
that they would be now. Totalitarian education may assign children to allotted tasks as free education will not do. It may screen
out the cleverest students and determine the field of specialization
appropriate to each one by processes not available to American
examiners. It may thus provide far larger numbers of young men

From "What Is a True University?" in the *Saturday Review*, January 31,
1959, p. 13. Used by permission of Archibald MacLeish and the *Saturday
Review*.

and women prepared to serve the State in predetermined capacities than the colleges and universities of a free society could produce. Indeed a free society, precisely because it is a free society, neither could compete, nor would compete in any such manipulation of human lives. But it does not necessarily follow that the totalitarian system is destined to overrun the earth. For in matters of human life and human intelligence, quantitative statistics do not measure differences.

. . . . .

What is required, if we are falling behind in scientific inventiveness, is not a different kind of education but a better education of our own kind—the kind suitable to our society. And the last thing that will give us a better education of our own kind is an education oriented to satisfy the personnel requirements of a social machine, whether a business corporation or a nation with a capital N. The service of the nation may have been an adequate educational goal fifty years ago when nation and community were more or less the same thing, but today, when the old American conception of the human community is one thing and the new American Nation is very rapidly becoming another, "the American University" must define its purpose for itself. It must choose the needs it proposes to satisfy, not on the basis of the Defense Department's priorities, but on the basis of the character of the community, which it is the University's duty to preserve and transmit.

Alfred Zimmern: *The pre-instruction stage in education provides the indispensable basis for all that follows.*

The first stage [in education] is that which precedes any regular instruction. It is the stage at which the young child is cared for in the family or, if in a public institution, in a kindergarten or

From *Learning and Leadership* (London: Oxford Univ. Press, 1928), pp. 29–30. Used by permission.

nursery school. It is the stage at which the human being becomes acquainted with his intimate environment, first with his own body, with his thumbs and toes, then with his family, with his home, his village or his town, and with his mother-tongue and the ancestral world opened up by it.

This is the most important stage in all education, and that in which the human mind makes the greatest advance. To pass from the womb and the cradle to the village, from the world of reverie and fancy to the world of social fact, from inarticulate crying to the expression of thoughts and wishes in a traditional and perfected mode of human intercourse, is to have achieved an advance far greater than that which is required of the modern world from literacy to international understanding.

But this earliest stage is all-important in another respect also. It provides a sure and indispensable basis for all that follows by integrating the growing citizen with his community and nation. 'A man without a city', said Aristotle, 'is either a god or a beast'. No one can render true service in the cause of international co-operation if he has not first thoroughly absorbed in his own mind and soul the meaning and value of nationality. And this experience cannot be acquired by a mere effort of the intellect: it is not to be found in books, still less in newspapers. It must be lived. It supplies the permanent element, what has been called on an earlier page the static element, in political appreciation and judgment. Without it, no political opinion is of value. It may correctly calculate the play of the ripples on the surface of public life. It cannot begin to understand the great hidden movement of the deep.

Too often, indeed, has the advocate of international co-operation been identified with the *déraciné*. In reality the two are at opposite poles. The *déraciné* may sometimes render good service in other fields of human achievement. In the sphere of politics he is not only useless but mischievous, for he is constitutionally incapable of entering into that which is the deepest element in all political and social experience—the attachment of a people to its home, its traditions, and its institutions.

Bertrand Russell: *Business managers are the aristocrats of the future.*

As regards the curriculum also, respect for wealth has had an effect, though this effect is less obvious than formerly. The Greeks, like all communities that employ slave labour, held the view that all manual work is vulgar. This led them to place a great emphasis upon such things as culture and philosophy and rhetoric, which could be studied without the use of the hands. They tended to think that all manipulation of matter was unworthy of a gentleman, and this probably had something to do with their partial lack of success in experimental science. Plutarch, relating the ingenious inventions of Archimedes during the siege of Syracuse, defends him from the charge of vulgarity on the ground that he was doing it for the benefit of his cousin the King. The Romans inherited the Greek view of culture, and down to our own day this view has been dominant in all countries of Western Europe. Culture is something which can be acquired by reading books, or by conversation. Whatever involves more than this is not culture in the Greek meaning of the term. And the Greek meaning of the term is still that adopted, at any rate in England, by most schoolmasters, many university teachers, and all old gentlemen with literary tastes. . . .

In matters of this sort, the United States is much ahead of Europe, owing to the fact that, in America, aristocracy was abolished with emphasis at a time when it still existed in every European country. But a new form of class distinction in education is growing up, which is the distinction between business management and the technical processes of manufacture. The man engaged in business management is the aristocrat of the future and the phrase "a great executive" has much the same connotations in modern America that the phrase "a great nobleman" had in the novels of Disraeli. The substitution of the great executive for the great nobleman as the type to be admired is having a considerable effect upon ideals of culture. A great nobleman, in the dithyrambic day-dreams of Disraeli, was, no doubt, a man possessed of power, but it was power which had come to him without his having had to seek it, and which he exercised somewhat lazily. He was possessed also of great wealth, but this, again, had come to him without exertion, and he affected to think little of it. The things upon which he prided himself were his exquisite manners, his knowledge of good wine, his familiarity with the great world of all civilised countries, his judgment in regard to Renaissance pictures, and his capacity for epigram.

It may be said generally that the accomplishments of aristocrats were frivolous, but innocent. The accomplishments of the great executives of our own time are very different. They are men whose position has been achieved by their powerful will, and their capacity for judging other men. Power is their ruling passion, organising is the activity in which they excel. They are men capable of doing the greatest good or the greatest harm, men who must be respected for their abilities and their importance, and loved or hated according to the nature of their work, but never viewed with indifference or condescension. In an industrial world men of this type must come to the fore. . . . But whether under capitalism or under communism, it is men of this type who must ultimately dominate an industrial civilisation, and the difference between their mentality and that of aristocrats of former times must have an important influence in making industrial culture different from that of feudal and commercial ages.

Ralph Barton Perry: *The teacher hesitates to exercise moral guidance.*

The idea that the purpose of education is the development of the individual's possibilities is a sound idea insofar as it springs from a recognition that education is for the benefit of the edu-

From *Realms of Value* (Cambridge, Mass.: Harvard Univ. Press, 1954), pp. 429–30. Used by permission.

cated and not the benefit of the educator. It is the learner and not the teacher who is the ultimate consumer. He is an end in himself, and he can be reshaped only through his own responses. The fact remains, however, that moral education implies guidance and control—external guidance as a means to internal control. The teacher hesitates to exercise this guidance. Some years ago a body of educational experts recommended that children be taught that "The things that bring all men together are greater than the things that keep them apart"; and that the teacher have "a firm grasp of moral principles even accepting the risk that these may be called prejudices." But the same report contained the reservation that "pupils must not be 'conditioned' to any set and determined ways of thinking." It is clear that the reservation defeats the recommendation.

The remark that the moral teacher must take the risk of being considered prejudiced is also revealing. Morality *is* a prejudice— a prejudice in favor of justice and benevolence. The use of this word suggests that it is a petty eccentricity, an arbitrary peculiarity, like preferring blondes to brunettes or French dressing to mayonnaise. But if morality means that "the things that bring all men together are greater than the things that keep them apart," as indeed it does, it underlies all human institutions, including education itself.

William James: *To be unable to recognize superiority is the very calamity of a higher education.*

What the colleges—teaching humanities by examples which may be special, but which must be typical and pregnant—should at least try to give us, is a general sense of what, under various disguises, *superiority* has always signified and may still signify. The feeling for a good human job anywhere, the admiration of

From "The Social Value of the College Bred" in *Memories and Studies* (New York: Longmans, Green & Co., Inc., 1911), pp. 314-15. Used by permission.

the really admirable, the disesteem of what is cheap and trashy and impermanent,—this is what we call the critical sense, the sense for ideal values. It is the better part of what men know as wisdom. Some of us are wise in this way naturally and by genius; some of us never become so. But to have spent one's youth at college, in contact with the choice and rare and precious, and yet still to be a blind prig or vulgarian, unable to scent out human excellence or to divine it amid its accidents, to know it only when ticketed and labelled and forced on us by others, this indeed should be accounted the very calamity and shipwreck of a higher education.

Albert Jay Nock: *At present one cannot afford to be educated.*

Education deprives a young person of one of his most precious possessions, the sense of co-operation with his fellows. He is like a pacifist in 1917, alone in spirit—a depressing situation, and especially, almost unbearably, depressing to youth. "After all," says Dumas's hero, "man is man's brother," and youth especially needs a free play of the fraternal sense; it needs the stimulus and support of association in common endeavour. The survivor of an older generation in America has had these benefits in some degree; he is more or less established and matured and can rub along fairly comfortably on his spiritual accumulations; and besides, as age comes on, emotions weaken and sensitiveness is dulled. In his day, from the spiritual and social point of view, one could afford to be educated—barely and with difficulty afford it perhaps, but education was not a flat liability. It netted enough to be worth its price. At present one can afford only to be trained. The young person's fellows are turning all their enregy into a single narrow channel of interest; they have set the whole current of their being in one direction. Education is all against his doing that, while training is all for it; hence training puts him in step

From *Free Speech and Plain Language*, pp. 214–17. Copyright 1937 by Albert Jay Nock, by permission of William Morrow & Co., Inc.

with his fellows, while education tends to leave him a solitary figure, spiritually disqualified.

For these reasons: education, in the first place, discloses other channels of interest and makes them look inviting. In the second place, it gives rise to the view that the interest which absorbs his fellows is not worth mortgaging one's whole self, body, mind and spirit, to carry on. In the third place, it shows what sort of people one's fellows inevitably become, through their exclusive absorption in this one interest, and makes it hard to reconcile oneself to the thought of becoming like them. Training, on the other hand, raises no such disturbances; it lets one go on one's chosen way, with no uncertainty, no loss of confidence, as a man of the crowd. Education is divisive, separatist; training induces the exhilarating sense that one is doing with others what others do and thinking the thoughts that others think.

Education, in a word, leads a person on to ask a great deal more from life than life, as at present organized, is willing to give him; and it begets dissatisfaction with the rewards that life holds out. Training tends to satisfy him with very moderate and simple returns. A good income, a home and family, the usual run of comforts and conveniences, diversions addressed only to the competitive or sporting spirit or else to raw sensation—training not only makes directly for getting these, but also for an inert and comfortable contentment with them. Well, these are all that our present society has to offer, so it is undeniably the best thing all round to keep people satisfied with them, which training does, and not to inject a subversive influence, like education, into this easy complacency. Politicians understand this—it is their business to understand it—and hence they hold up "a chicken in every pot and two cars in every garage" as a satisfying social ideal. But the mischief of education is its exorbitance. The educated lad may like stewed chicken and motor-cars as well as anybody, but his education has bred a liking for other things too, things that the society around him does not care for and will not countenance. It has bred tastes which society resents as culpably luxurious, and will not connive at gratifying. Paraphrasing the old saying, education sends him out to shift for himself with a champagne appetite amidst a gin-guzzling society.

Training, on the other hand, breeds no such tastes; it keeps him so well content with synthetic gin that a mention of champagne merely causes him to make a wry face. Not long ago I met a young acquaintance from the Middle West who has done well by himself in a business way and is fairly rich. He looked jaded and seedy, evidently from overwork, and as I was headed for Munich at the moment, I suggested he should take a holiday and go along. He replied, "Why, I couldn't sell anything in Munich—I'm a business man." For a moment or two I was rather taken aback by his attitude, but I presently recognized it as the characteristic attitude of trained proficiency, and I saw that as things are it was right. Training had kept his demands on life down to a strictly rudimentary order and never tended to muddle up their clear simplicity or shift their direction. Education would have done both; he was lucky to have had none.

Woodrow Wilson: *The parents and students desire something which the teacher has little thought of giving.*

What we should seek to impart in our colleges, therefore, is not so much learning itself as the spirit of learning. You can impart that to young men; and you can impart it to them in the three or four years at your disposal. It consists in the power to distinguish good reasoning from bad, in the power to digest and interpret evidence, in a habit of catholic observation and a preference for the non-partisan point of view, in an addiction to clear and logical processes of thought and yet an instinctive desire to interpret rather than to stick in the letter of the reasoning, in a taste for knowledge and a deep respect for the integrity of the human mind. It is citizenship of the world of knowledge, but not ownership of it. Scholars are the owners of its varied plots, in severalty.

From "The Spirit of Learning" in *Representative Phi Beta Kappa Orations* (2d ed.; New York: Elisha Parmele Press, 1930), pp. 472–74. Used by permission of Edith Bolling Wilson.

If we recognize and accept these ideas, this conception of the function and the possibilities of the college, there is hope of a general understanding and accommodation. At present there is a fundamental misunderstanding. The teachers in our colleges are men of learning and conceive it their duty to impart learning; but their pupils do not desire it; and the parents of their pupils do not desire it for them. They desire something else which the teacher has little thought of giving, generally thinks it no part of his function to give. Many of the parents of our modern under- graduates will frankly tell you that what they want for their sons is not so much what they will get in the classroom as something else, which they are at a loss to define, which they will get from the associations of college life: and many more would say the same thing if they were equally ingenuous. I know what they mean, and I am free to say that I sympathize with them. They understand that all that their boys get in the class-room is instruc- tion in certain definite bodies of knowledge; that all that they are expected to bring away from their lectures and recitations is items of learning. They have consorted with college men, if they are not college bred themselves, and know how very soon items of knowledge slip away from them, no matter how faithful and dili- gent they may have been in accumulating them when they were students. They observe that that part of the college acquisition is very soon lost. College graduates will tell you without shame or regret, within ten years of their graduation, that they remember practically nothing of what they learned in the class-room; and yet in the very same breath they will tell you that they would not have lost what they did get in college for anything in the world . . .

The processes of life, the contagions of association, are the only things that have ever got any real or permanent hold on men's minds. These are the conducting media for every effect we seek to work on the human spirit. The undergraduate should have scholars for teachers. They should hold his attention steadily upon great tested bodies of knowledge and should insist that he make himself acquainted with them, if only for the nonce. But they will give him nothing he is likely to carry with him through life if they stop with formal instruction, however thorough or exacting they may make it. Their permanent effects will be wrought upon his spirit. Their teaching will follow him through life only if they reveal to him the meaning, the significance, the essential validity of what they are about, the motives which prompt it, the processes which verify it. They will rule him, not by what they know and inform him of, but by the spirit of the things they expound. And that spirit they cannot convey in any formal manner. They can convey it only atmospherically, by making their ideals tell in some way upon the whole spirit of the place.

Randolph Bourne: *Every teacher knows this baffling resistance of the undergraduate mind.*

In these days of academic self-analysis, the intellectual caliber of the American undergraduate finds few admirers or defenders. Professors speak resignedly of the poverty of his background and imagination. Even the undergraduate himself in college editorials confesses that the student soul vibrates reluctantly to the larger intellectual and social issues of the day. The absorption in petty gossip, sports, class politics, fraternity life, suggests that too many undergraduates regard their college in the light of a glorified preparatory school where the activities of their boyhood may be worked out on a grandiose scale. They do not act as if they thought of the college as a new intellectual society in which one acquired certain rather definite scientific and professional attitudes, and learned new interpretations which threw experience and information into new terms and new lights. The average undergraduate tends to meet studies like philosophy, psychology, economics, general history, with a frankly puzzled wonder. A whole new world seems to dawn upon him, in its setting and vocabulary alien to anything in his previous life. Every teacher knows this baffling resistance of the undergraduate mind.

From *The History of a Literary Radical and Other Papers* (New York: S. A. Russell, 1956), pp. 147–49. Used by permission.

It is not so much that the student resists facts and details. He will absorb trusts and labor unions, municipal government and direct primaries, the poems of Matthew Arnold, and James's theory of the emotions. There is no unkindliness of his mind towards fairly concrete material. What he is more or less impervious to is points-of-view, interpretations. He seems to lack philosophy. The college has to let too many undergraduates pass out into professional and business life, not only without the germ of a philosophy, but without any desire for an interpretative clue through the maze. In this respect the American undergraduate presents a distinct contrast to the European. For the latter does seem to get a certain intellectual setting for his ideas which makes him intelligible, and gives journalism and the ordinary expression of life a certain tang which we lack here. Few of our undergraduates get from the college any such intellectual impress.

The explanation is probably not that the student has no philosophy, but that he comes to college with an unconscious philosophy so tenacious that the four years of the college in its present technique can do little to disintegrate it. The cultural background of the well-to-do American home with its "nice" people, its sentimental fiction and popular music, its amiable religiosity and vague moral optimism, is far more alien to the stern secular realism of modern university teaching than most people are willing to admit. The college world would find itself less frustrated by the undergraduate's secret hostility if it would more frankly recognize what a challenge its own attitudes are to our homely American ways of thinking and feeling. Since the college has not felt this dramatic contrast, or at least has not felt a holy mission to assail our American mushiness of thought through the undergraduate, it has rather let the latter run away with the college.

G. Reflections on Education: Means

Bertrand Russell: *There are two very different types of teachers.*

There are, in the teaching profession, two very different types. There are those who have an enthusiasm for some subject, and who love to teach it and implant their own enthusiasm in their pupils. On the other hand, there are those who enjoy the position of power and easy superiority, who like governing but have not enough skill to govern men. Some systems favour the former type, some the latter; modern efficiency tends more and more to favour the man who governs rather than teaches. I do not deny that the governing type has its uses: I once knew a lady who had taught in a public school in Texas, and had found it necessary always to come armed with a revolver. But except in remote and sparsely populated regions, boys or girls who are abnormally refractory can be isolated, with the result that those who remain, having lost their ringleader, will become amenable to less drastic methods. The teacher who is inspired by love of his subject combined with affection for children can, in most circumstances, achieve far more in the way of imparting knowledge and civilisation than can ever be achieved by the man who loves order and method and efficiency but lacks knowledge and hates children. Unfortunately, in any large school there is a considerable amount of administrative routine, which is generally done best by the worst teachers; and as the higher authorities see the administrative work but are apt not to see the teaching, there is a tendency for credit to be quite wrongly apportioned. Moreover, in any great administrative machine, the officials at the head of it naturally consider administra-

From *Education and the Modern World*, pp. 231–35. By permission of W. W. Norton & Company, Inc. and George Allen & Unwin, Ltd. Copyright 1932 by Bertrand Russell.

tion the most honourable and difficult kind of work, with the result that a better status and a higher salary are given to those who do the administrative work of schools than to those who actually teach. All this tends to produce the wrong type of teacher. It is the executive type that encourages uniformity, while the other type will rejoice in ability (which is in itself an eccentricity), and for the sake of ability will readily tolerate other forms of oddity. It is therefore very important, in combating the danger of uniformity, to encourage teachers who love teaching rather than those who love governing.

. . . . .

In the sphere of education, the danger of the administrator arises through his love of classification and statistics. It is impossible that he should not have this passion, since he must deal quickly with vast masses of material, which only classification will enable him to do. Now in some kinds of material, classification is fairly satisfactory; this occurs where there are well-marked natural kinds. The greengrocer sells peas and beans and spinach and cabbage, and is never obliged to stop and ask himself: "Is this object a pea or a cauliflower?" With children the matter is otherwise. The question whether a given child is mentally deficient is often a border-line question, to which, speaking scientifically, no precise answer can be given. But speaking administratively, a precise answer *must* be given: the child must either be sent to a special school, or kept in the ordinary school. The administrator, therefore, looks about for some means of reaching a precision which does not exist in nature; this is one of the reasons for which he tends to love intelligence tests. And what applies in the case of the mentally deficient applies also in the case of any other mental classification. The man who deals affectionately with a small group of children knows them as individuals, and feels things about them which it would be difficult to put into words; often it is what is peculiar to a child that such a man likes best. But the man who views children from a distance, through a mist of official reports, is impatient of this sort of thing. He wishes all children were exactly alike, since that would make his work easy, but he is compelled to admit classification by age, sex, nationality,

and religion. The most enlightened also admit classification by
intelligence tests. But even the most enlightened like everything
cut and dried, and forget the quality of individual life which
makes each human being different from every other. For this reason, there is a danger lest education officials should encourage
a uniformity towards which, in any case, the world is tending.

Ernest Nagel: *We ought to aim at something more than technical proficiency as the fruit of science instruction.*

I must . . . confess my conviction that unless the student of
science carries away with him from his technical studies a good
sense of the methodological structures of science, those studies
contribute little to his liberal education. Like many others, I have
been dismayed by the slowly rising tide of cynical irrationalism
that has engulfed so many influential writers, and not less dismayed because of the peculiar views they appear to hold concerning the nature of scientific reason—in spite of the fact that many
of them have been exposed at one time or another to a respectable
amount of instruction in the sciences. I have been especially dis-
couraged by the fact that distinguished contributors to the sciences have frequently (though perhaps unwittingly) encouraged
the debasement of the scientific enterprise—either through the
irrelevant use to which they put current scientific doctrine in support of some questionable metaphysics, *Lebensphilosophie*, or
political program, or through contrasting in disparaging but dubious manner the allegedly limited competence of scientific method
with the satisfying fullness of some other form of human experience as an avenue to knowledge. I can only infer from such facts
that it is possible to "do science" with reasonable proficiency,
without possessing a mature and cultivated understanding of what

From "The Methods of Science: What Are They? Can They Be Taught?"
Reprinted from *Scientific Monthly*, LXX (January 1950), 22–23, by permission of The American Association for the Advancement of Science.

one is doing and of how such doings are warranted. Nevertheless, we ought, I think, to aim at something more than technical proficiency as the fruit of science instruction. We certainly cannot afford to neglect technical proficiency; but we ought also to include as an essential part of our goal the development of that judiciously skeptical and yet tenaciously reasonable temper that characterizes at its best the continuum of inquiry that is science.

I am thus of the opinion that scientific method can be taught, and taught best not as a separate discipline or by precept, but in conjunction with the concrete materials of the sciences, and by example. The study of scientific method is a systematic reflection on the procedures of the sciences; and no greater pedagogic error can be committed than to give instruction in principles of method to students unfamiliar with scientific subject matter and practice. It is clear, however, that, if general courses in science are to be something else than training grounds for future specialists or preparations for parlor conversation, they must be so organized as to permit time for methodological reflection on the technical problems that are presented. There is a price that must be paid for such an organization, and in particular the conception that general courses in science should supply an encyclopedic compendium of useful knowledge must be abandoned. The essential point is that the materials to be included for study must be highly selected with a double end in view: to make the student competently familiar with some representative experimental and theoretical analyses of the natural sciences; and to provide him with clear examples of the operation of scientific method.

I feel confident that these are not incompatible principles of selection. . . . In any event, it seems to me that an adequate general course in science must contain a good variety of materials drawn from a number of departmentalized disciplines; for no one example of scientific analysis can adequately illustrate the various phases of scientific method. . . . What is essential, however, is that we keep our eyes on the goal of teaching science, not as a miscellaneous body of fixed doctrines, but as a series of intellectual achievements which are best understood as the products of a discriminating and flexible method of inquiry. Needless to say, complete success in such an enterprise is not easily achieved and may not be attainable. But, since even partial success is an important contribution to the development of a liberal intelligence, the prize is not unworthy of our best efforts.

Frank L. Lucas: *It is doubtful that critics have ever done very much good to the creative.*

Educators, indeed, are prone to believe too blindly in education. Chesterfield, for example, had the extraordinary notion that anyone could train himself to become 'a model of eloquence' and indeed anything else, except (he admits) a poet—'a drayman is probably born with as good organs as Milton, Locke, or Newton; but by culture they are much more above him than he is above his horse.' Similarly I once knew a clever man who fervently imagined that he could turn any normal child, if caught young enough, into a Trinity scholar. But my own experience is that firsts are born rather than made. In the same way, though painters have been and still are trained in schools, writers of value are not *taught* to write (though I believe something of the sort is advertised in London and in the United States)—they appear to teach themselves.

. . . . .

It is true that Antiquity made efforts, persisting for centuries, to train orators. But the results seem significantly insignificant. It began when some of the Greek sophists professed to make men eloquent; they were followed by generations of rhetoricians who eventually swarmed over the whole Greco-Roman world, till Juvenal could speak of them as finding employment even in furthest Thule. But in practice not even Aristotle's *Rhetoric* could prolong the great age of Attic oratory, then nearing its end; just as his *Poetics* brought no new life to dying Tragedy. As usual, critical theory could not procreate, it could only dissect. Cicero

From *Style* (London: Cassell & Co., Ltd., 1955), pp. 33–35. Available from The Macmillan Co., New York. Reprinted by permission of The Macmillan Co., and Cassell & Co., Ltd.

produced treatises on oratory, but no new Cicero. Writers like 'Longinus' or Quintilian, often interesting, often admirable, seem to have been equally barren of practical effect. And in the upshot, for the English (though not for the Scots) 'rhetoric' has become, ironically enough, a term of abuse. I cannot believe, despite Matthew Arnold, that critics have ever done very much good to the creative; though sometimes they have done a good deal of harm.

One is too often reminded of the man in Chekhov who set out to teach his kitten an improved method of catching mice, till it cowered at sight of one; or of that wise apologue uttered by Prince Mou of Wei, about the child from Shou-ling who was sent to Han-tan to learn the Han-tan walk—'he failed to master the steps, but spent so much time trying to acquire them, that in the end he forgot how one usually walks, and came home to Shou-ling on all fours.'

None the less, though education may be less infallible and more perilous than sanguine souls assume, it remains an inescapable necessity. It spoilt Chekhov's kitten: but it has to be imposed on every horse and hawk and hound. You cannot turn glass into diamonds; but diamonds can be polished; even glass can be cut. No one is born a writer. The greatest have had to learn. Only one learns most from trying to do things oneself. . . .

Ralph E. Ellsworth: *The lecture-textbook method does not teach students to develop judgment or taste in books.*

The teaching methods commonly used in colleges and universities too frequently produce nonreaders. Many courses are taught through a combination of formal class lectures and specific reading assignments in fairly rigid textbooks, just as they were before the rotary press made books plentiful. The professor who uses the

From "College Students and Reading" in *The American Scholar*, Autumn 1958, pp. 477–78. Used by permission.

lecture-textbook method is not concerned with the reading habits his method produces. He is concerned with the problem of teaching knowledge that his students can use in more advanced courses. Such courses are not intended to produce readers, and they certainly do not. A more serious result is that they do not require any real mental exertion on the part of the student. The thinking has been done by the professor and the author of the textbook. . . . The student is given no contact with source material, and so he does not learn what it means to evaluate facts and to draw conclusions from them. He merely learns the facts and principles others have developed from source materials. If this method of teaching were used only in introductory courses, the situation would not be so bad. But this is not the case; it permeates the entire college. This method does not teach students to develop judgment or taste in books for the very simple reason that it allows them no practice in handling or reading books. Why bother with reading several books if one textbook can present an adequate summary of current knowledge?

Reliance on the crutches of class lectures or on textbooks and other forms of passive learning is the worst possible kind of preparation for adult life in the America of today. Everyone is bombarded with one-sided, direct pressure statements in the form of magazines, radio and TV programs, house and trade journals, pamphlets and the like, and there is no professor around to say what the correct line is. He who has not formed the habit of evaluating sources is quite likely to be at the mercy of the special pleader.

Morris Kline: *Ignorance of mathematics has attained the status of a social grace.*

The object of this book is to advance the thesis that mathematics has been a major cultural force in Western civilization. Almost everyone knows that mathematics serves the very practi-

From *Mathematics in Western Culture* by Morris Kline, pp. ix–x. Copyright 1953 by Oxford Univ. Press, Inc. Reprinted by permission.

cal purpose of dictating engineering design. Fewer people seem to be aware that mathematics carries the main burden of scientific reasoning and is the core of the major theories of physical science. It is even less widely known that mathematics has determined the direction and content of much philosophic thought, has destroyed and rebuilt religious doctrines, has supplied substance to economic and political theories, has fashioned major painting, musical, architectural, and literary styles, has fathered our logic, and has furnished the best answers we have to fundamental questions about the nature of man and his universe. As the embodiment and most powerful advocate of the rational spirit, mathematics has invaded domains ruled by authority, custom, and habit, and supplanted them as the arbiter of thought and action. Finally, as an incomparably fine human achievement mathematics offers satisfactions and aesthetic values at least equal to those offered by any other branch of our culture.

Despite these by no means modest contributions to our life and thought, educated people almost universally reject mathematics as an intellectual interest. This attitude toward the subject is, in a sense, justified. School courses and books have presented 'mathematics' as a series of apparently meaningless technical procedures. Such material is as representative of the subject as an account of the name, position, and function of every bone in the human skeleton is representative of the living, thinking, and emotional being called man. Just as a phrase either loses meaning or acquires an unintended meaning when removed from its context, so mathematics detached from its rich intellectual setting in the culture of our civilization and reduced to a series of techniques has been grossly distorted. Since the layman makes very little use of technical mathematics, he has objected to the naked and dry material usually presented. Consequently, a subject that is basic, vital, and elevating is neglected and even scorned by otherwise highly educated people. Indeed, ignorance of mathematics has attained the status of a social grace.

Bertrand Russell: *The average educator kills imagination in the young.*

The first thing the average educator sets to work to kill in the young is imagination. Imagination *is* lawless, undisciplined, individual, and neither correct nor incorrect; in all these respects it is inconvenient to the teacher, especially when competition requires a rigid order of merit. The problem of the right treatment of imagination is rendered more difficult by the fact that, in most children, it decays spontaneously as interest in the real world increases. Adults in whom imagination remains strong are those who have retained from childhood something of its emancipation from fact; but if adult imagination is to be valuable, its emancipation from fact must not spring from ignorance, but from a certain lack of slavishness. . . .

To pass to more concrete considerations, take such a matter as children's drawing and painting. Most children, from about five years old to about eight, show considerable imagination of a pictorial kind if they are encouraged but otherwise left free. Some, though only a small minority, are capable of retaining the impulse to paint after they have become self-critical. But if they have been taught to copy carefully and to aim at accurate representation, they become increasingly scientific rather than artistic, and their painting ceases to show any imagination. If this is to be avoided, they must not be shown how to draw correctly except when they themselves ask for instruction, and they must not be allowed to think that correctness constitutes merit. This is difficult for the teacher, since artistic excellence is a matter of opinion and individual taste, whereas accuracy is capable of objective tests. The social element in school education, the fact of being one of a class, tends, unless the teacher is very exceptional, to lead to emphasis upon socially verifiable excellences rather than upon such as depend upon personal quality. If personal quality is to be preserved, definite teaching must be reduced to a minimum, and

Reprinted from *Education and the Modern World*, pp. 157–60. By permission of W. W. Norton & Co. Inc. and George Allen & Unwin, Ltd. Copyright 1932 by Bertrand Russell.

criticism must never be carried to such lengths as to produce timidity in self-expression. But these maxims are not likely to lead to work that will be pleasing to an inspector.

The same thing, at a slightly later age, applies to the teaching of literature. Teachers tend to teach too much, and to make up silly rules of style, such as that no sentence should begin with "and" or "but." Definite rules of grammar must of course be observed, though even grammar is more elastic than most teachers suppose. Any child who wrote:

And damned be him that first cries hold, enough

would be reproached not only for profanity but also for bad grammar. In regard to literature, as in regard to painting, the danger is lest correctness should be substituted for artistic excellence. The teaching of literature should be confined to reading, and the reading should be intensive rather than extensive. It is good to know by heart things from which one derives spontaneous pleasure, and it is totally useless, from the standpoint of education in literature, to read anything, however classical, which does not give actual delight to the reader. The literature that is read with avidity and known intimately moulds diction and style, whereas the literature that is read once coldly merely promotes pseudo-intelligent conversation. Pupils should, of course, write as well as read, but what they write should not be criticised, nor should they be shown how, in the teacher's opinion, they might have written it better. So far as writing is concerned, there should be no teaching.

Howard Mumford Jones: *It is difficult to invoke the arts as a medicine against narrowness.*

We universally agree that chemistry is hard work, and we expect students to grind away at it, just as we expect them to grind away at engineering. We cannot afford to have prescriptions filled

From *Reflections on Learning* (New Brunswick, N. J.: Rutgers Univ. Press, 1958), pp. 52–54. Used by permission.

by druggists whose knowledge of pharmacy is as vague as their capacity to write English, just as we cannot afford to have bridges built by engineers whose mastery of stresses and strains in materials is as vague as their mastery of spelling. Preparation for vocation or profession is therefore hard and demanding. The medical student or the future lawyer is so wrapped up in his studies that we have a certain degree of pride in saying that John never leaves the medical school until six o'clock and Joe is in the law school library until ten. We admire and we deplore this rigor. We admire it because it keeps American technology on top of the world; we deplore it because it is narrowing, and at this point we invoke the arts as a medicine against narrowness. Students are encouraged to take courses in literature on the ground that if they don't read literary masterpieces now, they will never read them hereafter—one of the most curious arguments for art I have ever heard. And in general, courses in the humanities are called upon by planners of programs in professional education to undo the damage which plans of professional education have done.

But difficulties arise. The first is that if the whole bent of a student's training, or four-fifths of that training, is in the direction of mastering highly specialized techniques, you cannot, as an annex or an afterthought, for one-fifth of his time somehow expect him to abandon the habits of thought that are the very pith and marrow of his professional training and simultaneously get up a quite different set of habits for the study of the humanities. If the pressure upon the student is, so to say, to learn how to solve problems by the use of a slide rule, he is bewildered when, confronted by a problem in literature or philosophy or painting, you tell him that not the slide rule but the written or spoken word is the instrument he is now expected to use. He is likely to take the position that since he is not clever with words, the problem is beyond him, or that since the problem is not soluble in his terms, it is essentially a frivolous problem. The harassed instructor has then to make an impossible choice: Either he flunks our young engineer or medical student or chemist; or he lowers his standards to the point where most of the engineers, medical students, and chemists can get by. Neither solution promises any mastery of the grammar of the art in question, and therefore both fail to produce any lasting basis of satisfaction in the art.

John B. Watson: *I'll guarantee to train him to become any kind of specialist, regardless of his talents.*

I should like to go one step further tonight and say, "Give me a dozen healthy infants, well-formed, and my own specified world to bring them up in and I'll guarantee to take any one at random and train him to become any type of specialist I might select—a doctor, lawyer, artist, merchant-chief and, yes, even into beggar-man and thief, regardless of his talents, penchants, tendencies, abilities, vocations and race of his ancestors." I am going beyond my facts and I admit it, but so have the advocates of the contrary and they have been doing it for many thousands of years. Please note that when this experiment is made I am to be allowed to specify the way they are to be brought up and the type of world they have to live in.

From "What the Nursery Has to Say about Instincts" in *Psychologies of 1925*, ed. Carl Murchison (Worcester, Mass.; Clark University, 1927), p. 19. Used by permission of The Journal Press.

Pitirim A. Sorokin: *We are living in an age of testocracy.*

At the present time in the Western countries almost every individual is tested from the cradle to the grave, before and after an important event in his life. We are living in an *age of testocracy*. By their tests of our intelligence, emotional stability, aptitude,

From "Physicalist and Mechanistic School" in *Contemporary Sociology*, ed. Joseph S. Roucek (New York: Philosophical Library, Inc., 1958), pp. 1143–44.

character, unconscious drives and of other traits of our personality the testocrats largely decide our vocation, occupation, social position, promotion or demotion, normality or abnormality, in brief, a large part of our life. At the present time, the testocrats have at their disposal a vast battery of supposedly scientific tests of all possible characteristics of personality or group. This evergrowing battery contains: (1) dozens of various intelligence tests; (2) tests of various traits of personality: aggressiveness, submission, caution, conformity, conscientiousness, originality, deception, suggestibility, and so on; (3) tests of instincts, "prepotent reflexes," and emotions; (4) tests of moods, temperament, will-power, extroversion-introversion, etc.; (5) tests of attitudes, interests, preferences; (6) tests of aptitudes, abilities, and leadership; (7) tests of ethical judgments and values; (8) tests of mental and moral normality or abnormality; (9) a legion of specific tests like: potential general and specific criminality, compatibility or incompatibility of prospective bridegroom and bride, loyalty and subversivity, successful or unsuccessful parole, etc.; (10) tests of the "basic type of personality"; (11) projective tests; (12) sociometric tests; and many others.

This sort of "test-centered" psychology and psychiatry are largely responsible for penetration and permeation of the recent sociology with the testomanic fashion. The use and administration of various tests of personality or group have become a sort of preliminary "must" in the bulk of the modern sociological studies. A large portion of this research consists mainly of a statistical summary of various tests given to the persons or groups studied, beginning with their intelligence test and ending with the Rorschach, or the sociometric, or the psycho-dramatic tests.

If these tests were scientific indeed, and if they tested the respective traits of the individuals or groups as accurately as, say, thermometer tests the body temperature or barometer tests the barometric pressure, such tests and researches could only be welcomed. Unfortunately, the real situation is quite different. Almost all of the numerous tests are very far from being adequate, reliable, or scientific tests. About all these tests one can say what one of the pioneers of intelligence tests, E. L. Thorndike, says about mental tests. "Just what they measure is not known; how far it

is proper to add, subtract, multiply, divide, and compute ratios
with the measures obtained is not known; just what the measures
obtained signify concerning the intelligence is not known." When
the tests are tested in their testing adequacy, the results often
show that they either do not test at all what they are supposed
to be testing, or they test a given characteristic in an unreliable,
sometimes in a misleading way, or they yield the "quotients,"
"indexes," and "scores" as enigmatic as some of the utterances of
the Pythia of Delphi or of the old tea-leaf tests.

ARTISTIC EXPERIENCE

A. The Nature of Art

Frederick J. E. Woodbridge: *Art tells us what life
really is.*

. . . it seems clear that Plato, and Greek philosophy generally,
thought that there was something salutary simply in seeing things
as they are. The spectacle of life fascinates. Caught in the turmoil
of affairs we do not see it clearly, for our eyes are fixed on other
things, our business, our wealth, our occupations, our reputation.
These give us a bias and a preoccupation which prevents our
seeing the spectacle we make of ourselves. But in moments of
leisure we flock to the theater or read stories of love, passion,
intrigue, and adventure. These, and not our experience, tell us
what life really is, for they transform us from participants in
action to spectators of it. This justifies our presence in the theater.
Surrounded by strangers and intimates we do not blush to look
at scenes in which we would never willingly be found in action,
or hear words we would never willingly be overheard using. We
have the happiness of detachment. We may laugh or cry without
having anything whatever at stake and without the moral obliga-
tion to interfere with what is going on. We see life without living
it. Like disembodied souls we enjoy the essences of joy and sorrow, love and hate, life and death, laughter and tears, without
the consequences they have in a society of bodies. Art, not business or work or morals or religion or science or philanthropy,
reveals what life is and reveals it to be viewed in freedom. By it
we escape from living. From it we may get pleasure and illumination. If we get the former only, the trouble is either with the art
or with ourselves.

From *The Son of Apollo* (Boston: Houghton Mifflin Company, 1929),
pp. 138–40. Used by permission.

Bernard Bosanquet: *The magic of art is that a copy of a thing is more splendid than the thing.*

I am . . . quoting . . . perhaps the earliest aesthetic judgment which Western literature contains. It is in the Homeric description of the metal-working deity's craftsmanship in the shield of Achilles. He has made upon it the representation of a deep fallow field with the ploughmen driving their furrows on it; and the poet observes, "And behind the plough the earth went black, and looked like ploughed ground, though it was made of gold; that was a very miracle of his craft."

Now what was the miracle here, that made Homer cry out at it with delight? It was not, surely, that when you have one bit of ploughed land you can make another like it. That goes on all day when a man ploughs a field. Or what made Dante say of the sculptures on the marble of Purgatory, that one who saw the reality would see no better than he did, and that the representation of some smoke set his eyes and nose at variance as to whether it was real?

Surely the miracle lies in what Homer accents when he says, "Though it was made of gold." It lies here; that without the heavy matter and whole natural process of the reality, man's mind possesses a magic by which it can extract the soul of the actual thing or event, and confer it on any medium which is convenient to him, the wall of a cave, or a plate of gold, or a scrap of paper. And when these great poets insist on the likeness of the imitation, I take it that the real underlying interest is in the conquest of the difference of the medium. So that really, in the naïve praise of successful imitation, we have, if we read it rightly, the germ of the fundamental doctrine of aesthetic semblance. That is to say, what matters is not the thing, but the appearance which you can carry off, and deal with apart from it, and recreate. And the real

From *Three Lectures on Aesthetics* (London: Macmillan & Co., Ltd., 1915), pp. 49–52. Reprinted by permission of Ellen Bosanquet.

sting of even the crudest glorification of copying is this wonder that you can carry off with you a thing's soul, and leave its body behind. . . . You can copy a thing so splendidly that your copy will be more beautiful than the thing.

Walter Pater: *Artistic genius is the power to put a world of its own creation in place of the familiar world.*

The basis of all artistic genius lies in the power of conceiving humanity in a new and striking way, of putting a happy world of its own creation in place of the meaner world of our common days, generating around itself an atmosphere with a novel power of refraction, selecting, transforming, recombining the images it transmits, according to the choice of the imaginative intellect. In exercising this power, painting and poetry have a variety of subject almost unlimited. The range of characters or persons open to them is as various as life itself; no character, however trivial, mis-shapen, or unlovely, can resist their magic. That is because those arts can accomplish their function in the choice and development of some special situation, which lifts or glorifies a character, in itself not poetical. To realise this situation, to define, in a chill and empty atmosphere, the focus where rays, in themselves pale and impotent, unite and begin to burn, the artist may have, in-deed, to employ the most cunning detail, to complicate and refine upon thought and passion a thousandfold. Let us take a brilliant example from the poems of Robert Browning. His poetry is pre-eminently the poetry of situations. The characters themselves are always of secondary importance; often they are characters in themselves of little interest; they seem to come to him by strange accidents from the ends of the world. His gift is shown by the way in which he accepts such a character, throws it into some situation, or apprehends it in some delicate pause of life, in which for a moment it becomes ideal. In the poem entitled *Le Byron de*

From *The Renaissance* (New York: Boni & Liveright, 1919), pp. 177–79.

nos Jours, in his *Dramatis Personae*, we have a single moment of
passion thrown into relief after this exquisite fashion. Those two
jaded Parisians are not intrinsically interesting: they begin to
interest us only when thrown into a choice situation. But to discriminate that moment, to make it appreciable by us, that we may
"find" it, what a cobweb of allusions, what double and treble re-
flexions of the mind upon itself, what an artificial light is con-
structed and broken over the chosen situation; on how fine a
needle's point that little world of passion is balanced! Yet, in spite
of this intricacy, the poem has the clear ring of a central motive.
We receive from it the impression of one imaginative tone, of a
single creative act.

Robert Louis Stevenson: *There will always be hours when we refuse to be put off by cold truth.*

There are moments when the mind refuses to be satisfied with
evolution, and demands a ruddier presentation of the sum of
man's experience. Sometimes the mood is brought about by laughter at the humorous side of life . . . Sometimes it comes by the
spirit of delight, and sometimes by the spirit of terror. At least,
there will always be hours when we refuse to be put off by the
feint of explanation, nicknamed science; and demand instead
some palpitating image of our estate, that shall represent the troubled and uncertain element in which we dwell, and satisfy reason
by the means of art. Science writes of the world as if with the
cold finger of a starfish; it is all true; but what is it when compared to the reality of which it discourses? where hearts beat
high in April, and death strikes, and hills totter in the earthquake,
and there is a glamour over all the objects of sight, and a thrill in
all noises for the ear, and Romance herself has made her dwelling
among men? So we come back to the old myth, and hear the goat-

From "Pan's Pipes." Available in *Virginibus Puerisque; Familiar Studies
of Men and Books* (London: J. M. Dent & Sons, Ltd.), pp. 108–9.

footed piper making the music which is itself the charm and terror of things; and when a glen invites our visiting footsteps, fancy that Pan leads us thither with a gracious tremolo; or when our hearts quail at the thunder of the cataract, tell ourselves that he has stamped his hoof in the nigh thicket.

Edith Franklin Wyatt: *Fiction enables us to become someone else.*

From time to time dialogues between enterprising reporters and authors visiting this country gladden the pages of the daily press. Among these I remember reading some years ago an opinion on novels which has always interested me.

The reporter mentioned to the visiting author a novel presenting a brilliant delineation of a newspaper-writer who becomes a drug-fiend.

"The book is greatly over-rated," the visiting author replied. "Why this newspaper-writer—the hero—is only a second-rate man! I should not care to ask him to my home to lunch."

Think of the "noted names of fiction" who could not survive this simple test. Consider the imaginary figures that you can not picture as enjoying lunch with your relatives, and with whom your relatives could not enjoy lunching. "I should not care to ask him (her) to my home to lunch." Goneril—or Regan either— Bill Sikes, Gilbert Osmond, Medea, Werther, Bradley Headstone, any of the people in *Wuthering Heights*—

Without indulging myself further in regarding this or other aspects of this quick test of the value of fiction I will hasten to say that the chief reason why it seems so dismal an absurdity is perhaps because it could only serve to cut off the visiting author from the most profoundly entertaining experience fiction offers. This is, for me at least, the experience of "dreaming true," the experience of being some one else, of being a hundred, a thousand other people.

From "Dreaming True" in *The Novel of Tomorrow*, pp. 137–38, by twelve American novelists, copyright 1922, 1950 The Bobbs-Merrill Company, Inc. Used by special permission of the publisher.

Irwin Edman: *Poetry rescues us from formulas and abstractions.*

There is another kind of sleep, too, from which the poet can awaken our promising youth, born to be fully aware. He rescues him from the abstractions in which the least abstract-minded of us live. By the time he is grown up, the young man will have come to live almost entirely in formulas. He will move, half dead, among logical conceptions. He thinks not of actual persons, with their induplicable voices, their individual gestures, their special note of comedy or pathos. He comes to think of peoples and polls and statistics; of populations and trends. He thinks not of actual hungering and suffering men and women, but of national groups, of geographical aggregations. It is not the water gleaming to the eye, soothing to the thirst, that he thinks of, but the chemical formula of H_2O by which its causes of production are identified; not the sadness and immediacy of death, but statistics and tables of mortality, occupy his mind. He sees not the actual processes of growth and life in flower or child, but the labels by which these are controlled and manipulated. He deals with the post-mortem formulas of a life he has never felt. It is the poet's function to waken him from these geometric torpors, to reinstate him in the living movement of nature itself, and the felt actuality of life. Poetry indeed reawakens rather than awakens. For when he was very young, the youth was once fully alive.

'Our birth is but a sleep and a forgetting,' one of our company once said. Rather is it our growing up that is a falling asleep and a gradual forgetting. Before we are fully creatures of habit and lethargy, the poet can rearouse us. To be fully awakened would be to be fully and continuously aware of reality. And is not reality, is not what is 'really real,' that which comes to us through no abstraction, no formulas, but in the vital immediacy of experience itself? Is it not the poet's special magic to find the

From *Philosopher's Quest*, pp. 236–37. Copyright 1947 by Irwin Edman. Reprinted by permission of The Viking Press, Inc.

words which call this quality into awareness again by the shining specificity, the electric directness, of his words?

Ludwig Lewisohn: *Myths, like dreams, are true.*

Dreaming and waking we today use the very techniques by which the antique fathers of the race created myth and lore and legend. Science and philosophy themselves derive from those magic formulae by which primordial souls sought to master the strange universe; all creative literature derives from the myths which were, always and at once, religion and poetry, faith and song, meaning and music, and to that mythic character all great and permanent literature tends in all ages to return.

How could it not be so? For myths, like dreams, are true not because they conform to outer fact but because they express the realities of the soul. Man made myths in his soul's image and believed them because he had made them thus. Therefore they were and have remained far truer to the essence of human life than stories merely invented by later men. This accounts for the well-known fact that the greatest artists from the Attic dramatists to Shakespeare and Milton, to Racine and Goethe, to Wagner and Thomas Mann, almost never invented their fables but used mythic and legendary material already deeply rooted in the consciousness both of their peoples and of mankind. Through these they expressed themselves to their fellows. Through these they could speak both for themselves and for all men. Immensely individualized as personalities themselves, they thus returned to that core of man's life at which myth and faith, shaped by man's essence, wrought in the image of his eternal self, are indissolubly one.

Most modern writers have struggled with so much anguish to achieve works so much more meager and so transitory because they were stranded, as it were, upon a bleak and empty shore.

From *The Magic Word*, pp. 22–25. Copyright 1950 by Ludwig Lewisohn. Reprinted by permission of the publishers, Farrar, Straus & Cudahy.

There were no longer either heroes or gods; great myth was reduced, until the other day, to empty fable. All ages but this were dark and ignorant. Faith and form were outmoded; the great game of equating man, the whole man, that fugitive from nature, with his biological make-up, set in. So the modern writer had no significant substance ready to his hand and had to wring substance from observation and personal experience. Instead of using his creative personality as the shaping principle of form and specific meaning, he had to make that personality itself both source and substance of his work. He had to try to be himself god, hero, priest and sacrifice, and to turn his own narrow life and experience into representative story, acceptable myth, into speech that would speak not only for himself but for all men. The lamentable results are all about us. The initial élan of the communication of personal experience and observation is stone dead. Each novel is a drearier or more contorted specimen of an exhausted mood and impulse. The unredeemed masses will inevitably mythologize not Thomas Mann but Taylor Caldwell. Poetry has withdrawn into a realm of sterile mumbling since, as Mark Van Doren said recently, even "music in words is suspect." We are in a desperate twilight region—a desert of melancholy muttering, unpierced by a single cry of man's heart, a single utterance of music or of aspiration.

It is this melancholy situation which justifies or, rather, renders imperative, an act of both scrutiny and recollection. When we turn our eyes once more upon man's real character and that of his expression we remember, undeterred by the materialist fool, that human language is a free and poetic creation by which this human being, torn out of the order of nature, knowing good and evil, stranded inscrutably upon this planet in the depth of space, spoke from the first of the mystery of himself and his being and cried out for his God. He created significant myth in rhythmic measures. Having done so, he achieved varying degrees of redemption from darkness and from guilt. In brief, he started, long before letters were invented, the composition of what was to be called literature. And literature will last as long as he himself lasts unchanged in character and purpose.

Gilbert Murray: *Art appeals to us by means of a common tradition.*

We have spoken of the tradition as a homogeneous thing, but for any poet or artist there are two quite different webs in it. There are the accepted conventions of this art and the accepted beliefs of his intellect, the one set aiming at the production of beauty, the others at the attainment of truth.

Now for every artist who is also a critic or rebel there is a difference of kind between these two sets of conventions. For the purposes of truth the tradition is absolutely indifferent. If, as a matter of fact, the earth goes round the sun, it does so not a whit the less because most ages have believed the opposite. The seeker for truth can, as far as truth is concerned, reject tradition without a qualm. But with art the case is different. Art has to give a message from one man to another. As you can only speak to a man in a language which you both know, so you can only appeal to his artistic side by means of some common tradition. His natural expectation, whether we try to satisfy or to surprise it, to surpass or to disappoint it, is always an essential element in the artistic effect. Consequently the tradition cannot be disregarded.

This distinction is often strongly marked in the practice of different artists. One poet may be both a pioneer of new roads in thought and a breaker of the laws of technique, like Walt Whitman—an enemy of the tradition in both kinds. Another may be slack and anarchical in his technique though quite conventional in his thought. I refrain from suggesting instances. Still more clearly there are poets, such as Shelley or Swinburne, whose works are full of intellectual rebellion while their technique is exquisite and elaborate. The thoughts are bold and strange. The form is the traditional form developed and made more exquisite.

From *Euripides and His Age*. One of the volumes in the Home University Library Series. (New York: Oxford Univ. Press, pp. 17–18.) Used by permission of Oxford University Press, London.

R. W. Livingstone: *The great writers of antiquity expressed emotions shared by all mankind.*

How 'troubled' would Homer or Sophocles be by the writings of Browning or Meredith, of Henry James or Conrad, in whom so many eddies and cross-currents of thought and experience unite.

Compare the story of Hector and Andromache with some famous passage from any of these writers. 'So spake glorious Hector and stretched out his arm to his boy. But the child shrunk crying to the bosom of his fair-girdled nurse, dismayed at the look of his dear father and in fear of the bronze and the horsehair crest that nodded fiercely from his helmet's top. Then his dear father and his lady mother laughed aloud: forthwith glorious Hector took the helmet from his head and laid it, all gleaming, on the earth; then kissed he his dear son and danced him in his arms, and spoke in prayer to Zeus and all the gods, "O Zeus and all ye gods, grant that this my son may be as I am, pre-eminent among the Trojans, and as valiant in might, and may he be a great king of Troy." So he spoke and laid his son in his dear wife's arms; and she took him to her fragrant bosom, smiling through tears. And her husband had pity to see her, and caressed her with his hand, and spoke and called her by her name: "Dear one, I pray thee be not of oversorrowful heart; no man against my fate shall send me to my death; but destiny, I ween, no man hath escaped." So spake glorious Hector and took up his horsehair-crested helmet; and his dear wife departed to her home, often looking back and letting fall great tears. And she came to the well-built house of man-slaying Hector, and found therein her many handmaidens, and stirred lamentation in them all. So they wept for Hector, while he yet lived, in his house; for they thought that he would no more come back to them from battle.' These are emotions shared by mankind twenty centuries before Christ and twenty centuries

From "Literature" in *The Legacy of Greece* (Oxford, England: The Clarendon Press, 1921), pp. 256–57. Used by permission.

after him, common equally to Shakespeare or Napoleon and to the stupidest and least educated of mankind; and these emotions are expressed with a simplicity as elemental as themselves. Subjects as simple may be found in our literature; expression as direct would be hard to find.

Bernard Bosanquet: *Aesthetic imagination and logical theory are coordinate powers.*

There is a tendency to think of imagination as a sort of separate faculty, creative of images; a tendency which puts a premium on the arbitrary and fantastic in beauty, rather than the logical and the penetrative. But this, I take it, is simply a blunder. The imagination is precisely the mind at work, pursuing and exploring the possibilities suggested by the connection of its experience. It may operate, of course, in the service of logical enquiry, and of exact science itself—the scientific use of the imagination is a well-known topic. The only difference is that when imagination is free, when the mind is operating, for instance, not in the service of theoretical truth, but in that of aesthetic feeling, then it altogether ceases to be bound by agreement with what we call reality as a whole. It cannot help starting from what we call experience, from what we have felt and seen, because there is nothing else to start from; but its guiding purpose is the satisfaction of feeling, and not the construction of a system in which every fact shall have its logically appropriate place. The only test is, whether it satisfies the feeling which inspires it. And its method need not be logical, though it often is so, and I incline to think is so in the best imaginative work. By saying it need not be logical, I mean that in following out a suggestion it need not adhere to the main thread of connection. It may start afresh on any incidental feature that presents itself. Practically, imagination is the mind working *under great*

From *Three Lectures on Aesthetics* (London: Macmillan & Co., Ltd., 1915), pp. 26–29, 54–56. Reprinted by permission of Ellen Bosanquet.

reservations which *set it free*; pursuing trains of images or ideas which comparison with the complete fabric of fact—from which its reservations protect it—would arrest or disfigure. . . . But the world of imagination is in no way subordinate to the total structure of real fact and truth. It is an alternative world, framed, no doubt, on the same ultimate basis, but with a method and purpose of its own, and having for its goal a different type of satisfaction from that of ascertained fact.

. . . though this imaginative experience is not within actual reality, and is not to be interpreted as theoretical truth, yet it may make a difference to our general theory of things, and our theory may make a difference to it. And so, for example, representation of nature and imitation and idealisation are very different things according as we hold that nature has in it a life and divinity which it is attempting to reveal,—so that idealisation is the positive effort to bring to apprehension the deeper beauty we feel to be there,—or as we hold that nature is at bottom a dead mechanical system, and idealisation therefore lies in some way of treating it which weakens or generalises its effect and makes it less and not more of what its fullest character would be. No doubt, theory seeking for truth does not accept imaginative expressions as logical conclusions, but it is bound to take account of the fact that imagination finds in experience the instrument of that immense embodiment of feeling which it constructs. Aesthetic imagination and logical theory are co-ordinate powers. Neither can do the work of the other. But both reveal something to us in their own way.

Irwin Edman: *The aesthetic mood is obviously at a discount in the world of action.*

Every human experience has its particular and curious æsthetic flavor, as an inevitable though undetected obligato. Æsthetic values enter into and qualify our estimates of persons and situa-

From *Human Traits and Their Social Significance* (Boston: Houghton Mifflin Co., 1920), pp. 342–44. Used by permission.

tions, and help to determine that general sympathy or revulsion, that love or hate for people, institutions, or ideas, which make the pervasive atmosphere of all human action. But in the world of action, we cannot emphasize these irrelevant æsthetic feelings. The appreciative and the practical moods are sharply contrasted. In the latter we are interested in results, and insist on the exclusion of all considerations that do not bear on their accomplishment. The appreciative or æsthetic mood is detached; it is interested not to act, but to pause and consider; it does not want to use the present as a point of departure. It wants to bask in the present perfection of color, word, or sound. The practical man is interested in a present situation for what can be done with it; he wants to know, in the vernacular, "What comes next?" "Where do we go from here?" The appreciator wishes to remain in the lovely interlude of perfection which he experiences in music, poetry, or painting.

The æsthetic mood is obviously at a discount in the world of action. To bask in the charm of a present situation, to linger and loiter, as it were, in the sun of beauty, is to accomplish nothing, to interrupt action. It is precisely for this reason that persons with extremely high æsthetic sensibilities are at such a discount in practical life. They are too easily dissolved in appreciation. They are too much absorbed, for practical efficiency, in the tragic, the whimsical, the beautiful, or the comic aspects of men and affairs. The same sensitivity to the innuendoes and colors of life that enable some of such men to give an exquisite and various portraiture of experience, incapacitates them for action. The practical man must not observe anything irrelevant to his immediate business. He must not be dissolved, at every random provocation, into ecstasy, laughter, or sorrow. There is too much to be done in business, government, mechanics, and the laboratory, to allow one's attention to wander dreamingly over the tragic, the beautiful, the pathetic, the comic, and the grotesque qualities of the day's work. To take an extreme case, it would, as Jane Harrison observes, be a monstrosity, when our friend was drowning, to note with lingering appreciation the fluent white curve of his arm in the glimmering waters of the late afternoon. The man to whom every event is flooded with imaginative possibilities and emotional suggestions is a useless or a dangerous character in situations where it is essential to discriminate the immediate and important bearings of facts.

R. W. Livingstone: *The ancients presented the essential interests of human nature uncomplicated by lesser issues.*

If a reader turned from Milton to Homer, from Shakespeare to Sophocles, from Plato or Aristotle to some modern work on ethics, politics, or literary criticism, he would find one point of difference between the earlier and the later writers in the greater simplicity of the former. They are briefer: the *Oedipus Tyrannus* has 1530 lines while the first two acts of *Hamlet* alone have more than 1600, and Greek histories and philosophical writings are correspondingly shorter than their modern counterparts. The whole of Thucydides could be printed in a twenty-four page issue of *The Times*, and leave room to spare; the essay of Aristotle on Poetry, which for generations dictated the principles of dramatic writing, has forty-five short pages; the *Republic* of Plato, which has influenced thought more than any other philosophic work, has a little over three hundred. Brevity indeed is not always simplicity, and it is possible to be at once simple and lengthy. But any one who examines these Greek writers will find that they are brief, because, avoiding bypaths and by-plots, elaborate or minute detail, they strike out the central features of their picture with an effortless economy of line. Their writing has a double quality. It shows a firm hold on the central and fundamental things: and it presents them unmixed with and unconfused by minor issues, so that they stand out like forest trees which no undergrowth of brushwood masks. It is important to make this distinction, for all great literature has the first of these qualities; the second is largely an accident of time. As civilization moves further from its origin,

From "Literature" in *The Legacy of Greece* (Oxford, England: The Clarendon Press, 1921), pp. 254–55. Used by permission.

it cannot but receive a thousand tributaries that continually augment its volume, and colour and confuse its streams: at the sources it flows clear and untroubled. The interests of an early age are the primal and essential interests of human nature and the literature of such an age presents them unalloyed and uncomplicated by lesser issues. In the thinkers the main and fundamental problems stand clearly out, and Plato and Thucydides take us straight to them. The poets make their poetry from emotions and interests that are as old as man, and have none of the refinements and complications which education and a long inheritance of culture superadd to the essential stuff of human nature. 'You Greeks are always children,' said the Egyptian priest to Solon; and he spoke the truth in a sense which he did not mean. The Greeks' feelings were not dulled or sophisticated by the *damnosa hereditas* of the past. Neither their life nor their mental atmosphere was complicated. They had not 'thought themselves into weariness'. They were the children of the world, and they united the startling acuteness, directness, and simplicity of children to the intellects of men.

Susanne K. Langer: *Music does not ordinarily influence behavior.*

Another kind of reaction to music, however, is more striking, and seems more significant: that is the *emotional* response it is commonly supposed to evoke. The belief that music arouses emotions goes back even to the Greek philosophers. It led Plato to demand, for his ideal state, a strict censorship of modes and tunes, lest his citizens be tempted by weak or voluptuous airs to indulge in demoralizing emotions. The same principle is often invoked to explain the use of music in tribal society, the lure of the African drum, the clarion call and the "Pibroch" calling armies or clans to battle, the world-old custom of lulling the baby to sleep with

Reprinted by permission of the publishers from *Philosophy in a New Key* (Cambridge, Mass.: Harvard Univ. Press, copyright 1942, 1951, 1957 by The President and Fellows of Harvard College), pp. 211–12.

slumber songs. The legend of the sirens is based on a belief in the narcotic and toxic effect of music, as also the story of Terpander's preventing civil war in Sparta, or of the Danish King Eric, who committed murder as a result of a harpist's deliberate experiment in mood-production. Despite the fact that there is, to my knowledge, not a single authentic record of any specific change of disposition or intention, or even the inhibition of a practical impulse in any person by the agency of music, this belief in the physical power of the art has come down to modern times. Music is known, indeed, to affect pulse-rate and respiration, to facilitate or disturb concentration, to excite or relax the organism, *while the stimulus lasts*; but beyond evoking impulses to sing, tap, adjust one's step to musical rhythm, perhaps to stare, hold one's breath or take a tense attitude, music does not ordinarily influence behavior. Its somatic influences seem to affect unmusical as well as musical persons (the selections usually employed in experimentation would be more likely to irritate than to soothe or inspire a musical person), and to be, therefore, functions of *sound* rather than of *music*. Experiments made with vocal music are entirely unreliable, since words and the pathos of the human voice are added to the musical stimulus. On the whole, the behavior of concert audiences after even the most thrilling performances makes the traditional magical influence of music on human actions very dubious. Its somatic effects are transient, and its moral hangovers or uplifts seem to be negligible.

B. H. Haggin: *A piece of music, like every other work of art, is a unique communication.*

I said that a piece of music is a communication. And if you are one of those to whom a Beethoven symphony is a lot of meaningless noises, you may say: "Tell me what it communicates"—meaning of course "Tell me in words." But the simple inescapable fact

From *The Listener's Musical Companion* (New Brunswick, N. J.: Rutgers Univ. Press, 1956), pp. 6–10. Used by permission.

of the situation is that what Beethoven says in those sounds cannot be told in words.

Someone observed once that art is not superfluous—by which
he meant that the artist produces it to communicate something he
can't communicate in any other way. You can see this most clearly
in poetry: the particular images and overtones of sense and feeling from the lines

> When to the Sessions of sweet silent thought
> I summon up remembrance of things past

are communicated only by this particular assemblage of words;
and you won't get them from a statement in other words like
"When in hours of meditation I recall the past."

So with painting. In one of his finest essays, *Music at Night*,
Aldous Huxley writes about two paintings of the Virgin, one by
Piero della Francesca, the other by Tura—about how they observe
the same current symbolical conventions but differ "in the forms
and their arrangement, in the disposition of the lines and planes
and masses," and how as a result of this pictorial difference they
"say" different things. Huxley describes what he thinks those
different things are; but the point of his essay is that words cannot really tell us what the two paintings "say," and that we can
learn this only from the paintings—from Piero's "welding together
of smooth and beautifully balanced solidities," from Tura's intricate lines and writhing surfaces—themselves.

This is true also of the grave, powerful, massive emotions to
which, says Roger Fry, we are compelled by a Cézanne still-life—
by the way a few apples and pears, commonplace objects entirely
without emotional associations, are "reduced to pure elements of
space and volume" and "coordinated and organized by the artist's
sensual intelligence." That is, Fry can describe those emotions as
grave, powerful and massive; but we can discover what they
really are only from that organization of elements of space and
volume on the canvas.

So with the piece of music, an organization of sounds which
don't, like words, refer to external objects, but do have internal
coherences that are meaningful to an ear sensitized to them. Huxley's example in his essay is the *Benedictus* of Beethoven's *Missa*

Solemnis; and he says correctly that it is a statement about the blessedness at the heart of things, but that no words can give us any knowledge of what Beethoven felt this blessedness to be—that we can learn this only from the music.

Actually, Cézanne compels us to those grave, powerful, massive emotions not just with one painting of apples and pears but with many; and the state of inner illumination and superearthly exaltation that Beethoven attained in his last years is communicated to us not just in one piano sonata or string quartet but in a number of works. And from this you may understand that our interest in a work of art is an interest not just in its meaning but in this meaning as embodied, made explicit in the organized detail of the work of art, and as newly and differently embodied and made explicit in the organized detail of each work of art. We are interested in those grave, powerful, massive emotions as they are communicated by each different painting of apples and pears by Cézanne; in that state of inner illumination and superearthly exaltation as it is communicated by each different piano sonata or string quartet of Beethoven.

If then you don't understand what Beethoven "says" it is because the sounds he uses are not a meaningful language for you; and the thing to do is to learn this language as you would any other. If you enjoy the music of Kern and Rodgers that is because its musical language is the one you do understand—the one you learned, as you did English, by hearing it from earliest childhood. Probably, if you had heard Beethoven as early, as much, and as long as Kern and Rodgers you would understand him as well; and if you want to acquire an understanding of Beethoven's vocabulary and ideas (for actually his language is the basic one of all Western music, popular and serious) you will have to live with them and get to know them as well as those of Kern and Rodgers.

Which is to say that you will have to listen to Beethoven's music, and keep listening. That, fortunately, is all you will have to do: . . . the meaning of a statement by Beethoven is an internal coherence of the sounds that you will apprehend directly from them by listening to them, or not at all.

And so try the experiment of listening to the beginning of the third movement of Beethoven's Trio Op. 97 (*Archduke*)—just the two statements of the piano that are echoed by the violin and cello, no more; and just once. Listen to it once again the next night, and every night for a week or two or as long as you care to continue the experiment. The passage may say as little to you after a month as it did the first night—in which case you will have to accept the fact that Beethoven and you are not for each other. But on the other hand it may, one of those nights, suddenly come alive for you and begin to make a definite though indefinable sense; and this will be the beginning of an understanding of music, the opening up of a new world of artistic experience as rich and stimulating as that of literature or painting. One thing is certain, however: if you don't get the meaning of Beethoven's statement from the statement, you won't get it from anything else. . . . whatever the biographical and historical influences involved in the process that produced the opening statement in the third movement of Beethoven's *Archduke* Trio, the result of the process was an organization of sounds with an effect which you can experience not by reading about the biographical and historical influences but only by listening to the organization of sounds in the statement.

To repeat: just as the way to understand a poem is to read it, and the way to understand a painting is to look at it, so the way —the only way—to understand a piece of music is to listen to it, and to keep listening.

Irwin Edman: *The master artist can achieve a perfection which cannot be obtained by the man of action.*

The industrial arts are . . . man's transformation of natural resources to ideal uses. In the same way political and social organization are human arts, enterprises, at their best, in the moulding of men's natures to their highest possible realization. But in the

From *Human Traits and Their Social Significance* (Boston: Houghton Mifflin Co., 1920), pp. 336–37. Used by permission.

world of action, whether political or industrial, there are incomparably greater hindrances to the realization in practice of imagined goods than there are, at least to the gifted, in the fine arts. Every ideal for which men attempt to find fulfillment in the world of action is subject to a thousand accidental deflections of circumstance. Every enterprise involves conflicting wills; the larger the enterprise, the more various and probably the more conflicting the interests involved. Social movements have their courses determined by factors altogether beyond the control of their originators. Statesmen can start wars, but cannot define their eventual fruits. A man may found a political party, and live to see it wander far from the ideal which he had framed. But in the fine arts, to the imaginatively and technically endowed, the materials are prepared and controllable. In the hands of a master, action does not wander from intent. Language to the poet, for example, is an immediate and responsible instrument; he can mould it precisely to his ideal intention. The enterprise of poetry is less dependent almost than any other undertaking on the accidents of circumstance, outside the poet's initial imaginative resources. In music, even so simple an instrument as a flute can yield perfection of sound. The composer of a symphony can invent a perpetual uncorroded beauty; the sculptor an immortality of irrefutably persuasive form. This explains in part why so many artists, of a reflective turn of mind, are pessimists in practical affairs. The world of action with its perpetual and pitiful frustrations, failures, and compromises, seems incomparably poor, paltry, and sordid, in comparison with the perfection that is attainable in art.

B. The Criticism of Art

George Santayana: *It is mere barbarism to feel that a thing is aesthetically good but morally evil.*

Never have art and beauty received a more glowing eulogy than is implied in Plato's censure. To him nothing was beautiful that was not beautiful to the core, and he would have thought to insult art—the remodelling of nature by reason—if he had given it a narrower field than all practice. As an architect who had fondly designed something impossible, or which might not please in execution, would at once erase it from the plan and abandon it for the love of perfect beauty and perfect art, so Plato wished to erase from pleasing appearance all that, when its operation was completed, would bring discord into the world. This was done in the ultimate interest of art and beauty, which in a cultivated mind are inseparable from the vitally good. It is mere barbarism to feel that a thing is æsthetically good but morally evil, or morally good but hateful to perception. Things partially evil or partially ugly may have to be chosen under stress of unfavourable circumstances, lest some worse thing come; but if a thing were ugly it would *thereby* not be wholly good, and if it were *altogether* good it would perforce be beautiful.

To criticise art on moral grounds is to pay it a high compliment by assuming that it aims to be adequate, and is addressed to a comprehensive mind. The only way in which art could disallow such criticism would be to protest its irresponsible infancy, and admit that it was a more or less amiable blatancy in individuals, and not *art* at all. Young animals often gambol in a delightful fashion, and men also may, though hardly when they intend to do so. Sportive self-expression can be prized because human nature contains a certain elasticity and margin for experiment, in which waste activity is inevitable and may be precious: for this license may lead, amid a thousand failures, to some real discovery and advance. Art, like life, should be free, since both are experimental. But it is one thing to make room for genius and to respect the sudden madness of poets through which, possibly, some god may speak, and it is quite another not to judge the result by rational standards. The earth's bowels are full of all sorts of rumblings; which of the oracles drawn thence is true can be judged only by the light of day. If an artist's inspiration has been happy, it has been so because his work can sweeten or ennoble the mind and because its total effect will be beneficent. Art being a part of life, the criticism of art is a part of morals.

John Ruskin: *You may read the character of men, and of nations, in their art.*

The faults of a work of art are the faults of its workman, and its virtues his virtues.

Great art is the expression of the mind of a great man, and mean art, that of the want of mind of a weak man. A foolish person builds foolishly, and a wise one, sensibly; a virtuous one, beautifully; and a vicious one, basely. If stone work is well put together, it means that a thoughtful man planned it, and a careful man cut it, and an honest man cemented it. If it has too much ornament, it means that its carver was too greedy of pleasure; if too little, that he was rude, or insensitive, or stupid, and the like. So that when once you have learned how to spell these most precious of all legends,—pictures and buildings,—you may read the characters of men, and of nations, in their art, as in a mirror; —nay, as in a microscope, and magnified a hundredfold; for the

From *The Queen of the Air* (New York: John Wiley & Son, 1869), pp. 105–6.

character becomes passionate in the art, and intensifies itself in all its noblest or meanest delights. Nay, not only as in a microscope, but as under a scalpel, and in dissection; for a man may hide himself from you, or misrepresent himself to you, every other way; but he cannot in his work: there, be sure, you have him to the inmost. All that he likes, all that he sees,—all that he can do, —his imagination, his affections, his perseverance, his impatience, his clumsiness, cleverness, everything is there. If the work is a cobweb, you know it was made by a spider; if a honeycomb, by a bee; a worm-cast is thrown up by a worm, and a nest wreathed by a bird; and a house built by a man, worthily, if he is worthy, and ignobly, if he is ignoble.

And always, from the least to the greatest, as the made thing is good or bad, so is the maker of it.

Leo Tolstoy: *Art is one of the conditions of human life.*

In order correctly to define art, it is necessary, first of all, to cease to consider it as a means to pleasure, and to consider it as one of the conditions of human life. Viewing it in this way, we cannot fail to observe that art is one of the means of intercourse between man and man.

Every work of art causes the receiver to enter into a certain kind of relationship both with him who produced, or is producing, the art, and with all those who, simultaneously, previously, or subsequently, receive the same artistic impression.

Speech, transmitting the thoughts and experiences of men, serves as a means of union among them, and art acts in a similar manner. The peculiarity of this latter means of intercourse, distinguishing it from intercourse by means of words, consists in this that whereas by words a man transmits his thoughts to another, by means of art he transmits his feelings.

The activity of art is based on the fact that a man, receiving through his sense of hearing or sight another man's expression of

From *What Is Art?* (New York: Thomas Y. Crowell & Co., 1899), pp. 47–49, 50.

feeling, is capable of experiencing the emotion which moved the man who expressed it. To take the simplest example: one man laughs, and another, who hears, becomes merry; or a man weeps, and another, who hears, feels sorrow. A man is excited or irritated, and another man, seeing him, comes to a similar state of mind. By his movements, or by the sounds of his voice, a man expresses courage and determination, or sadness and calmness, and this state of mind passes on to others. A man suffers, expressing his sufferings by groans and spasms, and this suffering transmits itself to other people; a man expresses his feeling of admiration, devotion, fear, respect, or love to certain objects, persons, or phenomena, and others are infected by the same feelings of admiration, devotion, fear, respect, or love to the same objects, persons, and phenomena.

And it is on this capacity of man to receive another man's expression of feeling, and experience those feelings himself, that the activity of art is based.

If a man infects another or others, directly, immediately, by his appearance, or by the sounds he gives vent to at the very time he experiences the feeling; if he causes another man to yawn when he himself cannot help yawning, or to laugh or cry when he himself is obliged to laugh or cry, or to suffer when he himself is suffering—that does not amount to art.

Art begins when one person, with the object of joining another or others to himself in one and the same feeling, expresses that feeling by certain external indications. To take the simplest example: a boy, having experienced, let us say, fear on encountering a wolf, relates that encounter; and, in order to evoke in others the feeling he has experienced, describes himself, his condition before the encounter, the surroundings, the wood, his own light-heartedness, and then the wolf's appearance, its movements, the distance between himself and the wolf, etc. All this, if only the boy, when telling the story, again experiences the feelings he had lived through and infects the hearers and compels them to feel what the narrator had experienced, is art. If even the boy had not seen a wolf but had frequently been afraid of one, and if, wishing to evoke in others the fear he had felt, he invented an encounter with a wolf, and recounted it so as to make his hearers share the feelings he experienced when he feared the wolf, that also would be art. And just in the same way it is art if a man, having experienced either the fear of suffering or the attraction of enjoyment (whether in reality or in imagination), expresses these feelings on canvas or in marble so that others are infected by them. And it is also art if a man feels or imagines to himself feelings of delight, gladness, sorrow, despair, courage, or despondency, and the transition from one to another of these feelings, and expresses these feelings by sounds, so that the hearers are infected by them, and experience them as they were experienced by the composer.

. . . . .

If only the spectators or auditors are infected by the feelings which the author has felt, it is art.

To evoke in oneself a feeling one has once experienced, and having evoked it in oneself, then, by means of movements, lines, colors, sounds, or forms expressed in words, so to transmit that feeling that others may experience the same feeling—this is the activity of art.

Art is a human activity, consisting in this, that one man consciously, by means of certain external signs, hands on to others feelings he has lived through, and that other people are infected by these feelings, and also experience them.

William Allen White: *One man's answer to the question "What is Art?" is as good as another's, and probably better.*

Any attempt to place the novel inside of definitions, setting its meets and bounds, brings us up sharply against the insistent question asked of old and never answered, "What is art?" And for himself, and his cosmos, one man's guess at the answer is as good

From "Splitting Fiction Three Ways" in *The Novel of Tomorrow*, pp. 123–24, by twelve American novelists, copyright 1922, 1950. The Bobbs-Merrill Company, Inc. Used by special permission of the publisher.

as another's, probably rather better. For every man has his own
scheme of creation. Every man is set down alone under the stars
and on the more or less solid earth, to build out of his conscious
experience the fabric of the dream in which he walks. If he sets
down some account of his dream, some definition of his universe
in terms of love or fear or hate or joy or any emotional medium
in which his conviction comes to him about life, what he makes,
for him is art. But it is of necessity not art for any one else. It
may be an obscure picture on the sand, drawn with a shell or
stick. It may be a Poem of Ecstasy or it may be a cathedral or a
large fat Mrs. Rubens in oil, or a patient Madame X. leisurely waiting for the laundry wagon to bring her first aid in the matter of
clothes! Whatever it may be, to some man the thing means a
conviction about the meaning of life. To its creator, if to no other
soul on earth, the thing created in joy or pain or fear or love or
whatever rise of pulse beat, means art. Others, of course, need not
accept it as art; being in ribald spirits they may laugh at it, or
otherwise, being mean and supercilious they may try to suppress
and censor the man's expression, which may seem to others ugly
or indecent, or stupid or wicked beyond tears. But whether they
censor it in laughter or in rage, they must not forget that for the
man who made it the thing was art. He has a right to issue his
challenge to the world and stand or fall by it.

Susanne K. Langer: *It is not enough to know why Leonardo's women smile mysteriously.*

What is artistic significance? What sort of meaning do "expressive forms" express?

Clearly they do not convey propositions, as literal symbols do.
We all know that a seascape (say) represents water and rocks,

Reprinted by permission of the publishers from *Philosophy in a New Key*
(Cambridge, Mass.: Harvard University Press, copyright 1942, 1951, 1957
by The President and Fellows of Harvard College), pp. 206–8.

boats and fish-piers; that a still-life represents oranges and apples, a vase of flowers, dead game or fish, etc. But such a content is not what makes the paint-patterns on the canvas "expressive forms." The mere notion of rabbits, grapes, or even boats at sunset is not the "idea" that inspires a painting. The artistic idea is always a "deeper" conception.

Several psychologists have ventured to unmask this "deeper" significance by interpreting pictures, poems, and even musical compositions as symbols of loved objects, mainly, of course, of a forbidden nature. Artistic activity, according to the psychoanalysts who have given it their attention, is an expression of primitive dynamisms, of unconscious wishes, and uses the objects or scenes represented to embody the secret fantasies of the artist.

This explanation has much to recommend it. It accounts for the fact that we are inclined to credit works of art with *significance,* although (by reason of the moral censorship which distorts the appearance of basic desires) we can never say what they signify. It does justice to the emotional interest, the seriousness with which we receive artistic experience. Above all, it brings this baffling department of human activity into the compass of a general psychological system—the so-called "dynamic psychology," based on the recognition of certain fundamental human needs, of the conflicts resulting from their mutual interference, and of the mechanism whereby they assert, disguise, and finally realize themselves. The starting-point of this psychology is the discovery of a previously unrecognized *symbolic mode,* typified in dream, and perfectly traceable in all works of fantasy. To assimilate art to the imaginative life in general is surely not a forced procedure . . .

These are strong recommendations for the psychoanalytic theory of aesthetics. But despite them all, I do not think this theory (though probably valid) throws any real light on those issues which confront artists and critics and constitute the philosophical problem of art. For the Freudian interpretation, no matter how far it be carried, never offers even the rudest criterion of *artistic* excellence. It may explain why a poem was written, why it is popular, what human features it hides under its fanciful imagery; what secret ideas a picture combines, and why Leonardo's women smile mysteriously. But *it makes no distinction between good and bad*

art. The features to which it attributes the importance and significance of a great masterpiece may all be found just as well in an
obscure work of some quite incompetent painter or poet. Wilhelm
Stekel, one of the leading Freudian psychologists interested in
artistic productions as a field for analysis, has stated this fact explicitly: "I want to point out at once," he says, "that it is irrelevant
to our purpose whether the poet in question is a great, universally
acknowledged poet, or whether we are dealing with a little
poetaster. For, after all, we are investigating only the impulse
which drives people to create."

An analysis to which the artistic merit of a work is irrelevant
can hardly be regarded as a promising technique of art-criticism,
for it can look only to a hidden *content* of the work, and not to
what every artist knows as the real problem—the *perfection of
form,* which makes this form "significant" in the artistic sense. We
cannot evaluate this perfection by finding more and more obscure
objects represented or suggested by the form.

Morris R. Cohen and Ernest Nagel: *May not logical tests enable us to find out whether some moral and aesthetic opinions have more evidence in their favor than others?*

Discussions of logic and scientific method are usually confined
to propositions about natural or other forms of existence. There
are, indeed, a great many writers who believe that scientific
method is inherently inapplicable to such judgments of estimation
or value, as "This is beautiful," "This is good," or "This ought to
be done." Now if we agree that all judgments of the latter type
express nothing but feelings, tastes, or individual preferences,
such judgments cannot be said to be true or false (except as de-
scriptions of the personal feelings of the one who utters them).

From *An Introduction to Logic and Scientific Method* by Morris R.
Cohen and Ernest Nagel, pp. 352–53. Copyright, 1934, by Harcourt, Brace
& Co., Inc.

Few, however, are willing to maintain this view consistently. Even those who urge the maxim *De gustibus non disputandum est* are not willing to maintain that there is neither truth nor falsity in the judgment which denies any beauty in the works of Shakespeare or Beethoven, or indiscriminately condemns as immoral all the doctrines of such diverse teachers as Confucius, Buddha, the Hebrew Prophets, Socrates, Epicurus, Mahomet, Nietzsche, and Karl Marx. Almost all human discourse would become meaningless if we took the view that every moral or esthetic judgment is no more true or false than any other.

This reflection is of course not in itself a logical proof that there is an element of objective truth in moral and esthetic judgments but it points to the necessity of a closer examination of the issue. There are, to be sure, great differences of opinion with regard to moral and esthetic issues. But this is also true, though to a lesser degree, about questions of existence in nature and in human affairs. Indeed there are no questions of natural science about which our information is so complete as to eliminate all differences of opinion. But the fact that certain issues cannot as yet be definitely settled does not mean that any opinion is as good as any other. Though we do not know the cause of cancer, we may know enough to say that some opinions on this point certainly have less evidence or rational ground than others. Hence even if moral and esthetic judgments are largely matters of opinion, may not logical tests enable us to clarify our opinions, discover their implications, and find out whether some of these opinions have more evidence in their favor than others?

John Ciardi: *All good poets write for the vertical audience.*

"What is the idea of 'the audience'? Is it enough to argue 'I have bought this book of poems [Wallace Stevens' *Collected Poems*] and therefore I have certain audience-rights'? I think, first, one must distinguish between two ideas of 'the audience.'

From "Dialogue with the Audience" in *Saturday Review*, November 22, 1958, p. 12. Used by permission of John Ciardi and the *Saturday Review*.

"One idea may be called the horizontal audience and the other the vertical audience. The horizontal audience consists of everybody who is alive at this moment. The vertical audience consists of everyone, vertically through time, who will ever read a given poem.

"Isn't it immediately obvious that Stevens can only 'be for' a tiny percentage of the horizontal audience? Even Frost, who is the most seemingly-clear and the most widely loved of our good poets, certainly does not reach more than a small percentage of the total population, or even of that part of the population that thinks of itself as literate—as at least literate enough to buy a best-seller. The fact is that no horizontal audience since the age of folk-poetry has been much interested in good poetry. And you may be sure that a few spokesmen sounding off in the name of that horizontal audience are not going to persuade the poets.

"All good poets write for the vertical audience. The vertical audience for Dante, for example, is now six centuries old. And it is growing. If the human race has any luck at all, part of Dante's audience is still thousands of years short of being born.

"Now try a flight of fancy. Imagine that you held an election tomorrow and asked the horizontal audience to vote for Dante as opposed to Eddie Guest. Guest would certainly swamp Dante in such an election. More people in the horizontal audience have read Guest and even, God save the mark, been moved by him— if only to their own inanition. But moved, nevertheless. And we're a democracy, aren't we? The majority rules: bless the majority?

"Not in art. Not horizontally at least. The verdict in art is vertical. Take the idea of majority vote a step further. Imagine that you held the same election on Judgment Day, calling for a total vote of the human race down through time. Can you fail to believe that Dante would then swamp Eddie Guest plus all the horizontalists from Robert Service to Carl Sandburg?

"The point is that the horizontal audience always outnumbers the vertical at any one moment, but that the vertical audience for good poetry always outnumbers the horizontal in time-enough. And not only for the greatest poets. Andrew Marvell is certainly a minor poet, but given time enough more people certainly will have read 'To His Coy Mistress' than will ever have subscribed to

Time, Life, and *Fortune.* Compared to what a good poem can do,
Luce is a piker at getting circulation."

Robert Lynd: *Indiscriminate praise is one of the deadly sins of criticism.*

Another argument which tells in favour of the theory that the
best criticism is praise is the fact that almost all the memorable
examples of critical folly have been denunciations. One remembers that Carlyle dismissed Herbert Spencer as a "never-ending
ass." One remembers that Byron thought nothing of Keats—"Jack
Ketch," as he called him. One remembers that the critics damned
Wagner's operas as a new form of sin. One remembers that Ruskin
denounced one of Whistler's nocturnes as a pot of paint flung in
the face of the British public. In the world of science we have a
thousand similar examples of new genius being hailed by the
critics as folly and charlatanry. Only the other day a biographer
of Lord Lister was reminding us how, at the British Association in
1869, Lister's antiseptic treatment was attacked as a "return to
the dark ages of surgery," the "carbolic mania," and "a professional criminality." The history of science, art, music and literature is strewn with the wrecks of such hostile criticisms. It is an
appalling spectacle for anyone interested in defending the intelligence of the human race. So appalling is it, indeed, that most of
us nowadays labour under such a terror of accidentally condemning something good that we have not the courage to condemn
anything at all. We think of the way in which Browning was once
taunted for his obscurity, and we cannot find it in our hearts to
censure Mr. Doughty. We recall the ignorant attacks on Manet
and Monet, and we will not risk an onslaught on the follies of
Picasso and the worse-than-Piscassos of contemporary art. We
grow a monstrous and unhealthy plant of tolerance in our souls,
and its branches drop colourless good words on the just and on
the unjust—on everybody, indeed, except . . . a few . . . whom

From *The Art of Letters* (London: Ernest Benn, Ltd., 1920), pp. 219–20.
Used by permission.

we know to be second-rate because they have large circulations. This is really a disastrous state of affairs for literature and the other arts. If criticism is, generally speaking, praise, it is, more definitely, praise of the right things. Praise for the sake of praise is as great an evil as blame for the sake of blame. Indiscriminate praise, in so far as it is the result of distrust of one's own judgment or of laziness or of insincerity, is one of the deadly sins in criticism. It is also one of the deadly dull sins.

Longinus: *Lofty genius is far removed from flawlessness.*

For my part, I am well aware that lofty genius is far removed from flawlessness; for invariable accuracy incurs the risk of pettiness, and in the sublime, as in great fortunes, there must be something which is overlooked. It may be necessarily the case that low and average natures remain as a rule free from failing and in greater safety because they never run a risk or seek to scale the heights, while great endowments prove insecure because of their very greatness. In the second place, I am not ignorant that it naturally happens that the worse side of human character is always the more easily recognised, and that the memory of errors remains indelible, while that of excellences quickly dies away. I have myself noted not a few errors on the part of Homer and other writers of the greatest distinction, and the slips they have made afford me anything but pleasure. Still I do not term them wilful errors, but rather oversights of a random and casual kind, due to neglect and introduced with all the heedlessness of genius. Consequently I do not waver in my view that excellences higher in quality, even if not sustained throughout, should always on a comparison be voted the first place, because of their sheer elevation of spirit if for no other reason.

From *On the Sublime*, ed. Charles Sears Baldwin. Published with Aristotle's *Poetics* (New York: The Macmillan Co., 1930), pp. 109–10. Used by permission.

Charles Morgan: *If art has anything to teach, it is that no one has a monopoly of vision.*

"By what means shall an artist enable men to imagine for themselves?" and, secondly: "What shall he enable them to imagine?" To the second question the authoritarian answer is simple: "The people shall not be enabled to imagine freely. They shall be compelled or persuaded or tempted to imagine what is good for them, and what is good for all is good for one and what is good for one is good for all." Sometimes the authoritarians dress up this answer in a more dignified and ancient dress, and say: "The people shall be made to imagine the Truth," and, when authority says that, we are on the way to the fire and the torture-chamber, to the death of Socrates, to the scourge and the crown of thorns. Why will men torment one another for the kingdom of this world, which is worthless when they have attained it? Why will they torment one another for the kingdom of God, which is within them? If art has anything to teach it is that these torments are vain, and that to mistake one supposed aspect of truth for Truth itself and so to imprison men's curiosity and aspiration in the dungeon of an ideology, is the unforgivable sin against the spirit of man.

An artist is bound by his vocation to recognize as sin the authoritarian's claim to be a monopolist of truth. For that very reason the word truth cannot be excluded from his answers to the two vital questions. When he is asked what he will enable men to imagine, he will answer, in summary: "Aspects of Truth." When he is asked by what means he will do this, he will answer, again in summary: "By communicating my own visions of Truth." You will observe that the word "visions" is in the plural: "visions," not "vision"; you will remember that Thomas Hardy called a volume of his poems *Moments of Vision*, and that he was careful to renounce all claim to a monopoly of truth. "I have no philosophy," he wrote, "merely what I have often explained to be a confused

From *Liberties of the Mind* (New York: The Macmillan Co. and London: Macmillan & Co., Ltd., 1951), pp. 90–92. Used by permission.

heap of impressions, like those of a bewildered child at a con-
juring show." And you will not have failed to notice that when
that giant among artists, Tolstoy, reached that stage of his life
which is called his "conversion"; when, that is to say, he ex-
changed his many visions of truth for one vision of it and established an ethical system; he became so much the less a practising
artist and indeed repudiated art altogether as he had formerly
understood it. But Hardy's saying that he had no philosophy is
not to be understood to mean that he had no point of view. He
stood on a hill-top and from it surveyed experience, and it was his
own hill-top; he was not inconsistent in the sense of being without
distinct individuality; he was not for ever blown hither and
thither by the opinions of others, joining leagues and clubs and
fashionable groups and peering out at life through their blinkers.
He preserved his integrity, guarded his individuality, looked out
from his own hill-top. But he did not look only north, or only
south, or only east or west. He did not fix upon a favourite view
and say: "This is Truth. There is no other." He surveyed the whole
landscape of experience with what eyes he had, and said to us:
"Look: what do you see with your different eyes?" And we looked,
and, though we did not see what he had seen, we saw what we
had not seen before and might never have seen but for his visionary flash.

Ralph Barton Perry: *It is proper to subject art to moral criticism.*

Art is subject to moral criticism, because morality is nothing
more nor less than the law which determines the whole order of
interests, within which art and every other good thing is possible.
It will scarcely be denied that art is an expression of interest, that
both its creation and its enjoyment are activities, moods, or phases
of life; and it follows that before this specific interest can be safely
or adequately satisfied, it is necessary to fulfil the general condi-

Reprinted with the permission of Charles Scribner's Sons from *The Moral
Economy*, pp. 174–76, copyright 1909 Charles Scribner's Sons; renewal
copyright 1937 Ralph Barton Perry.

tions that underlie the satisfaction of all interests. It is as absurd to speak of art for art's sake as it is to speak of drinking for drinking's sake, if you mean that this interest is entitled to entirely free play. Art, like all other interests, can flourish only in a sound and whole society, and the law of soundness and wholeness in life is morality.

The claim of art to exemption from moral criticism is commonly due to one or both of these two forms of misapprehension.

In the first place, it is assumed that morality, too, is a special interest; and that if the artist or connoisseur lets the moralist alone, it is no more than fair that the moralist should let him alone. But this assumption is false; as false as though the athlete were to chafe at the warnings of his medical adviser on the ground that general health was irrelevant to endurance or strength or agility. Now, doubtless, an athlete may for a time neglect his general health with no noticeable diminution of his skill; but that is only because he already possesses the health to abuse. It still remains true that the principles of health which the trainer represents are the principles upon which his skill is fundamentally based. Nature has made him healthy according to these principles, and he simply does not recognize his debt to them. Similarly, art may flourish in spite of the neglect of social and individual well-being, so that the pleadings of the moral advocate seem irrelevant; but this is possible only because the social order is already established, and the personality formed, according to the very principles which the moralist is announcing. Art may dissipate moral health, but it nevertheless lives only by virtue of such a source of supply. The basal condition of art is not the element of social evil or morbid temperament that may attract attention, but the measure of soundness that nevertheless remains.

The second misapprehension that lends plausibility to the excuses of art is the assumption that the moralist is proposing to *substitute* his canons for those of art. Now it is entirely true that moral insight in no way equips one for connoisseurship. There is a special aptitude and training that enables one to discriminate in such matters. But the moralist is judging art *on moral grounds.* Hence he does not say, "I see that your painting is ugly"; but he does say, "I see that your painting, which you esteem beautiful

(and I take your word for it), is *bad*." In the same way the moralist does not say to the self-indulgent man, "I see that you are not
having a good time" (the self-indulgent man is likely to know
better); but he says, "I see that it is bad for you to be having this
particular kind of good time." In other words, for the moralist
larger issues are at stake, and he is considering these on the
grounds proper to them. He is charged with defining and applying
the principles which determine the good of interests on the whole;
and while his conclusions can never replace those of the expert
within a special field, they will always possess authority to over-
rule them.

Aaron Copland: *Our concert halls have been turned into musical museums.*

Despite the attractions of phonograph and radio, which are
considerable, true music-lovers insist on hearing live performances
of music. An unusual and disturbing situation has gradually become all-pervasive at public performances of music: the universal
preponderance of old music on concert programs.

This unhealthy state of affairs, this obsession with old music,
tends to make all music listening safe and unadventurous since it
deals so largely in the works of the accepted masters. Filling our
halls with familiar sounds induces a sense of security in our audiences; they are gradually losing all need to exercise freely their
own musical judgment. Over and over again the same limited
number of bona fide, guaranteed masterpieces are on display; by
inference, therefore, it is mainly these works that are worth our
notice. This narrows considerably in the minds of a broad public
the very conception of how varied musical experience may be,
and puts all lesser works in a false light. It conventionalizes programs, obviously, and overemphasizes the interpreter's role, for
only through seeking out new "readings" is it possible to repeat
the same works year after year. Most pernicious of all, it leaves a

From *Music and Imagination* (Cambridge, Mass.: Harvard Univ. Press,
1952), pp. 17–19. Used by permission.

bare minimum of wall space for the showing of the works of new composers, without which the supply of future writers of master-works is certain to dry up.

This state of affairs is not merely a local or national one—it per-vades the musical life of every country that professes love for western music. Nine-tenths of the time a program performed in a concert hall in Buenos Aires provides an exact replica of what goes on in a concert hall of London or of Tel-Aviv. Music is no longer merely an international language, it is an international commodity.

This concentration on masterworks is having a profound influ-ence on present-day musical life. A solemn wall of respectability surrounds the haloed masterpieces of music and deadens their impact. They are written about too often out of a sticky sentiment steeped in conventionality. It is both exhilarating and depressing to think of them; exhilarating to think that great masses of people are put in daily contact with them, have the possibility of truly taking sustenance from them; and depressing to watch these same classics used to snuff out all liveliness, all immediacy from the contemporary scene.

. . . . .

The simple truth is that our concert halls have been turned into musical museums—auditory museums of a most limited kind. Our musical era is sick in that respect—our composers invalids who exist on the fringe of musical society, and our listeners impover-ished through a relentless repetition of the same works signed by a handful of sanctified names.

William Hazlitt: *The principle of universal suffrage is not applicable to matters of taste.*

The diffusion of taste is not the same thing as the improvement of taste; but it is only the former of these objects that is promoted by public institutions and other artificial means. The number of

From *The Complete Works of William Hazlitt* (London: J. M. Dent and Sons, Ltd., 1933), XVIII, 45–48.

candidates for fame, and of pretenders to criticism, is thus increased beyond all proportion, while the quantity of genius and feeling remains the same; with this difference, that the man of genius is lost in the crowd of competitors, who would never have become such but from encouragement and example; and that the opinion of those few persons whom nature intended for judges, is drowned in the noisy suffrages of shallow smatterers in taste. The principle of universal suffrage, however applicable to matters of government, which concern the common feelings and common interests of society is by no means applicable to matters of taste, which can only be decided upon by the most refined understandings. The highest efforts of genius, in every walk of art can never be properly understood by the generality of mankind: There are numberless beauties and truths which lie far beyond their comprehension. It is only as refinement and sublimity are blended with other qualities of a more obvious and grosser nature, that they pass current with the world. Taste is the highest degree of sensibility, or the impression made on the most cultivated and sensible of minds, as genius is the result of the highest powers both of feeling and invention. It may be objected, that the public taste is capable of gradual improvement, because, in the end, the public do justice to works of the greatest merit. This is a mistake. The reputation ultimately, and often slowly affixed to works of genius is stamped upon them by authority, not by popular consent or the common sense of the world. We imagine that the admiration of the works of celebrated men has become common, because the admiration of their names has become so. But does not every ignorant connoisseur pretend the same veneration, and talk with the same vapid assurance of Michael Angelo, though he has never seen even a copy of any of his pictures, as if he had studied them accurately,—merely because Sir Joshua Reynolds has praised him? Is Milton more popular now than when the *Paradise Lost* was first published? Or does he not rather owe his reputation to the judgment of a few persons in every successive period, accumulating in his favour, and overpowering by its weight the public indifference?

C. Literature and Science

James B. Conant: *Philosophers, writers, and artists affect our daily lives more profoundly than scholars and scientists.*

I have suggested on another occasion that one may group together under the heading "accumulative knowledge" subjects as diverse as mathematics, physics, chemistry, biology, anthropology, philology, and archaeology. One can state with assurance that great advances have been made in these subjects in the last three centuries. A similar statement cannot be made about philosophy, poetry, and the fine arts. If you are inclined to doubt this and raise the question of how progress even in academic matters can be defined, I would respond by asking you to perform an imaginary operation. Bring back to life the great figures of the past who were identified with the subjects in question. Ask them to view the present scene and answer whether or not in their opinion there has been an advance. No one can doubt how Galileo, Newton, Harvey, or the pioneers in anthropology and archaeology would respond. It is far otherwise with Michelangelo, Rembrandt, Dante, Milton, or Keats. It would be otherwise with Thomas Aquinas, Spinoza, Locke, or Kant. We might argue all day whether or not the particular artist or poet or philosopher would feel the present state of art or poetry or philosophy to be an advance or a retrogression from the days when he himself was a creative spirit. There would be no unanimity among us; and more significant still, no agreement between the majority view which might prevail and that which would have prevailed fifty years ago.

From *On Understanding Science* (New Haven: Yale Univ. Press, 1947), pp. 21–22. Used by permission.

I recognize how dangerous it is to introduce the concept of progress as a method of defining an area of intellectual activity. Therefore, I hasten to say that I am not implying any hierarchy in my classification. I put no halo over the words advance or progress; quite the contrary. In terms of their importance to each of us as human beings, I think the very subjects which fall outside of my definition of accumulative knowledge far outrank the others. To amplify this point would be to digress too far. I need only ask two questions: How often in our daily lives are we influenced in important decisions by the results of the scientific inquiries of modern times? How often do we act without reflecting the influence of the philosophy and poetry which we have consciously and unconsciously imbibed over many years? A dictator wishing to mold the thoughts and actions of a literate people could afford to leave the scientists and scholars alone, but he must win over to his side or destroy the philosophers, the writers and the artists.

John Hall Wheelock: *Words too often violate the innocent nobility of things.*

The knowledge of the objective universe that the scientist claims to have brought back with him from his explorations—whether as the result of a hypothesis, or of deduction from known facts, or of a new combination of such facts—can be tested empirically and, if proven valid, becomes a truth until such time as further knowledge calls for further adjustment and modification. What the poet feels he has discovered and made available in the process of his poem must stand the test of another kind of verification. The knowledge he claims to have revealed is a knowledge

From "The Two Knowledges: An Essay on a Certain Resistance" in *American Poetry at Mid-Century* by John Crowe Ransom, Delmore Schwartz, and John Hall Wheelock (Washington, D. C.: Library of Congress, 1958), p. 36. Included as the Introductory Essay to *Poets of Today* V (New York: Charles Scribner's Sons, 1958). Used by permission of author and publisher.

of the subjective universe of emotion and experience, and the touchstone here is the human spirit inhabiting that universe. To meet the test, to find acceptance as true knowledge, a poem must win the acquiescence in it of another mind. This is no easy matter. Reality so far transcends anything we can say about it as to make silence, for the most part, preferable. Silence says it better. Words too often violate the innocent nobility of things. Where our deepest feelings are concerned, only the spokesman supremely qualified will be tolerated. The statements of science, once checked with observable phenomena and found to embody true knowledge, are accepted as such and soon taken for granted. They are, moreover, as already remarked, subject to constant change as fresh findings make it necessary to amend or revise them. Not so the discoveries of the poet. These reach to the permanent heart of experience. They represent, always, a fresh revelation of an old, perhaps a forgotten, knowledge. We are not, ordinarily, receptive to having such a knowledge revived in us.

Gilbert Murray: *Unlike great works of science, great works of literature do not become obsolete.*

In philosophy, religion, poetry, and the highest kinds of art, the greatness of the author's mind seems as a rule to be all that matters; one almost ignores the date at which he worked. This is because in technical sciences the element of mere fact, or mere knowledge, is so enormous, the elements of imagination, character, and the like so very small. Hence, books on science, in a progressive age, very quickly become 'out of date,' and each new edition usually supersedes the last. It is the rarest thing for a work of science to survive as a text-book more than ten years or so. . . .

From "The Value of Greece to the Future of the World" in *The Legacy of Greece* (Oxford, England: The Clarendon Press, 1921), pp. 2, 5–7. Used by permission.

This is a simple point, but it is so important that we must dwell on it for a moment. If we read an old treatise on medicine or mechanics, we may admire it and feel it a work of genius, but we also feel that it is obsolete: its work is over; we have got beyond it. But when we read Homer or Aeschylus, if once we have the power to admire and understand their writing, we do not for the most part have any feeling of having got beyond them. We have done so no doubt in all kinds of minor things, in general knowledge, in details of technique, in civilization and the like; but hardly any sensible person ever imagines that he has got beyond their essential quality, the quality that has made them great.

Doubtless there is in every art an element of mere knowledge or science, and that element is progressive. But there is another element, too, which does not depend on knowledge and which does not progress but has a kind of stationary and eternal value, like the beauty of the dawn, or the love of a mother for her child, or the joy of a young animal in being alive, or the courage of a martyr facing torment. We cannot for all our progress get beyond these things; there they stand, like light upon the mountains. The only question is whether we can rise to them. And it is the same with all the greatest births of human imagination. As far as we can speculate, there is not the faintest probability of any poet ever setting to work on, let us say, the essential effect aimed at by Aeschylus in the Cassandra-scene of the *Agamemnon*, and doing it better than Aeschylus. The only thing which the human race has to do with that scene is to understand it and get out of it all the joy and emotion and wonder that it contains.

.   .   .   .   .

And here another point emerges, equally simple and equally important if we are to understand our relation to the past. Suppose a man says: 'I quite understand that Plato or Aeschylus may have had fine ideas, but surely anything of value which they said must long before this have become common property. There is no need to go back to the Greeks for it. We do not go back and read Copernicus to learn that the earth goes round the sun.' What is the answer? It is that such a view ignores exactly this difference between the progressive and the eternal, between knowledge and

imagination. If Harvey discovers that the blood is not stationary
but circulates, if Copernicus discovers that the earth goes round
the sun and not the sun round the earth, those discoveries can
easily be communicated in the most abbreviated form. If a me-
chanic invents an improvement on the telephone, or a social reformer puts some good usage in the place of a bad one, in a few
years we shall probably all be using the improvement without
even knowing what it is or saying Thank you. We may be as
stupid as we like, we have in a sense got the good of it.

But can one apply the same process to *Macbeth* or *Romeo and
Juliet*? Can any one tell us in a few words what they come to?
Or can a person get the good of them in any way except one—the
way of vivid and loving study, following and feeling the author's
meaning all through? To suppose, as I believe some people do,
that you can get the value of a great poem by studying an abstract
of it in an encyclopaedia or by reading cursorily an average trans-
lation of it, argues really a kind of mental deficiency, like deafness
or colour-blindness. The things that we have called eternal, the
things of the spirit and the imagination, always seem to lie more
in a process than in a result, and can only be reached and enjoyed
by somehow going through the process again. If the value of a
particular walk lies in the scenery, you do not get that value by
taking a short cut or using a fast motor-car.

Walter Pater: *Art and literature bring a sense of free-
dom into a world ruled by natural laws.*

What modern art has to do in the service of culture is so to
rearrange the details of modern life, so to reflect it, that it may
satisfy the spirit. And what does the spirit need in the face of
modern life? The sense of freedom. That naïve, rough sense of
freedom, which supposes man's will to be limited, if at all, only by
a will stronger than his, he can never have again. The attempt to
represent it in art would have so little verisimilitude that it would

From *The Renaissance* (New York: Boni & Liveright, 1919), pp. 192–93.

be flat and uninteresting. The chief factor in the thoughts of the
modern mind concerning itself is the intricacy, the universality of
natural law, even in the moral order. For us, necessity is not, as
of old, a sort of mythological personage without us, with whom
we can do warfare. It is rather a magic web woven through and
through us, like that magnetic system of which modern science
speaks, penetrating us with a network, subtler than our subtlest
nerves, yet bearing in it the central forces of the world. Can art
represent men and women in these bewildering toils so as to give
the spirit at least an equivalent for the sense of freedom? Certainly, in Goethe's romances, and even more in the romances of
Victor Hugo, we have high examples of modern art dealing thus
with modern life, regarding that life as the modern mind must
regard it, yet reflecting upon it blitheness and repose. Natural
laws we shall never modify, embarrass us as they may; but there
is still something in the nobler or less noble attitude with which
we watch their fatal combinations. In those romances of Goethe
and Victor Hugo, in some excellent work done *after* them, this
entanglement, this network of law, becomes the tragic situation,
in which certain groups of noble men and women work out for
themselves a supreme *Dénouemènt*. Who, if he saw through all,
would fret against the chain of circumstance which endows one
at the end with those great experiences?

J. Bronowski: *In the moment of creation—in art or in science—the heart misses a beat.*

The discoveries of science, the works of art are explorations—
more, are explosions, of a hidden likeness. The discoverer or the
artist presents in them two aspects of nature and fuses them into
one. This is the act of creation, in which an original thought is
born, and it is the same act in original science and original art.
But it is not therefore the monopoly of the man who wrote the

Reprinted by permission of Julian Messner, Inc. from *Science and Human Values*, copyright 1956 by J. Bronowski, pp. 30–32.

poem or who made the discovery. On the contrary, I believe this view of the creative act to be right because it alone gives a meaning to the act of appreciation. The poem or the discovery exists in two moments of vision: the moment of appreciation as much as that of creation; for the appreciator must see the movement, wake to the echo which was started in the creation of the work. In the moment of appreciation we live again the moment when the creator saw and held the hidden likeness. When a simile takes us aback and persuades us together, when we find a juxtaposition in a picture both odd and intriguing, when a theory is at once fresh and convincing, we do not merely nod over someone else's work. We re-enact the creative act, and we ourselves make the discovery again. At bottom, there is no unifying likeness there until we too have seized it, we too have made it for ourselves.

How slipshod by comparison is the notion that either art or science sets out to copy nature. If the task of the painter were to copy for men what they see, the critic could make only a single judgment: either that the copy is right or that it is wrong. And if science were a copy of fact, then every theory would be either right or wrong, and would be so forever. There would be nothing left for us to say but this is so or is not so. No one who has read a page by a good critic or a speculative scientist can ever again think that this barren choice of yes or no is all that the mind offers.

Reality is not an exhibit for man's inspection, labeled: "Do not touch." There are no appearances to be photographed, no experiences to be copied, in which we do not take part. We re-make nature by the act of discovery, in the poem or in the theorem. And the great poem and the deep theorem are new to every reader, and yet are his own experiences, because he himself re-creates them. They are the marks of unity in variety; and in the instant when the mind seizes this for itself, in art or in science, the heart misses a beat.

Thomas Love Peacock: *As science and knowledge advance, poetry becomes increasingly unnecessary and increasingly inferior.*

The highest inspirations of poetry are resolvable into three ingredients: the rant of unregulated passion, the whining of exaggerated feeling, and the cant of factitious sentiment: and can therefore . . . never make a philosopher, nor a statesman, nor in any class of life an useful or rational man. It cannot claim the slightest share in any one of the comforts and utilities of life of which we have witnessed so many and so rapid advances. But though not useful, it may be said it is highly ornamental, and deserves to be cultivated for the pleasure it yields. Even if this be granted, it does not follow that a writer of poetry in the present state of society is not a waster of his own time, and a robber of that of others. Poetry is not one of those arts which, like painting, require repetition and multiplication, in order to be diffused among society. There are more good poems already existing than are sufficient to employ that portion of life which any mere reader and recipient of poetical impressions should devote to them, and these having been produced in poetical times, are far superior in all the characteristics of poetry to the artificial reconstructions of a few morbid ascetics in unpoetical times. To read the promiscuous rubbish of the present time to the exclusion of the select treasures of the past, is to substitute the worse for the better variety of the same mode of enjoyment.

But in whatever degree poetry is cultivated, it must necessarily be to the neglect of some branch of useful study: and it is a lamentable spectacle to see minds, capable of better things, running to seed in the specious indolence of these empty aimless mockeries of intellectual exertion. Poetry was the mental rattle that awak-

From "The Four Ages of Poetry" in *Peacock's Four Ages of Poetry, Shelley's Defense of Poetry, Browning's Essay on Shelley* (Boston: Houghton Mifflin Company, 1921), pp. 17–19.

ened the attention of intellect in the infancy of civil society: but for the maturity of mind to make a serious business of the play-things of its childhood, is as absurd as for a full-grown man to rub his gums with coral, and cry to be charmed to sleep by the jingle of silver bells.

. . . . .

Now when we consider that it is not the thinking and studious, and scientific and philosophical part of the community, not to those whose minds are bent on the pursuit and promotion of per-manently useful ends and aims, that poets must address their minstrelsy, but to that much larger portion of the reading public, whose minds are not awakened to the desire of valuable knowl-edge, and who are indifferent to any thing beyond being charmed, moved, excited, affected, and exalted: charmed by harmony, moved by sentiment, excited by passion, affected by pathos, and exalted by sublimity: harmony, which is language on the rack of Procrustes; sentiment, which is canting egotism in the mask of refined feeling; passion, which is the commotion of a weak and selfish mind; pathos, which is the whining of an unmanly spirit; and sublimity, which is the inflation of an empty head: when we consider that the great and permanent interests of human society become more and more the main spring of intellectual pursuit; that in proportion as they become so, the subordinacy of the orna-mental to the useful will be more and more seen and acknowl-edged; and that therefore the progress of useful art and science, and of moral and political knowledge, will continue more and more to withdraw attention from frivolous and unconducive, to solid and conducive studies: that therefore the poetical audience will not only continually diminish in the proportion of its number to that of the rest of the reading public, but will also sink lower and lower in the comparison of intellectual acquirement: when we consider that the poet must still please his audience, and must therefore continue to sink to their level, while the rest of the community is rising above it: we may easily conceive that the day is not distant, when the degraded state of every species of poetry will be as generally recognized as that of dramatic poetry has long been: and this not from any decrease either of intellectual power, or intellectual acquisition, but because intellectual power and intellectual acquisition have turned themselves into other and better channels, and have abandoned the cultivation and the fate of poetry to the degenerate fry of modern rhymesters, and their olympic judges, the magazine critics, who continue to debate and promulgate oracles about poetry, as if it were still what it was in the Homeric age, the all-in-all of intellectual progression, and as if there were no such things in existence as mathematicians, astronomers, chemists, moralists, metaphysicians, historians, politicians, and political economists, who have built into the upper air of intelligence a pyramid, from the summit of which they see the modern Parnassus far beneath them, and, knowing how small a place it occupies in the comprehensiveness of their prospect, smile at the little ambition and the circumscribed perceptions with which the drivellers and mountebanks upon it are contending for the poetical palm and the critical chair.

Percy Bysshe Shelley: *For want of the poetical faculty, man, having enslaved the elements, remains himself a slave.*

. . . poets have been challenged to resign the civic crown to reasoners . . . It is admitted that the exercise of the imagination is most delightful, but it is alleged that that of reason is more useful. Let us examine . . . this . . .

. . . . .

. . . it exceeds all imagination to conceive what would have been the moral condition of the world if neither Dante, Petrarch, Boccaccio, Chaucer, Shakspeare, Calderon, Lord Bacon, nor Milton, had ever existed; if Raphael and Michael Angelo had never been born; if the Hebrew poetry had never been translated; if a

From "A Defence of Poetry" in *Peacock's Four Ages of Poetry, Shelley's Defense of Poetry, Browning's Essay on Shelley* (Boston: Houghton Mifflin Company, 1921), pp. 49, 51–53.

revival of the study of Greek literature had never taken place; if no monuments of ancient sculpture had been handed down to us; and if the poetry of the religion of the ancient world had been extinguished together with its belief. The human mind could never, except by the intervention of these excitements, have been awakened to the invention of the grosser sciences, and that application of analytical reasoning to the aberrations of society, which it is now attempted to exalt over the direct expression of the inventive and creative faculty itself.

We have more moral, political, and historical wisdom, than we know how to reduce into practice; we have more scientific and economical knowledge than can be accommodated to the just distribution of the produce which it multiplies. The poetry, in these systems of thought, is concealed by the accumulation of facts and calculating processes. There is no want of knowledge respecting what is wisest and best in morals, government, and political economy, or at least what is wiser and better than what men now practise and endure. But we let "*I dare not* wait upon *I would*, like the poor cat in the adage." We want the creative faculty to imagine that which we know; we want the generous impulse to act that which we imagine; we want the poetry of life: our calculations have outrun conception; we have eaten more than we can digest. The cultivation of those sciences which have enlarged the limits of the empire of man over the external world, has, for want of the poetical faculty, proportionally circumscribed those of the internal world; and man, having enslaved the elements, remains himself a slave. To what but a cultivation of the mechanical arts in a degree disproportioned to the presence of the creative faculty, which is the basis of all knowledge, is to be attributed the abuse of all invention for abridging and combining labour, to the exasperation of the inequality of mankind? From what other cause has it arisen that the discoveries which should have lightened, have added a weight to the curse imposed on Adam? Poetry, and the principle of Self, of which money is the visible incarnation, are the God and Mammon of the world.

The functions of the poetical faculty are twofold; by one it creates new materials of knowledge, and power, and pleasure; by the other it engenders in the mind a desire to reproduce and arrange them according to a certain rhythm and order, which may be called the beautiful and the good. The cultivation of poetry is never more to be desired than at periods when, from an excess of the selfish and calculating principle, the accumulation of the materials of external life exceed the quantity of the power of assimilating them to the internal laws of human nature. The body has then become too unwieldy for that which animates it.

George Santayana: *Where it is believed that only experimental science can yield knowledge, poetry will be rather despised.*

I know that the distinctively American philosophy, pragmatism or instrumentalism, warms to the praise of experimental science, and even asserts that there is no other sort of valid knowledge. This opinion is itself symptomatic. The word "knowledge" (like the word "truth," sometimes used by pragmatists as if synonymous with "knowledge") is commonly a eulogistic word; and if all other intellectual possessions save strictly experimental science are denied the title of knowledge, we may suspect that, even if admitted as forms of feeling or of poetry, they will be rather despised. Yet before experimental science had made much progress, perception, familiarity, and insight, on the human scale and in pictorial and dramatic terms, had richly furnished the mind, and sufficed to guide it pertinently in all indispensable matters. All the mechanical arts which experiment has created are luxuries, luxuries in which the poor are now compelled to indulge, instead of in their ancient luxuries, such as religion, story-telling, piping, ribaldry, dancing, and fine holiday clothes. Doubtless those legends and sports kept them scientifically ignorant and unprogressive. Yet considered intellectually, or as furniture for the mind, the artificial abstractions which modern science substitutes for the

From *The Idler and His Works*, published by George Braziller, 1957, pp. 45–47. Copyright © Daniel Cory 1957.

natural symbols of the senses and fancy have no greater value. They are not truth substituted for illusion, but one language substituted for another. And what a language! Essentially vacant, thin, dark, and unintelligible, it has only one merit: it is a vehicle of power—of power, I mean, over matter. For the purposes of dealing with the flux of matter, far removed in its dynamic texture from the human scale, this experimental and mathematical science is alone relevant: the old arts were only customs, and treated natural things almost as if they were persons, and the sailor steered his ship as if he were driving a horse. When that rude acquaintance gave out, the prayers, oracles, and incantations of the classic mind were nothing to the purpose. The essential darkness of modern science goes naturally with its utility: how should matter not be dark to spirit? A pragmatic knowledge of it is knowledge enough. Such knowledge contains the most expeditious methods of doing business, with the greatest safety and the least possible expense of thought. After business is dispatched (or while it is carried on, if such doubleness does not involve too much distraction) the mind is free to enjoy the sensations, the vistas, the hopes which its contacts with nature are capable of arousing. If geography, history, letters, and worldly wisdom are no longer called "knowledge," they are not absolutely forbidden to survive: they remain a part of experience, idle in so far as not useful in material work, but admissible, perhaps, as by-play and recreation.

G. H. Hardy: *The mathematician's patterns, like the painter's or the poet's, must be beautiful.*

A mathematician, like a painter or a poet, is a maker of patterns. If his patterns are more permanent than theirs, it is because they are made with *ideas*. A painter makes patterns with shapes

From *A Mathematician's Apology* (Cambridge, England: The University Press, 1940), pp. 24–25. Used by permission of the Cambridge Univ. Press.

and colours, a poet with words. A painting may embody an 'idea,' but the idea is usually commonplace and unimportant. In poetry, ideas count for a good deal more; but, as Housman insisted, the importance of ideas in poetry is habitually exaggerated: 'I cannot satisfy myself that there are any such things as poetical ideas. . . . Poetry is not the thing said but a way of saying it.'

> Not all the water in the rough rude sea
> Can wash the balm from an anointed King.

Could lines be better, and could ideas be at once more trite and more false? The poverty of the ideas seems hardly to affect the beauty of the verbal pattern. A mathematician, on the other hand, has no material to work with but ideas, and so his patterns are likely to last longer, since ideas wear less with time than words.

The mathematician's patterns, like the painter's or the poet's, must be *beautiful*; the ideas, like the colours or the words, must fit together in a harmonious way. Beauty is the first test: there is no permanent place in the world for ugly mathematics . . . It may be very hard to *define* mathematical beauty, but that is just as true of beauty of any kind—we may not know quite what we mean by a beautiful poem, but that does not prevent us from recognizing one when we read it.

Appendix A: Guide to Major Ideas in the Selections

1. How does progress in science threaten civilization? Brandt, 13; Bridgman, 7; Broad, 32; Bronowski, 3, 17, 19, 25, 74; Fosdick, 5; Langer, 16; Zimmern, 9

2. How does science contribute to the development of civilization? Bronowski, 17, 25; Fosdick, 5; Merz, 14; Peacock, 254; Russell, 34; Shelley, 256

3. How is science shaping the intellectual life of our time? Arendt, 26; Broad, 32; Bronowski, 17; Conant, 247; Falckenberg, 149; Jones, 201; Merz, 14; Oppenheimer, 18; Peacock, 254; Russell, 34; Shelley, 256; Whitehead, 15

4. Does science favor the development of liberal culture? Bronowski, 25, 53; Burroughs, 37; Conant, 21; Eddington, 46; Huxley, 35, 176; James, 86; Jones, 201; Merz, 14; Nagel, 194; Nunn, 45; Ortega y Gasset, 27; Peacock, 254; Russell, 34; Santayana, 258; Shelley, 256; Snow, 30; Wheelock, 248; Woodbridge, 41

5. Does science have an unsettling effect on society? Brandt, 13; Broad, 32; Bronowski, 3; Fosdick, 5; Langer, 16; Oppenheimer, 18; Shelley, 256; Wheelock, 248; Whitehead, 15

6. How does dissent contribute to progress in the arts, science, and social life? Bronowski, 17, 74; Cohen, 71; Mill, 144; Murray, 144; Russell, 175; Whitehead, 75

7. Are scientists wiser than nonscientists in human affairs? Arendt, 26; Conant, 21, 33, 247; Lucas, 108; MacIver, 124; Nagel, 194; Ogburn, 158; Ortega y Gasset, 27; Snow, 30; Zimmern, 9

8. Can the moral life be based entirely on reason? Balfour, 147; Burroughs, 37; Clifford, 85; Cohen and Nagel, 236; Edman, 101; Fosdick, 5; Friedrich, 125; Fullerton, 94; Haldane, 119;

261

Hobhouse, 98; James, 86; Johnson, 103; Santayana, 96; Shelley, 256

9. Should curbs be placed on scientific inquiry? Bridgman, 7, 93; Bronowski, 3; Fosdick, 5

10. What is the role of reason in politics? Bryce, 106; Burns, 91; Clifford, 85; Edman, 101; Fullerton, 94; James, 86; Lecky, 105; Lippmann, 92; Munro, 111; Ogburn, 158; Robinson, 171; Russell, 175; Shelley, 256; Smith, 118; Woodbridge, 113

11. Is everyday experience unreal? Andrade, 69; Burroughs, 37; Eddington, 43, 46, 51; Edman, 48, 214; Krutch, 66; Nunn, 45; Russell, 34; Santayana, 258; Stevenson, 212; Woodbridge, 209

12. What is the nature of truth in art? Bosanquet, 219; Brinton, 99; Bronowski, 252; Edman, 220, 227; Hardy, 259; Macaulay, 169; Morgan, 241; Santayana, 258; Stevenson, 212; Wheelock, 248; Woodbridge, 209

13. Should the scientist assume social responsibility for the use of his discoveries? Arendt, 26; Brandt, 13; Bridgman, 7; Bronowski, 3, 19; Fosdick, 5; Meier, 20; Zimmern, 9

14. Can a specialist be educated? Broad, 32; Huxley, 35; MacLeish, 180; Ortega y Gasset, 27; Robinson, 171; Snow, 30

15. Is mathematics a tool of cultural force? Hardy, 259; Huxley, 35; Kline, 59, 198; Santayana, 258

16. What is the relation of impulse and reason? Balfour, 147; Eddington, 51; Fullerton, 153; Hobhouse, 98; Lippmann, 92; Ogburn, 158; Russell, 34, 175; Santayana, 258

17. Should the scientist take an active part in public affairs? Arendt, 26; Brandt, 13; Bridgman, 93

18. How does the progress of science tend to enrich and impoverish man's spiritual life? Bronowski, 17, 25; Burns, 150; Burroughs, 37; Edman, 131; Huxley, 35; Jones, 201; Langer, 16; Mumford, 132; Oppenheimer, 18; Ortega y Gasset, 27; Peacock, 254; Russell, 34; Santayana, 258; Shelley, 256; Snow, 30; Stevenson, 212; Zimmern, 9

19. Should art be judged by moral standards? Cohen and Nagel, 236; Langer, 234; Morgan, 241; Perry, 242; Ruskin, 230; Santayana, 229; Shelley, 256

20. What is the nature of truth in science? Andrade, 77; Arendt, 26; Brinton, 99; Bronowski, 17, 25, 74, 252; Cohen, 71; Fos-

dick, 5; James, 86; MacLeish, 180; Murray, 249; Nagel, 73; Oppenheimer, 18; Santayana, 49, 258; Stevenson, 212; Wheelock, 248

21. How does knowledge in science differ from knowledge in the arts? Brinton, 99; Burroughs, 37; Conant, 247; Livingstone, 218; Murray, 249; Santayana, 146; Whitehead, 15

22. Is science indifferent to moral values? Bronowski, 17, 19; Fosdick, 5; James, 86; Meier, 20; Snow, 30; Zimmern, 9

23. Are the realities of science really real? Andrade, 57, 69; Arendt, 26; Burroughs, 37; Cohen and Nagel, 60; Eddington, 43, 46, 51; Edman, 48, 214; Kline, 59; Krutch, 66; Nunn, 45; Santayana, 258; Stevenson, 212

24. What is the role of imagination in science? Andrade, 57; Balfour, 147; Bosanquet, 219; Bronowski, 25, 53, 252; Conant, 33; Eddington, 43, 46, 51; Edman, 48; Langer, 16; MacLeish, 180; Moore, 148; Nunn, 61; Peirce, 152; Russell, 175; Santayana, 49; Singer, 40

25. Does art reflect the spirit of an age? Burroughs, 37; Lewisohn, 215; Livingstone, 218, 222; Murray, 217; Ruskin, 230

26. What are the sources of artistic satisfactions? Bosanquet, 219; Bronowski, 252; Eddington, 51; Edman, 214, 227; Haggin, 224; Langer, 223; Lewisohn, 215; Livingstone, 218, 222; Longinus, 240; Morgan, 241; Pater, 211, 251; Peacock, 254; Ruskin, 230; Shelley, 256; Stevenson, 212; Tolstoy, 231; Wyatt, 213; Woodbridge, 209

27. What is the distinction between the physical and social sciences? Bridgman, 93; Bronowski, 25; Conant, 21; McKeon, 162; Meier, 20; Nagel, 23; Ogburn, 158

28. Does art have any practical value? Conant, 247; Edman, 220, 227; Lucas, 108; Mumford, 132; Peacock, 254; Russell, 34; Shelley, 256; Wheelock, 248; Woodbridge, 209

29. What are "laws" in science? Andrade, 77; Bronowski, 3, 25; Butler, 79; Chesterton, 64; Krutch, 66; Pater, 251; Tolstoy, 102

30. How is excellence in art determined? Ciardi, 237; Cohen and Nagel, 236; Haggin, 224; Hazlitt, 245; Langer, 234; Longinus, 240; Lucas, 196; Lynd, 239; Ruskin, 230; Russell, 200; Tolstoy, 231; Wheelock, 248; White, 233

31. What is the relation of poetry and science? Burroughs, 37; Conant, 247; Hardy, 259; Langer, 16; Livingstone, 218; Murray, 249; Peacock, 254; Russell, 34; Shelley, 256; Woodbridge, 209

32. Is scientific method the only way to achieve true knowledge? Burroughs, 37; Cohen, 71; Fullerton, 153; Hardy, 259; Moore, 148; Nagel, 73; Peirce, 152; Santayana, 258; Snow, 30; Stevenson, 212; Wheelock, 248

33. What is the nature of art? Bosanquet, 210; Bronowski, 252; Haggin, 224; Hardy, 259; Langer, 234; Morgan, 241; Peacock, 254; Santayana, 229; Tolstoy, 231; White, 233

34. What is the relation of art and politics? MacIver, 124; Morgan, 241

35. What are some of the problems of leadership in a democracy? Bridgman, 127; Bryce, 115; Eliot, 117; Hook, 114, 120; Krutch, 129; Ritchie, 139

36. What is the role of imagination in the arts? Bosanquet, 219; Brinton, 99; Bronowski, 252; Collingwood, 167; Edman, 227; Hardy, 259; MacLeish, 180; Ross Williamson, 168; Russell, 200; Shelley, 256; Woodbridge, 41, 161; Wyatt, 213

37. What makes a great leader? Edman, 101; Eliot, 117; Haldane, 119; Hook, 120; Schlesinger, 122

38. What accounts for the isolation of science from society? Arendt, 26; Brandt, 13; Bronowski, 3, 25; Conant, 33; Lucas, 108; Merz, 14; Ortega y Gasset, 27; Santayana, 258; Snow, 30; Zimmern, 9

39. What is a historical fact? Collingwood, 160; McKeon, 162; May, 164; Macaulay, 169; Woodbridge, 172

40. Is science adequate for solving human problems? Broad, 32; Bronowski, 17, 19, 25, 74; Conant, 21, 247; Fosdick, 5; James, 86; Langer, 16; Lucas, 108; Meier, 20; Nagel, 23, 73; Ogburn, 158; Oppenheimer, 18; Ortega y Gasset, 27; Russell, 34; Santayana, 49; Shelley, 256; Whitehead, 15

41. What is the role of imagination in the writing of history? Collingwood, 167; Macaulay, 169; Ross Williamson, 168; Woodbridge, 161

42. Does science offer a satisfactory way of life? Bridgman, 93; Bronowski, 17, 25, 74; Fosdick, 5; Nagel, 194

43. What is man's relation to the natural world? Langer, 16; Mumford, 132; Santayana, 49; Thoreau, 134

44. Is science free from irrational elements? Bridgman, 93; Bronowski, 3, 25, 252; Conant, 21, 33; Fosdick, 5; Fullerton, 153; Hobhouse, 98; James, 86; Meier, 20; Russell, 34

45. Why must history be rewritten? Collingwood, 160; Macaulay, 169; McKeon, 162; May, 164; Robinson, 171; Woodbridge, 172

46. What is the role of music in our lives? Copland, 244; Haggin, 224; Langer, 223; Lynd, 239

47. How can we make the best use of leisure? Bronowski, 17; Edman, 131; Mumford, 132; Woodbridge, 209

48. Does education prepare adequately for life in modern society? Bourne, 190; Ellsworth, 197; James, 185; Krutch, 129; MacLeish, 180; Nock, 186; Oppenheimer, 18; Perry, 184; Russell, 143, 175, 183, 192, 200; Zimmern, 181

49. Can the historian be impartial? Collingwood, 167; Crump, 166; Macaulay, 169; Ross Williamson, 168; Woodbridge, 161

50. What are the marks of progress? Bridgman, 127; Broad, 32; Conant, 247; Muller, 155; Murray, 249; Santayana, 146; Smith, 118; Wilson, 110

51. How should the arts be taught? Jones, 201; Lucas, 196; Russell, 200

52. What is the nature of political liberty? Burke, 138; Ritchie, 137

53. Does a belief in the "common man" invite the triumph of mediocrity? Arnold, 127; Bridgman, 7, 127; Friedrich, 125; Krutch, 129; James, 185; MacIver, 124; Schlesinger, 122; Wilson, 110

54. How does psychology answer some of man's problems? Broad, 32; Hobhouse, 98; Langer, 234; Lippmann, 92; Ogburn, 158; Sorokin, 203; Watson, 203

55. How should mathematics and science be taught? Kline, 198; Nagel, 194

56. Of what use is philosophy? Balfour, 147; Burns, 150; Descartes, 156; Falckenberg, 149; Fullerton, 153; Moore, 148; Peirce, 152; Santayana, 146

57. Are language and science playing compatible roles? Arendt, 26; Brandt, 13; Bronowski, 3; Conant, 33; Kline, 59; Langer, 16; Lucas, 108; Santayana, 258; Zimmern, 9

58. Has philosophy progressed? Burns, 150; Conant, 247; Santayana, 146

59. What good are visions and visionaries? Brinton, 99; Burns, 91; Child, 89; Edman, 101; Haldane, 119; Hook, 141; Morgan, 241; Munro, 111; Woodbridge, 113

60. Must man always live with war? Brandt, 13; Bridgman, 7; Broad, 32; Bronowski, 3; Child, 89; Fosdick, 5; Hook, 141; Mumford, 132; Zimmern, 9

61. What are some of the problems of teaching and administration? Ellsworth, 197; Kline, 198; Russell, 192; Wilson, 188

62. What are the uses of and defenses against propaganda? Bryce, 106; Child, 89; Eliot, 117; Ellsworth, 197; Hook, 120; Lecky, 105; Lucas, 108; Ogburn, 158; Russell, 175

63. Why do philosophers disagree? Balfour, 147; Descartes, 156; Falckenberg, 149; Fullerton, 153; Moore, 148; Peirce, 152

Appendix B: Some Suggested Exercises

1. Compare two selections in the book which deal with the same or similar ideas. Indicate which selection you think the better, and why.
2. Compare the treatment of an idea in this book with the treatment of the same idea in a standard textbook. Analyze similarities and differences in treatment. If you should find that the idea you have selected is not treated in a textbook in what appears to be the relevant field, tell how you would account for this omission and what conclusions you draw.
3. Arrange a symposium based on a group of selections in the book. Ask all students except the participants to do outside reading on the subject of the symposium, and to join in the general class discussion at the close of the symposium.
4. Arrange two symposia on the same subject. The participants in the first discussion are to be majors in the arts and humanities; those in the second, majors in science and mathematics.
5. Choose a selection for critical consideration by the entire class.

    a. Ask each student who agrees with the point of view expressed in the selection to gather and present concrete evidence and other supporting material (not derived from the book) which tend to amplify and strengthen the original statement.

    b. For the hour which follows, ask each student who disagrees with the point of view expressed in the selection to gather and present concrete evidence and other materials which tend to weaken or nullify the original statement.

6. Ask the students majoring in a given field to arrange a symposium or panel discussion on a topic taken up in the selections which deal with the subject matter of their field. Arrange a discussion for the majors in each area.

7. Paraphrase the thought of a selection which attracts you. Put the paraphrase aside. After an interval of two weeks, reread the original selection; and without looking at your first paraphrase, write a second paraphrase. Read your paraphrases to the class. Tell which you consider the better and why.

8. Pick out a selection (or a passage in a selection) which you consider unusually good. Read the selection to the class and tell why you consider it good by identifying and analyzing the elements which account for its power.

9. Compare one of the selections in the book with an article (not in the book) which deals with the same idea. Prepare a speech for delivery in class in which you tell (1) what the two selections have in common, (2) how they differ, and (3) the merit and shortcomings of each.

Appendix C: Sentences and Expressions for Use as Topics

1. Economics is an imperfect science. Anyone who claims that his economic judgments are emotionally detached, politically impartial, and otherwise objective is himself suspect.—John Kenneth Galbraith
2. A scientist should examine an idea as an artist might look at a delicately enameled vase—in many different lights and positions so as to bring out all its beauty and value.—Ian Stevenson
3. If the country is to be governed with the consent of the governed, then the governed must arrive at opinions about what their governors want them to consent to.—Walter Lippmann
4. If you can measure that of which you speak, and can express it by a number, you know something of your subject. If you cannot measure it, your knowledge is meager and unsatisfactory.—Lord Kelvin
5. Bad logic and pretended facts are more dangerous than imagination and opinion. Even the simple-minded do not believe a thing just because a poet says so. But they seldom doubt what they are told that "science proves."—Joseph Wood Krutch
6. The purpose of science is to know, but periodically man becomes so persistent in his search for documented knowledge that he mistakes the documentation for the knowledge itself. Repeatedly man has so engulfed himself in facts that he has lost sight of their meaning.—Hal Borland
7. Government by the multitude is a contradiction in terms. Were it conducted by the multitude it would not be government.—William Bennett Munro

8. Nonsense which it would be shameful for a reasonable being to write, speak or hear spoken, can be sung or listened to by that same rational being with pleasure and even with a kind of intellectual conviction.—Aldous Huxley

9. Every reform, however necessary, will by weak minds be carried to an excess, which will itself need reforming.—Samuel Taylor Coleridge

10. If the idols of scientists were piled on top of one another in the manner of a totem pole, the topmost one would be a grinning fetish called Measurement.—Anthony Standen

11. An unexciting truth may be eclipsed by a thrilling falsehood. —Aldous Huxley

12. The firmness of the American's faith in the blessings of education is equalled only by the vagueness of his ideas as to the kind of education to which these blessings are annexed. —Irving Babbitt

13. It cannot be too often repeated, line upon line, precept upon precept, until it comes into the currency of a proverb, *to innovate is not to reform.*—Edmund Burke

14. It is a matter of colossal and tragic irony that man, in his scientific genius, has learned how to harness nature, how to control the relations among the elements and direct them as he sees fit, but has never yet learned how to live with himself.—Ralph Bunche

15. Artists treat facts as stimuli for imagination, whereas scientists use imagination to coordinate facts.—Arthur Koestler

16. Happy families are all alike; every unhappy family is unhappy in its own way.—Leo Tolstoy

17. One can generally tell a man's special field of investigation by the words which he uses carefully and the words he uses carelessly.—Ralph Barton Perry

18. I abhor averages. I like the individual case. A man may have six meals one day and none the next, making an average of three per day, but that is not a good way to live.—Louis Brandeis

19. History in general is a collection of crimes, follies, and misfortunes, among which we have now and then met with a

few virtues, and some happy times; as we sometimes see scattered huts in a barren desert.—Voltaire

20. There are two spiritual dangers in not owning a farm. One is the danger of supposing that breakfast comes from the grocery, and the other that heat comes from the furnace.—Aldo Leopold

21. I have no belief in panaceas and almost none in sudden ruin. I believe with Montesquieu that if the chance of a battle—I may add, the passage of a law—has ruined a state, there was a general cause at work that made the state ready to perish by a single battle or a law.—Oliver Wendell Holmes, Jr.

22. Western civilization, wherever it penetrates, brings with it water-taps, sewers, and police; but it brings also an ugliness, an insincerity, a vulgarity never before known to history, unless it be under the Roman Empire.—G. Lowes Dickinson

23. Ours is probably the only poetry in history that has had to be *taught* in its own time. A contemporary art that must be taught to adults before it can be enjoyed is sick.—Karl Shapiro

24. Voting is a more orderly process than rioting, but has only an even chance of producing the right answer.—C. Northcote Parkinson

25. The art of politics, in the sense of gaining and retaining power, is easier than the art of statesmanship: there is a proved technology of the first, but not of the second.—Ralph Barton Perry

26. If knowledge is limited to what is defined with exactitude, it appears to be doomed to be hypothetical, provisional, and uncertain.—Theodore Merz

27. Few conceptions are more remote from experience than those by which ordinary experience is scientifically explained. —Arthur James Balfour

28. Documents are a great embarrassment to the conscientious historian.—Edward A. Singer

29. There are two kinds of things which we are likely to take as undoubtedly real. We take physical objects to be real, and we take states of mind to be real. We might say, anything is real if it is as real as a rock, or as real as pain. . . . The history of thought has been very largely controlled by the fact

that to some men the rock is the impressive and sufficient type of reality, to others the feeling or 'the mind.'—Ernest Hocking

30. . . . the best way to judge a culture is to see what kind of people are in the jails.—John Dewey

31. To guess what the history of Europe would have been, had this or that man of genius not been born, may be utterly idle; but it is not venturesome to assert that our civilization would never have arisen, had some superhuman agent destroyed in each generation all the children whose inborn mental nature ranked among the highest ten per cent in excellence.—Walter T. Marvin

32. In life human beings return from a distracting variety of interests to a few simple things; or, if they do not return, run the risk of losing their souls. In literature, which is the shadow of life, they need to do the same.—R. W. Livingstone

33. Metaphor and simile are the poet's rebellion against routine impressions.—Irwin Edman

34. If I wished to punish a province, I would have it governed by philosophers.—Frederick the Great

35. . . . written history too seldom shows that ordinary men have always had to suffer the history their leaders were making. —Herbert J. Muller

36. There is, in truth, no such thing as an exact fact in the whole realm of the beautiful.—H. L. Mencken

37. A liberal arts education . . . is a relatively harmless adornment to a solid education if one has the time and the money for it in normal times. But these are not normal times.— George Tichenor

38. . . . science would be far less advanced than she is if the passionate desires of individuals to get their own faiths confirmed had been kept out of the game.—William James

39. . . . do not be a fool and learn by experience.—Plato

40. A man's mind stretched by a new idea can never go back to its original dimensions.—Oliver Wendell Holmes

41. Most of the defects of modern psychosocial sciences are due to the clumsy imitation of the physical sciences.—Pitirim A. Sorokin

42. Being well informed about science is not the same thing as understanding science, though the two propositions are not antithetical.—James B. Conant

43. A novel is an impression, not an argument.—Thomas Hardy

44. There must be a new world, if there is to be any world at all.—Thomas Carlyle

45. The case has still to be proved that professors are more rational in their politics than ditch-diggers.—Samuel Lubell

46. If I read a book and it makes my whole body so cold no fire can ever warm me, I know that is poetry. If I feel physically as if the top of my head were taken off, I know that is poetry. These are the only ways I know it. Is there any other way? —Emily Dickinson

47. Before the days of Kepler the heavens declared the glory of the Lord; and we needed no calculation of stellar distances, no fancies about a plurality of worlds, no image of infinite spaces, to make the stars sublime.—George Santayana

48. All life is an experiment. Every year, if not every day, we have to wager our salvation upon some prophecy based upon imperfect knowledge.—Oliver Wendell Holmes

49. Can there be any doubt that contact with a great character, a great soul through literature, immensely surpasses in educational value, in moral and spiritual stimulus, contact with any of the forms or laws of physical nature, through science?— John Burroughs

50. I know that all beings, if only they can count, must find that three and two make five. Perhaps the angels can't count; but if they can, this axiom is true for them. If I met an angel who declared that his experience had occasionally shown him a three or a two that did *not* make five, I should know at once what sort of an angel he was. But now *why* am I so sure of this?—Josiah Royce